CASENOTE® Legal Briefs

CONSTITUTIONAL LAW

Keyed to Courses Using

**Stone, Seidman, Sunstein, Tushnet, and Karlan's
Constitutional Law
Eighth Edition**

Authored by: Publisher's Editorial Staff

Wolters Kluwer

This publication is designed to provide accurate and authoritative information in regard to the subject matter covered. It is sold with the understanding that the publisher is not engaged in rendering legal, accounting, or other professional services. If legal advice or other expert assistance is required, the services of a competent professional person should be sought.

— From a Declaration of Principles adopted jointly
by a Committee of the American Bar Association
and a Committee of Publishers and Associates

Printed in the United States of America.

1 2 3 4 5 6 7 8 9 0

ISBN 978-1-4548-9860-3

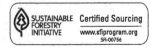

About Wolters Kluwer Legal & Regulatory U.S.

Wolters Kluwer Legal & Regulatory U.S. delivers expert content and solutions in the areas of law, corporate compliance, health compliance, reimbursement, and legal education. Its practical solutions help customers successfully navigate the demands of a changing environment to drive their daily activities, enhance decision quality and inspire confident outcomes.

Serving customers worldwide, its legal and regulatory portfolio includes products under the Aspen Publishers, CCH Incorporated, Kluwer Law International, ftwilliam.com and MediRegs names. They are regarded as exceptional and trusted resources for general legal and practice-specific knowledge, compliance and risk management, dynamic workflow solutions, and expert commentary.

Format for the Casenote® Legal Brief

Nature of Case: This section identifies the form of action (e.g., breach of contract, negligence, battery), the type of proceeding (e.g., demurrer, appeal from trial court's jury instructions), or the relief sought (e.g., damages, injunction, criminal sanctions).

Fact Summary: This is included to refresh your memory and can be used as a quick reminder of the facts.

Rule of Law: Summarizes the general principle of law that the case illustrates. It may be used for instant recall of the court's holding and for classroom discussion or home review.

Facts: This section contains all relevant facts of the case, including the contentions of the parties and the lower court holdings. It is written in a logical order to give the student a clear understanding of the case. The plaintiff and defendant are identified by their proper names throughout and are always labeled with a (P) or (D).

Palsgraf v. Long Island R.R. Co.

Injured bystander (P) v. Railroad company (D)

N.Y. Ct. App., 248 N.Y. 339, 162 N.E. 99 (1928).

NATURE OF CASE: Appeal from judgment affirming verdict for plaintiff seeking damages for personal injury.

FACT SUMMARY: Helen Palsgraf (P) was injured on R.R.'s (D) train platform when R.R.'s (D) guard helped a passenger aboard a moving train, causing his package to fall on the tracks. The package contained fireworks which exploded, creating a shock that tipped a scale onto Palsgraf (P).

🏛 RULE OF LAW
The risk reasonably to be perceived defines the duty to be obeyed.

FACTS: Helen Palsgraf (P) purchased a ticket to Rockaway Beach from R.R. (D) and was waiting on the train platform. As she waited, two men ran to catch a train that was pulling out from the platform. The first man jumped aboard, but the second man, who appeared as if he might fall, was helped aboard by the guard on the train who had kept the door open so they could jump aboard. A guard on the platform also helped by pushing him onto the train. The man was carrying a package wrapped in newspaper. In the process, the man dropped his package, which fell on the tracks. The package contained fireworks and exploded. The shock of the explosion was apparently of great enough strength to tip over some scales at the other end of the platform, which fell on Palsgraf (P) and injured her. A jury awarded her damages, and R.R. (D) appealed.

ISSUE: Does the risk reasonably to be perceived define the duty to be obeyed?

HOLDING AND DECISION: (Cardozo, C.J.) Yes. The risk reasonably to be perceived defines the duty to be obeyed. If there is no foreseeable hazard to the injured party as the result of a seemingly innocent act, the act does not become a tort because it happened to be a wrong as to another. If the wrong was not willful, the plaintiff must show that the act as to her had such great and apparent possibilities of danger as to entitle her to protection. Negligence in the abstract is not enough upon which to base liability. Negligence is a relative concept, evolving out of the common law doctrine of trespass on the case. To establish liability, the defendant must owe a legal duty of reasonable care to the injured party. A cause of action in tort will lie where harm,

though unintended, could have been averted or avoided by observance of such a duty. The scope of the duty is limited by the range of danger that a reasonable person could foresee. In this case, there was nothing to suggest from the appearance of the parcel or otherwise that the parcel contained fireworks. The guard could not reasonably have had any warning of a threat to Palsgraf (P), and R.R. (D) therefore cannot be held liable. Judgment is reversed in favor of R.R. (D).

DISSENT: (Andrews, J.) The concept that there is no negligence unless R.R. (D) owes a legal duty to take care as to Palsgraf (P) herself is too narrow. Everyone owes to the world at large the duty of refraining from those acts that may unreasonably threaten the safety of others. If the guard's action was negligent as to those nearby, it was also negligent as to those outside what might be termed the "danger zone." For Palsgraf (P) to recover, R.R.'s (D) negligence must have been the proximate cause of her injury, a question of fact for the jury.

▶ ANALYSIS
The majority defined the limit of the defendant's liability in terms of the danger that a reasonable person in defendant's situation would have perceived. The dissent argued that the limitation should not be placed on liability, but rather on damages. Judge Andrews suggested that only injuries that would not have happened but for R.R.'s (D) negligence should be compensable. Both the majority and dissent recognized the policy-driven need to limit liability for negligent acts, seeking, in the words of Judge Andrews, to define a framework "that will be practical and in keeping with the general understanding of mankind." The Restatement (Second) of Torts has accepted Judge Cardozo's view.

━━

Quicknotes
FORESEEABILITY A reasonable expectation that change is the probable result of certain acts or omissions.

NEGLIGENCE Conduct falling below the standard of care that a reasonable person would demonstrate under similar conditions.

PROXIMATE CAUSE The natural sequence of events without which an injury would not have been sustained.

━━

Party ID: Quick identification of the relationship between the parties.

Concurrence/Dissent: All concurrences and dissents are briefed whenever they are included by the casebook editor.

Analysis: This last paragraph gives you a broad understanding of where the case "fits in" with other cases in the section of the book and with the entire course. It is a hornbook-style discussion indicating whether the case is a majority or minority opinion and comparing the principal case with other cases in the casebook. It may also provide analysis from restatements, uniform codes, and law review articles. The analysis will prove to be invaluable to classroom discussion.

Issue: The issue is a concise question that brings out the essence of the opinion as it relates to the section of the casebook in which the case appears. Both substantive and procedural issues are included if relevant to the decision.

Holding and Decision: This section offers a clear and in-depth discussion of the rule of the case and the court's rationale. It is written in easy-to-understand language and answers the issue presented by applying the law to the facts of the case. When relevant, it includes a thorough discussion of the exceptions to the case as listed by the court, any major cites to the other cases on point, and the names of the judges who wrote the decisions.

Quicknotes: Conveniently defines legal terms found in the case and summarizes the nature of any statutes, codes, or rules referred to in the text.

Note to Students

Wolters Kluwer Legal & Regulatory U.S. is proud to offer *Casenote*® *Legal Briefs*—continuing thirty years of publishing America's best-selling legal briefs.

Casenote® *Legal Briefs* are designed to help you save time when briefing assigned cases. Organized under convenient headings, they show you how to abstract the basic facts and holdings from the text of the actual opinions handed down by the courts. Used as part of a rigorous study regimen, they can help you spend more time analyzing and critiquing points of law than on copying bits and pieces of judicial opinions into your notebook or outline.

Casenote® *Legal Briefs* should never be used as a substitute for assigned casebook readings. They work best when read as a follow-up to reviewing the underlying opinions themselves. Students who try to avoid reading and digesting the judicial opinions in their casebooks or online sources will end up shortchanging themselves in the long run. The ability to absorb, critique, and restate the dynamic and complex elements of case law decisions is crucial to your success in law school and beyond. It cannot be developed vicariously.

Casenote® *Legal Briefs* represents but one of the many offerings in Legal Education's Study Aid Timeline, which includes:

- *Casenote*® *Legal Briefs*
- *Emanuel*® *Law Outlines*
- *Emanuel*® *Law in a Flash* Flash Cards
- *Emanuel*® *CrunchTime*® Series

Each of these series is designed to provide you with easy-to-understand explanations of complex points of law. Each volume offers guidance on the principles of legal analysis and, consulted regularly, will hone your ability to spot relevant issues. We have titles that will help you prepare for class, prepare for your exams, and enhance your general comprehension of the law along the way.

To find out more about our law school tools for success, visit us at *www.WKLegaledu.com* or email us at *legaledu@wolterskluwer.com*. We'll be happy to assist you.

How to Brief a Case

A. Decide on a Format and Stick to It

Structure is essential to a good brief. It enables you to arrange systematically the related parts that are scattered throughout most cases, thus making manageable and understandable what might otherwise seem to be an endless and unfathomable sea of information. There are, of course, an unlimited number of formats that can be utilized. However, it is best to find one that suits your needs and stick to it. Consistency breeds both efficiency and the security that when called upon you will know where to look in your brief for the information you are asked to give.

Any format, as long as it presents the essential elements of a case in an organized fashion, can be used. Experience, however, has led *Casenote® Legal Briefs* to develop and utilize the following format because of its logical flow and universal applicability.

NATURE OF CASE: This is a brief statement of the legal character and procedural status of the case (e.g., "Appeal of a burglary conviction").

There are many different alternatives open to a litigant dissatisfied with a court ruling. The key to determining which one has been used is to discover *who is asking this court for what.*

This first entry in the brief should be kept as *short as possible.* Use the court's terminology if you understand it. But since jurisdictions vary as to the titles of pleadings, the best entry is the one that addresses who wants what in this proceeding, not the one that sounds most like the court's language.

RULE OF LAW: A statement of the general principle of law that the case illustrates (e.g., "An acceptance that varies any term of the offer is considered a rejection and counteroffer").

Determining the rule of law of a case is a procedure similar to determining the issue of the case. Avoid being fooled by red herrings; there may be a few rules of law mentioned in the case excerpt, but usually only one is *the* rule with which the casebook editor is concerned. The techniques used to locate the issue, described below, may also be utilized to find the rule of law. Generally, your best guide is simply the chapter heading. It is a clue to the point the casebook editor seeks to make and should be kept in mind when reading every case in the respective section.

FACTS: A synopsis of only the essential facts of the case, i.e., those bearing upon or leading up to the issue.

The facts entry should be a short statement of the events and transactions that led one party to initiate legal proceedings against another in the first place. While some cases conveniently state the salient facts at the beginning of the decision, in other instances they will have to be culled from hiding places throughout the text, even from concurring and dissenting opinions. Some of the "facts" will often be in dispute and should be so noted. Conflicting evidence may be briefly pointed up. "Hard" facts must be included. Both must be *relevant* in order to be listed in the facts entry. It is impossible to tell what is relevant until the entire case is read, as the ultimate determination of the rights and liabilities of the parties may turn on something buried deep in the opinion.

Generally, the facts entry should not be longer than three to five *short* sentences.

It is often helpful to identify the role played by a party in a given context. For example, in a construction contract case the identification of a party as the "contractor" or "builder" alleviates the need to tell that that party was the one who was supposed to have built the house.

It is always helpful, and a good general practice, to identify the "plaintiff" and the "defendant." This may seem elementary and uncomplicated, but, especially in view of the creative editing practiced by some casebook editors, it is sometimes a difficult or even impossible task. Bear in mind that the *party presently* seeking something from this court may not be the plaintiff, and that sometimes only the cross-claim of a defendant is treated in the excerpt. Confusing or misaligning the parties can ruin your analysis and understanding of the case.

ISSUE: A statement of the general legal question answered by or illustrated in the case. For clarity, the issue is best put in the form of a question capable of a "yes" or "no" answer. In reality, the issue is simply the Rule of Law put in the form of a question (e.g., "May an offer be accepted by performance?").

The major problem presented in discerning what is *the* issue in the case is that an opinion usually purports to raise and answer several questions. However, except for rare cases, only one such question is really the issue in the case. Collateral issues not necessary to the resolution of the matter in controversy are handled by the court by language known as *"obiter dictum"* or merely *"dictum."* While dicta may be included later in the brief, they have no place under the issue heading.

To find the issue, ask *who wants what* and then go on to ask *why did that party succeed or fail in getting it.* Once this is determined, the "why" should be turned into a question.

The complexity of the issues in the cases will vary, but in all cases a single-sentence question should sum up the issue. *In a few cases,* there will be two, or even more rarely, three issues of equal importance to the resolution of the case. Each should be expressed in a single-sentence question.

Since many issues are resolved by a court in coming to a final disposition of a case, the casebook editor will reproduce the portion of the opinion containing the issue or issues most relevant to the area of law under scrutiny. A noted law professor gave this advice: "Close the book; look at the title on the cover." Chances are, if it is Property, you need not concern yourself with whether, for example, the federal government's treatment of the plaintiff's land really raises a federal question sufficient to support jurisdiction on this ground in federal court.

The same rule applies to chapter headings designating sub-areas within the subjects. They tip you off as to what the text is designed to teach. The cases are arranged in a casebook to show a progression or development of the law, so that the preceding cases may also help.

It is also most important to remember to *read the notes and questions* at the end of a case to determine what the editors wanted you to have gleaned from it.

HOLDING AND DECISION: This section should succinctly explain the rationale of the court in arriving at its decision. In capsulizing the "reasoning" of the court, it should always include an application of the general rule or rules of law to the specific facts of the case. Hidden justifications come to light in this entry: the reasons for the state of the law, the public policies, the biases and prejudices, those considerations that influence the justices' thinking and, ultimately, the outcome of the case. At the end, there should be a short indication of the disposition or procedural resolution of the case (e.g., "Decision of the trial court for Mr. Smith (P) reversed").

The foregoing format is designed to help you "digest" the reams of case material with which you will be faced in your law school career. Once mastered by practice, it will place at your fingertips the information the authors of your casebooks have sought to impart to you in case-by-case illustration and analysis.

B. Be as Economical as Possible in Briefing Cases

Once armed with a format that encourages succinctness, it is as important to be economical with regard to the time spent on the actual reading of the case as it is to be economical in the writing of the brief itself. This does not mean "skimming" a case. Rather, it means reading the case with an "eye" trained to recognize into which "section" of your brief a particular passage or line fits and having a system for quickly and precisely marking the case so that the passages fitting any one particular part of

the brief can be easily identified and brought together in a concise and accurate manner when the brief is actually written.

It is of no use to simply repeat everything in the opinion of the court; record only enough information to trigger your recollection of what the court said. Nevertheless, an accurate statement of the "law of the case," i.e., the legal principle applied to the facts, is absolutely essential to class preparation and to learning the law under the case method.

To that end, it is important to develop a "shorthand" that you can use to make marginal notations. These notations will tell you at a glance in which section of the brief you will be placing that particular passage or portion of the opinion.

Some students prefer to underline all the salient portions of the opinion (with a pencil or colored underliner marker), making marginal notations as they go along. Others prefer the color-coded method of underlining, utilizing different colors of markers to underline the salient portions of the case, each separate color being used to represent a different section of the brief. For example, blue underlining could be used for passages relating to the rule of law, yellow for those relating to the issue, and green for those relating to the holding and decision, etc. While it has its advocates, the color-coded method can be confusing and time-consuming (all that time spent on changing colored markers). Furthermore, it can interfere with the continuity and concentration many students deem essential to the reading of a case for maximum comprehension. In the end, however, it is a matter of personal preference and style. Just remember, whatever method you use, underlining must be used sparingly or its value is lost.

If you take the marginal notation route, an efficient and easy method is to go along underlining the key portions of the case and placing in the margin alongside them the following "markers" to indicate where a particular passage or line "belongs" in the brief you will write:

N (NATURE OF CASE)
RL (RULE OF LAW)
I (ISSUE)
HL (HOLDING AND DECISION, relates to the RULE OF LAW behind the decision)
HR (HOLDING AND DECISION, gives the RATIONALE or reasoning behind the decision)
HA (HOLDING AND DECISION, applies the general principle(s) of law to the facts of the case to arrive at the decision)

Remember that a particular passage may well contain information necessary to more than one part of your brief, in which case you simply note that in the margin. If you are using the color-coded underlining method instead of marginal notation, simply make asterisks or checks in the margin next to the passage in question in the colors that indicate the additional sections of the brief where it might be utilized.

The economy of utilizing "shorthand" in marking cases for briefing can be maintained in the actual brief writing process itself by utilizing "law student shorthand" within the brief. There are many commonly used words and phrases for which abbreviations can be substituted in your briefs (and in your class notes also). You can develop abbreviations that are personal to you and which will save you a lot of time. A reference list of briefing abbreviations can be found on page x of this book.

C. Use Both the Briefing Process and the Brief as a Learning Tool

Now that you have a format and the tools for briefing cases efficiently, the most important thing is to make the time spent in briefing profitable to you and to make the most advantageous use of the briefs you create. Of course, the briefs are invaluable for classroom reference when you are called upon to explain or analyze a particular case. However, they are also useful in reviewing for exams. A quick glance at the fact summary should bring the case to mind, and a rereading of the rule of law should enable you to go over the underlying legal concept in your mind, how it was applied in that particular case, and how it might apply in other factual settings.

As to the value to be derived from engaging in the briefing process itself, there is an immediate benefit that arises from being forced to sift through the essential facts and reasoning from the court's opinion and to succinctly express them in your own words in your brief. The process ensures that you understand the case and the point that it illustrates, and that means you will be ready to absorb further analysis and information brought forth in class. It also ensures you will have something to say when called upon in class. The briefing process helps develop a mental agility for getting to the *gist* of a case and for identifying, expounding on, and applying the legal concepts and issues found there. The briefing process is the mental process on which you must rely in taking law school examinations; it is also the mental process upon which a lawyer relies in serving his clients and in making his living.

Abbreviations for Briefs

acceptance	acp		offer	O
affirmed	aff		offeree	OE
answer	ans		offeror	OR
assumption of risk	a/r		ordinance	ord
attorney	atty		pain and suffering	p/s
beyond a reasonable doubt	b/r/d		parol evidence	p/e
bona fide purchaser	BFP		plaintiff	P
breach of contract	br/k		prima facie	p/f
cause of action	c/a		probable cause	p/c
common law	c/l		proximate cause	px/c
Constitution	Con		real property	r/p
constitutional	con		reasonable doubt	r/d
contract	K		reasonable man	r/m
contributory negligence	c/n		rebuttable presumption	rb/p
cross	x		remanded	rem
cross-complaint	x/c		res ipsa loquitur	RIL
cross-examination	x/ex		respondeat superior	r/s
cruel and unusual punishment	c/u/p		Restatement	RS
defendant	D		reversed	rev
dismissed	dis		Rule Against Perpetuities	RAP
double jeopardy	d/j		search and seizure	s/s
due process	d/p		search warrant	s/w
equal protection	e/p		self-defense	s/d
equity	eq		specific performance	s/p
evidence	ev		statute	S
exclude	exc		statute of frauds	S/F
exclusionary rule	exc/r		statute of limitations	S/L
felony	f/n		summary judgment	s/j
freedom of speech	f/s		tenancy at will	t/w
good faith	g/f		tenancy in common	t/c
habeas corpus	h/c		tenant	t
hearsay	hr		third party	TP
husband	H		third party beneficiary	TPB
injunction	inj		transferred intent	TI
in loco parentis	ILP		unconscionable	uncon
inter vivos	I/v		unconstitutional	unconst
joint tenancy	j/t		undue influence	u/e
judgment	judgt		Uniform Commercial Code	UCC
jurisdiction	jur		unilateral	uni
last clear chance	LCC		vendee	VE
long-arm statute	LAS		vendor	VR
majority view	maj		versus	v
meeting of minds	MOM		void for vagueness	VFV
minority view	min		weight of authority	w/a
Miranda rule	Mir/r		weight of the evidence	w/e
Miranda warnings	Mir/w		wife	W
negligence	neg		with	w/
notice	ntc		within	w/i
nuisance	nus		without	w/o
obligation	ob		without prejudice	w/o/p
obscene	obs		wrongful death	wr/d

Table of Cases

The Constitution and the Supreme Court

Quick Reference Rules of Law

Marbury v. Madison

Justice (P) v. Secretary of State (D)

5 U.S. (1 Cranch) 137 (1803).

NATURE OF CASE: Writ of mandamus to compel delivery of commission.

FACT SUMMARY: President Jefferson's Secretary of State, Madison (D), refused to deliver a commission granted to Marbury (P) by former President Adams.

🏛 RULE OF LAW
The Supreme Court has the power, implied from Article VI, § 2 of the Constitution, to review acts of Congress and if they are found repugnant to the Constitution, to declare them void.

FACTS: On March 2, 1801, the outgoing President of the United States, John Adams, named 42 justices of the peace for the District of Columbia under the Organic Act passed the same day by Congress. William Marbury (P) was one of the justices named. The commissions of Marbury (P) and other named justices were signed by Adams on his last day in office, March 3, and signed and sealed by the Acting Secretary of State, John Marshall. However, the formal commissions were not delivered by the end of the day. The new President, Thomas Jefferson, treated those appointments that were not formalized by delivery of the papers of commission prior to Adams leaving office as a nullity. Marbury (P) and other affected colleagues brought this writ of mandamus to the Supreme Court to compel Jefferson's Secretary of State, James Madison (D), to deliver the commissions. John Marshall, the current Chief Justice of the Supreme Court, delivered the opinion.

ISSUE: Does the Constitution give the Supreme Court the authority to review acts of Congress and declare them, if repugnant to the Constitution, to be void?

HOLDING AND DECISION: (Marshall, C.J.) Yes. The Supreme Court has the power, implied from Article VI, § 2 of the Constitution, to review acts of Congress and if they are found repugnant to the Constitution, to declare them void. The government of the United States is a government of laws, not of men. The President, bound by these laws, is given certain political powers by the Constitution that he may use at his discretion. To aid him in his duties, he is authorized to appoint certain officers to carry out his orders. Their acts as officers are his acts and are never subject to examination by the courts. However, where these officers are given by law specific duties on which individual rights depend, any individual injured by breach of such duty may resort to his country's laws for a remedy. Here, Marbury (P) had a right to the commission, and Madison's (D) refusal to deliver it violated that right. The present case is clearly one for mandamus.

However, should the Supreme Court be the court to issue it? The Judiciary Act of 1789 established and authorized United States courts to issue writs of mandamus to courts or persons holding office under U.S. authority. Secretary of State Madison (D) comes within the Act. If the Supreme Court is powerless to issue the writ of mandamus to him, it must be because the Act is unconstitutional. Article III of the Constitution provides that the Supreme Court shall have original jurisdiction in all cases affecting ambassadors, other public ministers and consuls, and where a state is a party. In all other cases, the Supreme Court shall have appellate jurisdiction. Marbury (P) urged that since Article III contains no restrictive words, the power to assign original jurisdiction to the courts remains in the legislature. But if Congress is allowed to distribute the original and appellate jurisdiction of the Supreme Court, as in the Judiciary Act, then the constitutional grant of Article III is form without substance. But no clause in the Constitution is presumed to be without effect. For the Court to issue a mandamus, it must be an exercise of appellate jurisdiction. The grant of appellate jurisdiction is the power to revise and correct proceedings already instituted; it does not create the cause. To issue a writ of mandamus ordering an executive officer to deliver a paper is to create the original action for that paper. This would be an unconstitutional exercise of original jurisdiction beyond the power of the Court. It is the province and duty of the judicial department to say what the law is. And any law, including acts of the legislature, which is repugnant to the Constitution, is void. Mandamus denied.

▶ ANALYSIS

Judicial review of legislative acts was a controversial subject even before the Constitution was ratified and adopted. Alexander Hamilton upheld the theory of judicial review in the Federalist Papers. He argued that the judiciary, being the most vulnerable branch of the government, was designed to be an intermediary between the people and the legislature. Since the interpretation of laws was the responsibility of the judiciary, and the Constitution the supreme law of the land, any conflict between legislative acts and the Constitution were to be resolved by the court in favor of the Constitution. But other authorities have attacked this position. In the case of *Eakin v. Raub*, 12 Serg. & Rawle 330, 353 (Pa. 1825), Justice Gibson dissented, stating that the judiciary's function was limited to interpreting the laws and should not extend to scrutinizing the legislature's authority to enact them. Judge Learned

Continued on next page.

Hand felt that judicial review was inconsistent with the separation of powers. But history has supported the authority of judicial review of legislative acts. The United States survives on a tripartite government. Theoretically, the three branches should be strong enough to check and balance the others. To limit the judiciary to the passive task of interpretation would be to limit its strength in the tripartite structure. *Marbury* served to buttress the judiciary branch making it equal to the executive and legislative branches.

Quicknotes

APPELLATE JURISDICTION The power of a higher court to review the decisions of lower courts.

JUDICIAL REVIEW The authority of the courts to review decisions, actions or omissions committed by another agency or branch of government.

ORIGINAL JURISDICTION The power of a court to hear an action upon its commencement.

WRIT OF MANDAMUS A court order issued commanding a public or private entity, or an official thereof, to perform a duty required by law.

Martin v. Hunter's Lessee

British citizen (P) v. U.S. citizen (D)

14 U.S. (1 Wheat.) 304 (1816).

NATURE OF CASE: Appeal of land title dispute in state court involving issues of federal law.

FACT SUMMARY: The Virginia Court of Appeals held that the Supreme Court did not have jurisdiction to decide matters of federal law in state courts.

RULE OF LAW
The Supreme Court has jurisdiction over issues of federal law in state courts.

FACTS: Martin (P), a British subject, claimed certain land. Hunter (D) claimed the land under a grant from the state. Martin (P) claimed that certain treaties between the United States and England gave him the land. The state trial court found for Martin (P); the state appellate court reversed. The Supreme Court reversed on the basis of the treaties and matters of federal law and directed the state court to enter judgment for Martin (P). The state court refused. The Supreme Court reached the issue of its jurisdiction in the matter.

ISSUE: Does the Supreme Court have jurisdiction over issues of federal law in state courts?

HOLDING AND DECISION: (Story, J.) Yes. The Supreme Court has jurisdiction over issues of federal law in state courts. The Constitution grants power to the Court in all cases arising under the Constitution or federal laws, irrespective of the tribunal of origin. It cannot be said that Supreme Court review of state court decisions is overly intrusive on state power, since it is accepted that Congress can supersede state laws, and this is equally intrusive. Finally, the laws of the United States require national uniformity, and only by having one final arbiter of federal law may this be achieved. Reversed.

ANALYSIS

This action was a landmark in American judicial history. It is difficult to envision what the American legal system would be like today if this decision had gone the other way. It would seem that the federal system in that case would have been little different than the state systems.

Quicknotes

APPELLATE JURISDICTION The power of a higher court to review the decisions of lower courts.

JURISDICTION The authority of a court to hear and declare judgment in respect to a particular matter.

McCulloch v. Maryland

Bank cashier (D) v. State (P)

17 U.S. (4 Wheat.) 316 (1819).

NATURE OF CASE: Action arising out of violation of a state statute.

FACT SUMMARY: McCulloch (D), the cashier of the Baltimore branch of the U.S. Bank, issued bank notes in violation of a Maryland (P) statute providing that no bank, without authority from the state, could issue bank notes except on stamped paper issued by the state.

RULE OF LAW
(1) Certain federal powers giving Congress the discretion and power to choose and enact the means to perform the duties imposed upon it are to be implied from the Necessary and Proper Clause.
(2) The federal Constitution and the laws made pursuant to it are supreme and control the constitutions and the laws of the states.

FACTS: A Maryland (P) statute prohibited any bank operating in the state without state authority from issuing bank notes except upon stamped paper issued by the state. The law specifies the fees payable for the paper and provides for penalties for violators. An Act of Congress established a U.S. Bank. McCulloch (D), the U.S. Bank's cashier for its Baltimore branch, issued bank notes without complying with the Maryland (P) law.

ISSUE:
(1) Does Congress have the power to incorporate a bank?
(2) Does a state have the power to impose fees on the operation of an institution created by Congress pursuant to its constitutional powers?

HOLDING AND DECISION: (Marshall, C.J.)
(1) Yes. Certain federal powers giving Congress the discretion and power to choose and enact the means to perform the duties imposed upon it are to be implied from the Necessary and Proper Clause. It's true that this government is one of enumerated powers. However, the Constitution does not exclude incidental or implied powers. It does not require that everything be granted expressly and minutely described. To have so required would have entirely changed the character of the Constitution and made it into a legal code. The enumerated powers given to the government imply the ordinary means of execution. The power of creating a corporation may be implied as incidental to other powers or used as a means of executing them. The Necessary and Proper Clause gives Congress the power to make "all laws which shall be necessary and proper for carrying into execution" the powers vested by the Constitution

in the U.S. Government. Maryland (P) argues that the word "necessary" limits the right to pass laws for the execution of the granted powers to those that are indispensable. However, in common usage "necessary" frequently means convenient, useful, and essential. Considering the word's common usage, its usage in another part of the Constitution (Article 1, section 10), and its inclusion among the powers given to Congress, rather than among the limitations upon Congress, it cannot be held to restrain Congress. The sound construction of the Constitution must allow Congress the discretion to choose the means to perform the duties imposed upon it. So long as the end is legitimate and within the scope of the Constitution, any means that are appropriate, that are plainly adapted to that end, and that are not prohibited by the Constitution, but are consistent with its spirit, are constitutional. A bank is a convenient, useful, and essential instrument for handling national finances. Hence, it is within Congress's power to enact a law incorporating a U.S. bank.
(2) No. The federal Constitution and the laws made pursuant to it are supreme and control the constitutions and the laws of the states. Maryland (P) was incorrect in its contention that the powers of the federal government are delegated by the states, which alone are truly sovereign. The Constitution derives its authority from the people, not from the states. Here, Maryland's (P) statute in effect taxes the operation of the U.S. Bank, a bank properly created within Congress's power. The power to tax involves the power to destroy. Here it is in opposition to the supreme congressional power to create a bank. Also, when a state taxes an organization created by the U.S. Government, it acts upon an institution created by people over whom it claims no control. The states have no power, by taxation or otherwise, to impede, burden, or in any manner control the operations of constitutional laws enacted by Congress. The Maryland (P) statute is, therefore, unconstitutional and void. Reversed.

ANALYSIS

Federalism is the basis of the Constitution's response to the problem of governing large geographical areas with diverse local needs. The success of federalism depends upon maintaining the balance between the need for the supremacy and sovereignty of the federal government and the interest in maintaining independent state government

Continued on next page.

and curtailing national intrusion into intrastate affairs. The U.S. federal structure allocates powers between the nation and the states by enumerating the powers delegated to the national government and acknowledging the retention by the states of the remainder. The Articles of Confederation followed a similar scheme. The Constitution expanded the enumerated national powers to remedy weaknesses of the Articles. The move from the Articles to the Constitution was a shift from a central government with fewer powers to one with more powers.

Quicknotes

ENUMERATED POWERS Those powers expressly delegated by the Constitution to a particular branch of government.

FEDERALISM A scheme of government whereby the power to govern is divided between a central and localized governments.

IMPLIED POWERS Powers impliedly delegated to the various branches of government that, while not expressly stated in the Constitution, are necessary to effectuate the enumerated powers.

Ex parte McCardle

Federal government (P) v. Newspaper editor (D)

74 U.S. (7 Wall.) 506 (1869).

NATURE OF CASE: Appeal from denial of habeas corpus.

FACT SUMMARY: McCardle (D) appealed from a denial of habeas corpus to the Supreme Court, but Congress passed an act forbidding the Court jurisdiction.

🏛 RULE OF LAW
Although the Supreme Court derives its appellate jurisdiction from the Constitution, the Constitution also gives Congress the express power to make exceptions to that appellate jurisdiction.

FACTS: After the Civil War, Congress imposed military government on many former Confederate states under authority of the Civil War Reconstruction Acts. McCardle (D), a Mississippi newspaper editor, was held in military custody on charges of publishing libelous and incendiary articles. McCardle (D) brought a habeas corpus writ based on a congressional act passed on February 5, 1867. The act authorized federal courts to grant habeas corpus to persons held in violation of Constitutional rights, and also gave authority for appeals to the Supreme Court. The circuit court denied McCardle's (D) habeas corpus writ, but the Supreme Court sustained jurisdiction for an appeal on the merits. However, after arguments were heard, Congress passed an act on March 27, 1868, that repealed that much of the 1867 act that allowed an appeal to the Supreme Court from the circuit court and the exercise by the Supreme Court by jurisdiction on any such appeals, past or present.

ISSUE: Does Congress have the power, under the Constitution, to make exceptions to the appellate jurisdiction of the Supreme Court?

HOLDING AND DECISION: (Chase, C.J.) Yes. Although the Supreme Court derives its appellate jurisdiction from the Constitution, the Constitution also gives Congress the express power to make exceptions to that appellate jurisdiction. The appellate jurisdiction of the Supreme Court is not derived from acts of Congress but is conferred by the Constitution with such exceptions and regulations as Congress shall make. And though Congress has affirmatively described in the act of 1789 the regulations governing the exercise of the Supreme Court's appellate jurisdiction, with the implication that any exercise of that jurisdiction not within the purview of the act would be negated, the exception to the appellate jurisdiction in the present case is not to be inferred from such affirmations. The exceptions in this case are express. That part of the 1867 act giving the Court appellate jurisdiction in habeas corpus cases is expressly repealed. The effect is to take away the court's jurisdiction, dismissing the cause. When a legislative act is repealed, it is as if it had never existed except to transactions past and closed. Thus, no judgment can be rendered in a suit after repeal of the act under which it was brought. But this does not deny forever the Court's appellate power in habeas corpus cases. The act of 1868 affects only such appeals from circuit courts brought under the act of 1867. Appeal dismissed.

▶ ANALYSIS

McCardle is clearly an example of judicial restraint. The authority of Congress to control the jurisdiction of the Supreme Court is not unlimited. This was proved in *Marbury v. Madison*, 5 U.S. (1 Cranch) 137 (1803), where the Court, faced with an extension by Congress of its original jurisdiction as granted under the Constitution, refused to accept the constitutionality of the congressional act. While this specifically limited the Supreme Court's original jurisdiction, it provided Marshall with the ideal arena to assert the doctrine of judicial review. But in *McCardle*, the Court backed away from confrontation with Congress due to current-day political crises that followed the Civil War. Thereafter, the Court sought to limit congressional power by the power of judicial review announced in *Marbury*. The Court held on several occasions that certain congressional attempts to delimit its jurisdiction were unconstitutional attempts to invade the judicial province. Such congressional actions were considered a violation of the separation of powers. Today, it is doubtful that *McCardle* would be sustained.

Quicknotes

APPELLATE JURISDICTION The power of a higher court to review the decisions of lower courts.

ORIGINAL JURISDICTION The power of a court to hear an action upon its commencement.

Lujan v. Defenders of Wildlife

Federal government (D) v. Members (P)

504 U.S. 555 (1992).

NATURE OF CASE: Appeal from denial of motion to dismiss action seeking declaratory judgment and injunction against administrative rule.

FACT SUMMARY: Defenders of Wildlife (P) sought a declaratory judgment and injunction to extend application of the Endangered Species Act to government actions taken in foreign nations.

RULE OF LAW
Only individuals who have suffered concrete harm have standing to seek judicial review of agency rules.

FACTS: The U.S. Interior Department (D) reinterpreted the Endangered Species Act (ESA) to apply only to government actions taken in the United States or on the high seas, and not in foreign nations. Two Defenders of Wildlife members (P) had visited separate sites abroad and claimed harm by such reinterpretation. The members (P) planned to return sometime to observe endangered animals in the sites they had previously visited, but the Interior Department's (D) new interpretation would probably increase the extinction rate of the endangered species they planned to study. The members (P) sought a declaratory judgment and an injunction requiring the Interior Department (D) to apply the ESA to actions taken in foreign nations.

ISSUE: Do individuals who have suffered no concrete harm have standing to seek judicial review of agency rules?

HOLDING AND DECISION: (Scalia, J.) No. Only individuals who have suffered concrete harm have standing to seek judicial review of agency rules. That Defenders of Wildlife members (P) intend to return "someday" to wildlife sites does not constitute "actual or imminent" injury caused by the Interior Department's (D) reinterpretation of the ESA. Further, it is unclear applying the ESA to actions in foreign nations will effect the redress sought by Defenders (P). Reversed.

CONCURRENCE: (Kennedy, J.) While the ESA permits citizen suits, it fails to establish injury in "any person" by virtue of any "violation." Since standing is not established, the redressability issue should not be reached.

CONCURRENCE: (Stevens, J.) While the Interior Department's (D) reinterpretation of the ESA is correct, an injury is suffered whenever action is taken that harms the interest in studying animals in natural habitats.

DISSENT: (Blackmun, J.) The professional backgrounds of the Defenders of Wildlife members (P) make it reasonable to assume the members (P) will soon return to the foreign sites, thus satisfying the "actual or imminent" injury requirement for standing. Requiring a specific return date in the future is an empty formality. Such rigid principles as enunciated by the plurality are likely to apply only in environmental claims. Environmental plaintiffs should not be held to have special standing disabilities.

ANALYSIS

Minimally, showing "standing" requires three elements: (1) plaintiff suffers an injury; (2) the injury is caused by the conduct complained of; and (3) a favorable decision is likely to redress the injury. In *Northeastern Fla. Chapter of Assn. Gen. Contractors v. Jacksonville*, 508 U.S. 656 (1993), the Supreme Court held a nonminority group had standing to challenge a city's minority set-aside program. The Court held the group need only show it was ready and able to bid on contracts but was prevented from doing so on an equal basis; no actual loss of contract need be shown.

■■■

Quicknotes

DECLARATORY JUDGMENT A judgment of the court establishing the rights of the parties.

INJUNCTION A court order requiring a person to do or prohibiting that person from doing a specific act.

■■■

Massachusetts v. EPA

State (P) v. Federal agency (D)

549 U.S. 497 (2007).

NATURE OF CASE: Appeal challenging a federal agency's alleged refusal to enforce the federal Clean Air Act against motor-vehicle emissions.

FACT SUMMARY: A state and several other parties challenged the Environmental Protection Agency's (D) failure to enforce the Clean Air Act against motor-vehicle emissions.

🏛 RULE OF LAW
A plaintiff has standing if it demonstrates a concrete injury that is both fairly traceable to the defendant and redressable by judicial relief.

FACTS: The Environmental Protection Agency (EPA) (D) refused to enforce the Clean Air Act against motor-vehicle emissions. Massachusetts (P) and several other parties appealed the EPA's (D) refusal [by petitioning the U.S. Court of Appeals for the District of Columbia Circuit to review the EPA's (D) decision. The appellate court did not affirmatively hold that Massachusetts (P) had standing, but a majority of that court did uphold the EPA's (D) decision. Massachusetts (P) petitioned the Supreme Court for further review.]

ISSUE: Does a plaintiff have standing if it demonstrates a concrete injury that is both fairly traceable to the defendant and redressable by judicial relief?

HOLDING AND DECISION: (Stevens, J.) Yes. A plaintiff has standing if it demonstrates a concrete injury that is both fairly traceable to the defendant and redressable by judicial relief. The jurisdiction of federal courts is limited to "cases" and "controversies," and Massachusetts (P) has satisfied that threshold hurdle here. As a State, Massachusetts (P) proceeds in its quasi-sovereign capacity, and case law supports applying different standards of justiciability for such litigants. The particularized injury for Massachusetts (P) in this case is the damage to the State's (P) coastline that will, and will continue to, occur. Further, the injury to that coastline is fairly traceable to the EPA's (D) inaction; even small effects on an injury in fact satisfy the causation requirement in federal standing analysis. Finally, Massachusetts' (P) injury can be redressed judicially, even though the outcome of a judicial remedy might be delayed while new motor-vehicle emissions are implemented. Accordingly, Massachusetts (P) has standing. [Reversed and remanded.]

DISSENT: (Roberts, C.J.) Any redress of the injuries in this case should be left to the political branches. Relaxing standing requirements for a state exists nowhere in this Court's precedents. Under normal standing analysis, Massachusetts's (P) injury fails to satisfy the requirement of a "concrete and particularized" injury; injuries to "humanity at large" do not suffice. Also, any causal connection between the EPA's (D) inaction and damage to the coastlines is so tenuous and speculative that it cannot support a finding of standing. Further, Massachusetts (P) cannot satisfy the redressability factor because emissions from other countries are likely to dwarf any reduction in emissions that might result from the EPA's (D) enforcement of the Clean Air Act. Diluting the appropriate standing requirements only permits courts to encroach upon authority that is properly committed to Congress and the President.

▶ ANALYSIS

The three factors in the standing analysis announced by *Lujan v. Defenders of Wildlife*, 504 U.S. 555 (1992), are very clear: the complaining party must have suffered (1) an injury in fact (2) that is fairly traceable to the defendant and (3) that can be redressed by judicial relief. As the Court's 5-4 decision in this case shows, however, what is not so clear is how those three factors should apply to any specific dispute. The fundamental importance of justiciability, as Chief Justice Roberts notes in dissent, resides in the most basic questions about the kinds of disputes that courts should—and should not—hear.

■■■

Quicknotes

REDRESSABILITY Requirement that in order for a court to hear a case there must be an injury that is redressable or capable of being remedied.

■■■

Clapper v. Amnesty International USA

Federal official (D) v. Organization communicating with foreigners located outside the U.S. (P)

133 S. Ct. 1138 (2013).

NATURE OF CASE: Appeal from ruling that plaintiffs had Article III standing to challenge the constitutionality of Section 702 of the Foreign Intelligence Surveillance Act of 1978 (FISA), 50 U.S.C. § 1881a. [The complete procedural posture of the case is not presented in the casebook extract.]

FACT SUMMARY: United States individuals and entities (P), including attorneys and human rights, labor, legal, and media organizations, contended that they had Article III standing to bring suit challenging the constitutionality of Section 702 of the Foreign Intelligence Surveillance Act (FISA), 50 U.S.C. § 1881a, which allows the surveillance of individuals who are not "United States persons" and who are reasonably believed to be located outside the United States. These plaintiffs (P) asserted that they had standing because (1) there was an "objectively reasonable likelihood" that their communications would be intercepted at some time in the future, and (2) that they were suffering present injuries resulting from costly and burdensome measures they believed they had to take to protect the confidentiality of their international communications from possible § 1881a surveillance.

🏛 RULE OF LAW

A plaintiff does not have Article III standing to challenge a statute where the plaintiff can demonstrate neither that future injury the plaintiff fears will flow to it from the statute is certainly impending, nor that countermeasures the plaintiff has taken to avert such feared injury are based on anything more than speculation of non-imminent harm.

FACTS: Section 702 of the Foreign Intelligence Surveillance Act of 1978 (FISA), 50 U.S.C. § 1881a, added by the FISA Amendments Act of 2008, permits the Attorney General and the Director of National Intelligence to acquire foreign intelligence information by jointly authorizing the surveillance of individuals who are not "United States persons" and are reasonably believed to be located outside the United States. Before doing so, the Attorney General and the Director of National Intelligence normally must obtain the Foreign Intelligence Surveillance Court's (FISC) approval. Surveillance under § 1881a is subject to statutory conditions, judicial authorization, congressional supervision, and compliance with the Fourth Amendment. United States individuals and entities (P), including attorneys and human rights, labor, legal, and media organizations, claimed that they engaged in sensitive international communications with individuals who they

believed were likely targets of § 1881a surveillance, including colleagues, clients, sources, and other individuals located abroad. On the day that the FISA Amendments Act was enacted, they filed suit, seeking a declaration that § 1881a is facially unconstitutional, as well as a permanent injunction against § 1881a-authorized surveillance. These plaintiffs (P) asserted that they had standing because (1) there was an "objectively reasonable likelihood" that their communications would be intercepted at some time in the future, and (2) that they were suffering present injuries resulting from costly and burdensome measures they believed they had to take to protect the confidentiality of their international communications from possible § 1881a surveillance. The court of appeals held that the plaintiffs (P) had Article III standing to bring their suit. The Supreme Court granted certiorari. [The complete procedural posture of the case is not presented in the casebook extract.]

ISSUE: Does a plaintiff have Article III standing to challenge a statute where the plaintiff can demonstrate neither that future injury the plaintiff fears will flow to it from the statute is certainly impending, nor that countermeasures the plaintiff has taken to avert such feared injury are based on anything more than speculation of non-imminent harm?

HOLDING AND DECISION: (Alito, J.) No. A plaintiff does not have Article III standing to challenge a statute where the plaintiff can demonstrate neither that future injury the plaintiff fears will flow to it from the statute is certainly impending, nor that countermeasures the plaintiff has taken to avert such feared injury are based on anything more than speculation of non-imminent harm. Plaintiffs (P) assert that they have suffered injury in fact that is fairly traceable to § 1881a because there is an objectively reasonable likelihood that their communications with their foreign contacts will be intercepted under § 1881a at some point. This argument fails. Plaintiffs' (P) standing theory rests on a speculative chain of possibilities that does not establish that their potential injury is certainly impending or is fairly traceable to § 1881a. First, it is highly speculative whether the Government (D) will imminently target communications to which plaintiffs (P) are parties. Since plaintiffs (P), as U.S. persons, cannot be targeted under § 1881a, their theory necessarily rests on their assertion that their foreign contacts will be targeted. Yet they have no actual knowledge of the Government's (D) § 1881a targeting practices. Second, even if plaintiffs (P) could demonstrate that the targeting of their foreign

Continued on next page.

contacts is imminent, they can only speculate as to whether the Government (D) will seek to use § 1881a-authorized surveillance instead of one of the Government's (D) numerous other surveillance methods, which are not challenged here. Third, even if plaintiffs (P) could show that the Government (D) will seek FISC authorization to target plaintiffs' foreign contacts under § 1881a, they can only speculate as to whether the FISC will authorize the surveillance. This Court is reluctant to endorse standing theories that require guesswork as to how independent decisionmakers will exercise their judgment. Fourth, even if the Government (D) were to obtain the FISC's approval to target plaintiffs' (P) foreign contacts under § 1881a, it is unclear whether the Government (D) would succeed in acquiring those contacts' communications. Fifth and finally, even if the Government (D) were to target plaintiffs' (P) foreign contacts, plaintiffs (P) can only speculate as to whether their own communications with those contacts would be incidentally acquired. For these reasons, plaintiffs (P) have failed to show that their potential injury is certainly impending or is fairly traceable to § 1881a. Plaintiffs' (P) second argument, that they suffer ongoing injuries that are fairly traceable to § 1881a because the risk of § 1881a surveillance requires them to take costly and burdensome measures to protect the confidentiality of their communications, is also unavailing. Plaintiffs (P) cannot manufacture standing by choosing to make expenditures based on hypothetical future harm that is not certainly impending. Because they do not face a threat of certainly impending interception under § 1881a, their costs are simply the product of their fear of surveillance, which is insufficient to create standing. Accordingly, any ongoing injuries that respondents are suffering are not fairly traceable to § 1881a. If the law were otherwise, an enterprising plaintiff would be able to secure a lower standard for Article III standing simply by making an expenditure based on a nonparanoid fear. Still another reason that plaintiffs' (P) present injuries are not fairly traceable to § 1881a is that even before § 1881a was enacted, they had a similar incentive to engage in many of the countermeasures that they are now taking. Plaintiffs' (P) other arguments are similarly unpersuasive. Contrary to their claim, their alleged injuries are not the same kinds of injuries that supported standing in other cases, which are readily distinguishable from the case at bar. Moreover, their suggestion that they should be held to have standing because otherwise the constitutionality of § 1881a will never be adjudicated is both legally and factually incorrect. First, the assumption that if they have no standing to sue, no one would have standing, is not a reason to find standing, and, second, the holding in this case by no means insulates § 1881a from judicial review. For example, if the Government (D) intends to use or disclose information obtained or derived from a § 1881a acquisition in judicial or administrative proceedings, it must provide advance notice of its intent, and the affected person may challenge the lawfulness of the acquisition. Additionally, any elec-

tronic communications service provider that the Government (D) directs to assist in § 1881a surveillance may challenge the lawfulness of that directive before the FISC. Reversed and remanded.

DISSENT: (Breyer, J.) The key issue presented here is whether the injury, i.e., the interception of a private telephone or e-mail conversation, is "actual or imminent." Given the structure of § 1881a, there is a high likelihood of injury to the plaintiffs (P). This statute changed this prior law in three important ways. First, it eliminated the requirement that the Government (D) describe to the FISC each specific target and identify each facility at which its surveillance would be directed, thus permitting surveillance on a programmatic, not necessarily individualized, basis. Second, it eliminated the requirement that a target be a "foreign power or an agent of a foreign power." Third, it diminished the court's authority to insist upon, and eliminated its authority to supervise, instance-specific privacy-intrusion minimization procedures (though the Government (D) still must use court-approved general minimization procedures). Thus, using the authority of § 1881a, the Government (D) can now obtain court approval for its surveillance of electronic communications between places within the United States and targets in foreign territories by showing the court (1) that "a significant purpose of the acquisition is to obtain foreign intelligence information," and (2) that it will use general targeting and privacy-intrusion minimization procedures of a kind that the court had previously approved. First, plaintiffs (P) have engaged, and continue to engage, in electronic communications of a kind that § 1881a, but not the prior Act, authorizes the Government (D) to intercept. Second, plaintiffs (P) have a strong motive to engage in, and the Government (D) has a strong motive to listen to, conversations of the kind described. Third, the Government's (D) past behavior shows that it has sought, and hence will in all likelihood continue to seek, information about alleged terrorists and detainees through means that include surveillance of electronic communications. Fourth, the Government (D) has the capacity to conduct electronic surveillance of the kind at issue. To some degree this capacity rests upon technology available to it. This capacity also includes the Government's (D) authority to obtain the kind of information here at issue from private carriers, and the Government (D) is expanding that capacity. Although the Government (D) must have FISC authorization to use such capacity, the Government (D) rarely files requests that fail to meet the statutory criteria, and § 1881a simplifies, and thus expedites, the approval process, making it more likely that the Government (D) will use § 1881a to obtain the necessary approval. Thus, there is a high probability that the Government (D) will intercept at least some electronic communication to which at least some of the plaintiffs (P) are parties, and the majority therefore is wrong

Continued on next page.

when it describes the harm threatened plaintiffs (P) as "speculative." The majority more plausibly says that the plaintiffs (P) have failed to show that the threatened harm is "certainly impending," but, as the majority appears to concede, certainty is not, and never has been, the touchstone of standing. The future is inherently uncertain, yet federal courts frequently entertain actions for injunctions and for declaratory relief aimed at preventing future activities that are reasonably likely or highly likely, but not absolutely certain, to take place; that degree of certainty is all that is needed to support standing here. The Court's holdings in standing cases show that standing exists here, as the Court has often found standing where the occurrence of the relevant injury was far less certain than here. In some standing cases, the Court has found that a reasonable probability of future injury comes accompanied with present injury that takes the form of reasonable efforts to mitigate the threatened effects of the future injury or to prevent it from occurring, and those are the circumstances present here. In sum, the word "certainly" in the phrase "certainly impending" does not refer to absolute certainty. As our case law demonstrates, what the Constitution requires is something more akin to "reasonable probability" or "high probability." The use of some such standard is all that is necessary here to ensure the actual concrete injury that the Constitution demands, and, therefore, the plaintiffs (P) should be granted standing to bring their action.

▶ ANALYSIS

Although the majority conceded that the Court's precedents do not uniformly require plaintiffs to demonstrate that it is literally certain that the harms they identify will come about, and, in some instances have found standing based on a "substantial risk" that the harm will occur, which may prompt plaintiffs to reasonably incur costs to mitigate or avoid that harm, the majority nevertheless made clear that to the extent that the "substantial risk" standard is relevant and is distinct from the "clearly impending" requirement, the plaintiffs (P) here fell short of even that standard, in light of the attenuated chain of inferences necessary to find harm here. In addition, the majority emphasized that plaintiffs (P) bear the burden of pleading and proving concrete facts showing that the defendant's actual action has caused the substantial risk of harm and cannot rely on speculation about the unfettered choices made by independent actors not before the court.

■═■

Quicknotes

PERMANENT INJUNCTION A remedy imposed by the court ordering a party to cease the conduct of a specific activity until the final disposition of the cause of action.

STANDING The right to commence suit against another party because of a personal stake in the resolution of the controversy.

Baker v. Carr

Voters (P) v. State (D)

369 U.S. 186 (1962).

NATURE OF CASE: Appeal from denial of challenge to state apportionment system.

FACT SUMMARY: A 60-year-old Tennessee apportionment system was attacked as obsolete.

🏛 RULE OF LAW
Reapportionment issues present justiciable questions.

FACTS: A 1901 statute apportioned members of the Tennessee Assembly among the state's counties. By 1961, the population had experienced substantial redistribution. Certain individuals (P) filed a district court action challenging the apportionment system as arbitrary and capricious, seeking reapportionment. The court of appeals held that the issue was nonjusticiable.

ISSUE: Do reapportionment issues present justiciable questions?

HOLDING AND DECISION: (Brennan, J.) Yes. Reapportionment issues present justiciable questions. Nonjusticiable or "political" questions are those properly left to other branches of government, either because courts do not have the resources to handle them or because they are best decided through the political process. Examples include foreign relations and the validity of enactments (other than the constitutionality thereto). The issue here, however, is whether the guarantees of equal protection found in the Constitution are being met. Thus, in this issue, the Court is being called upon to judge the constitutionality of the system under attack, something squarely within the Court's power and duty. Reversed and remanded.

DISSENT: (Frankfurter, J.) The Court should not interject itself into political disagreements, as it has done here. Also, it is doubtful that the Court is adequately equipped to handle the subtleties of reapportionment issues. Finally, the structure of state institutions should be given great respect.

▶ ANALYSIS

It is important to understand the difference between a nonjusticiable political question and a political issue. Political issues with constitutional dimensions generally are fair game for judicial review. Political questions are issues that may have constitutional dimensions but are of a nature that they should be resolved in the political arena. The classic example is foreign relations.

■■■

Quicknotes

JUSTICIABILITY An actual controversy that is capable of determination by the court.

■■■

Bush v. Gore

Candidate (D) v. Candidate (P)

531 U.S. 98 (2000).

NATURE OF CASE: Suit seeking stay of state supreme court order.

FACT SUMMARY: Bush (D) sought a stay of the Florida Supreme Court's order permitting a manual recount of ballots in the 2000 presidential election.

🏛 RULE OF LAW
Having once granted the right to vote on equal terms, the state may not, by later arbitrary and disparate treatment, value one person's vote over that of another.

FACTS: After a machine count and recount of ballots in the 2000 Florida presidential election, Gore (P) trailed Bush (D) by less than 1,000 votes. Gore (P) sought further recounts in certain Florida counties. The U.S. Supreme Court vacated a decision of the Florida Supreme Court extending the deadline for the completion of recounts. The Florida Supreme Court ordered a manual recount of all "undervotes"—those ballots on which the machine did not record any presidential choice. Bush (D) sought a stay of the Florida Supreme Court ruling. The U.S. Supreme Court stayed the Florida Supreme Court's order three days before the statutory deadline for the completion of proceedings bearing on the final certification of the state's electors.

ISSUE: Having once granted the right to vote on equal terms, may the state, by later arbitrary and disparate treatment, value one person's vote over that of another?

HOLDING AND DECISION: (Per curiam) No. Having once granted the right to vote on equal terms, the state may not, by later arbitrary and disparate treatment, value one person's vote over that of another. The right to vote is protected both in its allocation as well as its exercise. The recount mechanism implemented here does not satisfy the minimum requirement for non-arbitrary treatment of voters necessary to secure the fundamental right. The standards for accepting or rejecting contested ballots vary not only from county to county but within the county from team to team of recounters. Because any recount seeking to meet the December 12 date will be unconstitutional without substantial additional work, the decision of the Florida Supreme Court ordering the recount to proceed is reversed and the case is remanded.

CONCURRENCE: (Rehnquist, C.J.) There are grounds for reversal in addition to those in the per curiam opinion. (1) Where the election of the President is involved, and the Constitution imposes a duty on a branch of state government, the text of the state's election law, and not just its interpretation by the state courts, takes on independent significance. Therefore, 3 U.S.C. § 5 informs the application of the Constitution's mandate in Art. II, § 1, cl. 2 the state legislature shall appoint electors to the electoral college in a manner of its choosing to the state's electoral scheme. Section 5 provides that the state's selection of electors will be conclusive if the selection is accomplished pursuant to laws enacted prior to the election and is complete six days prior to the meeting of the electoral college. To respect the legislature's powers, post-election state-court actions must not be allowed to frustrate the legislative desire to attain the "safe harbor" provided by § 5, and, to determine whether a state court has infringed upon the legislature's Article II authority, the Court must examine the state's election law. (2) Here, the Florida court's interpretation of "legal vote" and, therefore, its decision to order a contest-period recount, plainly departed from the legislative scheme. The election code does not require the counting of improperly marked ballots, and for the court to reject this established practice, prescribed by the Secretary of State, was also a departure from the legislative scheme. (3) The Florida Supreme Court's order jeopardizes the "legislative wish" to take advantage of the safe harbor provided by 3 U.S.C. § 5. The state court ordered a massive recount four-days before the last date for a final determination that will satisfy § 5. However, no one claims that the ballots the court seeks to have recounted were not previously tabulated. Those ballots were initially read by voting machines at the time of the election, and then reread pursuant to the state's automatic recount provision. There is also no claim of fraud.

DISSENT: (Stevens, J.) While the use of differing sub-standards for determining voter intent in different counties employing similar voting systems may raise serious concerns, those concerns are alleviated by the fact that a single impartial magistrate will ultimately adjudicate all objections arising from the recount process. The loser in this Presidential election is the Nation's confidence in the judge as an impartial guardian of the rule of law.

DISSENT: (Souter, J.) The case should be remanded to the Florida courts with instructions to establish uniform standards in any further recounting.

DISSENT: (Ginsburg, J.) The Court contradicts the basic principle that a state may organize itself as it sees fit. Article II does not call for the scrutiny taken by this Court.

Continued on next page.

DISSENT: (Breyer, J.) This Court should resist the temptation to resolve tangential legal disputes, where doing so threatens to determine the outcome of the election.

▶ *ANALYSIS*

The Court here does not challenge the Florida Supreme Court's authority to resolve election disputes or to define a legal vote or order a manual recount. The Court rejects the standard employed, which was the "intent of the voter," and the absence of specific standards to ensure its equal application.

■══■

Quicknotes

DUE PROCESS CLAUSE Clauses found in the Fifth and Fourteenth Amendments to the United States Constitution providing that no person shall be deprived of "life, liberty, or property, without due process of law."

EQUAL PROTECTION A constitutional guarantee that no person shall be denied the same protection of the laws enjoyed by other persons in like circumstances.

■══■

Federalism at Work: Congress and the National Economy

Quick Reference Rules of Law

Gibbons v. Ogden

Ship operator (D) v. Ship operator (P)

22 U.S. (9 Wheat.) 1 (1824).

NATURE OF CASE: Action seeking an injunction to protect an exclusive right to operate ships between New York City and New Jersey.

FACT SUMMARY: Ogden (P), after acquiring a monopoly right from the State of New York to operate ships between New York City and New Jersey, sought to enjoin Gibbons (D) from operating his ships, licensed by the federal government, between the same points.

RULE OF LAW

If a state law conflicts with a congressional act regulating commerce, the congressional act is controlling.

FACTS: In 1803, the New York legislature granted an exclusive right to Robert Livingston and Robert Fulton to operate ships powered by fire or steam in New York waters for twenty years. The right was subsequently extended for another ten years. Ogden (P) obtained an assignment from Livingston and Fulton to operate his ships between Elizabethtown, New Jersey, and New York City. Gibbons (D) was also running two boats between these points and his boats had been enrolled and licensed under the laws of the United States for carrying on the coasting trade. Ogden (P) obtained an injunction stopping Gibbons (D) from operating his ships between the points for which Ogden (P) had received an exclusive right to operate his own ships. The case was appealed to the Supreme Court. Ogden (P) claimed that the federal government did not have exclusive jurisdiction over commerce but that the states had retained power by which they could regulate commerce within their own states and that the exclusive right to operate his ships only concerned intrastate commerce. Gibbons (D) contended that Congress had exclusive power to regulate interstate commerce and that New York had attempted to regulate interstate commerce by granting the exclusive right and enforcing it with the injunction.

ISSUE: If a state law conflicts with a congressional act regulating commerce, is the congressional act controlling?

HOLDING AND DECISION: (Marshall, C.J.) Yes. If a state law conflicts with a congressional act regulating commerce, the congressional act is controlling. Congress has the power to regulate navigation within the limits of every state and, therefore, the regulations that Congress passed controlling navigation within the boundaries of New York were valid. Ogden (P) argued that the states through the Tenth Amendment have the power to regulate commerce with foreign nations and among the states because the power that the states gave up to Congress to regulate commerce wasn't absolute and the residue of that power remained with the states. But Congress was given all the power to regulate interstate commerce, although it is possible for the states to pass regulations that may affect some activity associated with interstate commerce. In that case, states must base such regulations on some other source of power than the commerce power (such as the police power of the state). Regardless of the source of the state power, anytime a state regulation conflicts with a federal regulation, the state regulation must yield to the federal law. Since in this case the law of New York conflicted with a federal regulation dealing with interstate commerce, the New York law is not valid. Accordingly, the Court dismissed Ogden's (P) suit to obtain an injunction against Gibbons (D).

ANALYSIS

The federal commerce power is concurrent with state power over commerce within the state. Hence, the Court has been asked many times to define the line between federal and state power to regulate commerce. During the early history of the United States, the court was not often called upon to determine the scope of federal power under the Commerce Clause. Instead, the early cases generally involved some state action that was claimed to discriminate against or burden interstate commerce. Hence, the Commerce Clause operated as a restraint upon state powers. Most of these cases did not involve any exercise of the commerce power by Congress at all. Large-scale regulatory action by Congress began with the Interstate Commerce Act in 1887 and the Sherman Antitrust Act in 1890. Challenges to these statutes initiated the major modern confrontations between the Court and congressional authority regarding commerce.

Quicknotes

INJUNCTION A court order requiring a person to do, or prohibiting that person from doing, a specific act.

RESIDUUM The leftover balance; surplus or residue.

Hammer v. Dagenhart (The Child Labor Case)

U.S. Attorney General (D) v. Parent (P)

247 U.S. 251 (1918).

NATURE OF CASE: Appeal from a decree enjoining enforcement of the Child Labor Act.

FACT SUMMARY: Congress passed a law prohibiting the shipment in interstate commerce of any products of any mills, mines, or factories that employed children.

🏛 RULE OF LAW
The making of goods and the mining of coal are not commerce, nor does the fact that these things are to be afterwards shipped or used in interstate commerce make their production a part of such commerce.

FACTS: A congressional act prohibited the shipment in interstate commerce of the product of any mine or quarry that employed children under the age of 16. It prohibited the shipment in such commerce of the product of any mill, cannery, workshop, or factory that employed children under the age of 14 or employed children between the ages of 14 and 16 for more than eight hours a day or more than six days a week or before 6 a.m. or after 7 p.m. Dagenhart (P) brought this action on behalf of his two minor children after being informed by the company where they worked of their impending discharge on the effective date of the Act. Hammer (D), the U.S. Attorney General, and the company that had employed Dagenhart's (P) children were named as defendants.

ISSUE: Can Congress, under its commerce power, pass a law prohibiting the transportation in interstate commerce of products of companies that employed children as laborers in violation of the terms of the law?

HOLDING AND DECISION: (Day, J.) No. It is argued that the power of Congress to regulate commerce includes the power to prohibit the transportation of ordinary products in commerce. However, in cases such as *The Lottery Case*, 188 U.S. 321 (1903), the power to prohibit the carrying of lottery tickets is to those particular objects the same as the exertion of the power to regulate. In those cases, the use of interstate commerce was necessary to the accomplishment of harmful results. Regulation over commerce could only be accomplished by prohibiting the use of interstate commerce to affect the evil intended. Here, the thing intended to be accomplished by this Act is the denial of interstate commerce facilities to those employing children within the prohibited ages. The goods shipped are of themselves harmless. The production of articles intended for interstate commerce is a matter of local regulation. The making of goods and the mining of coal are not commerce,

nor does the fact that these things are to be afterwards shipped or used in interstate commerce make their production a part thereof. It is also argued that congressional regulation is necessary because of the unfair advantage possessed by manufacturers in states that have less stringent child labor laws. However, Congress has no power to require states to exercise their police powers to prevent possible unfair competition. The Act is unconstitutional, and the decree enjoining its enforcement is affirmed.

DISSENT: (Holmes, J.) *The Lottery Case* and others following it establish that a law is not beyond Congress's commerce power merely because it prohibits certain transportation. There is no legal distinction between the evils sought to be controlled in those cases and the evil of premature and excessive child labor. The Court has no right to substitute its judgment of which evils may be controlled.

▶ ANALYSIS

After the *Hammer* decision, Congress sought to regulate child labor through the taxing power; that law was invalidated in *Bailey v. Drexel Furnishing Co.*, 259 U.S. 20 (1922). Subsequently, Congress submitted a proposed constitutional amendment to the states that authorized a national child labor law. The amendment has not been ratified, but the need for it has largely disappeared in view of *U.S. v. Darby*, 312 U.S. 100 (1941), which overruled *Hammer*.

◼▤◼

Quicknotes

COMMERCE POWER The power delegated to Congress by the Constitution to regulate interstate commerce.

◼▤◼

Wickard v. Filburn

Department of Agriculture (P) v. Farmer (D)

317 U.S. 111 (1942).

NATURE OF CASE: Action to enjoin enforcement of penalty provisions of the Agricultural Adjustment Act.

FACT SUMMARY: Filburn (D) was ordered to pay a penalty imposed by the Agriculture Adjustment Act for producing wheat in excess of his assigned quota. He argued that the federal regulations could not be constitutionally applied to his crops because part of his crop was intended for his own consumption, not for interstate commerce.

> **RULE OF LAW**
> Farm production that is intended for consumption on the farm is subject to Congress's commerce power, since it may have a substantial economic effect on interstate commerce.

FACTS: The purpose of the Agriculture Adjustment Act ("the Act") was to control the volume of wheat moving in interstate commerce to avoid surpluses and shortages that would result in abnormally high or low prices and thereby obstruct commerce. Under the Act, the Secretary of Agriculture would set a national acreage allotment for wheat production, which would be divided into allotments for individual farms. Filburn (D) was the owner and operator of a small farm. In the past he had grown a small amount of wheat of which he sold part, fed part to poultry and livestock (some of the livestock were later sold), used part in making flour for home consumption, and kept the rest for seeding the next year. In 1940, his wheat production exceeded the maximum he was allowed under the Act and he was assessed a penalty for the excess. Filburn (D) refused to pay on the ground the Act was unconstitutional in that it attempted to regulate purely local production and consumption, which at most, had an indirect effect on interstate commerce. The Government (P) argued the Act regulated not production and consumption, but only marketing (which was defined in the Act to include the feeding of the wheat to livestock that was later sold), and even if interpreted to include production and consumption, it was a legitimate exercise of the Commerce Clause and the Necessary and Proper Clause.

ISSUE: Does Congress, under the Commerce Clause, have the power to regulate the production of wheat that is grown for home consumption purposes rather than for sale in interstate commerce?

HOLDING AND DECISION: (Jackson, J.) Yes. Farm production that is intended for consumption on the farm is subject to Congress's commerce power, since it may have a substantial economic effect on interstate commerce.

A local activity, such as production, may be reached under the Commerce Clause if it exerts a substantial economic effect on interstate commerce. The Agriculture Adjustment Act was enacted because of the problems of the wheat market: there had been a decrease in export in recent years, causing surpluses that in turn caused congestion in the market and lower prices. It has been repeatedly held that the commerce power of Congress includes the power to regulate prices and practices affecting prices. Wheat destined for home consumption has an effect on the interstate price of wheat and is, therefore, subject to regulation. As the market price of wheat climbs, farmers will sell more of their crop that was intended for home consumption on the market causing a decrease in prices. Even if the wheat is never sold, there still is a substantial effect on interstate commerce because it reduces demand for wheat; that wheat which Filburn (D) produces for his own use means he will buy less wheat on the market. Although the actual effect of Filburn's (D) overproduction will be small, the combination of all such producers does cause a substantial effect on commerce. Reversed.

▶ **ANALYSIS**

Wickard is yet another application of the "affectation doctrine." The Court focuses not on the nature of the regulated activity (e.g., whether it is local) but on the final economic effect of that activity. Here, although the effect of Filburn's (D) excess wheat production was insignificant on the national market, there still was some effect, at least in theory, so regulation was allowed. The Court in *Wickard* expressly rejected the old formulas for determining the extent of the commerce power such as direct/indirect and production/commerce.

Quicknotes

LOCAL ACTIVITY An activity such as mining or manufacturing that has only an indirect effect in interstate commerce because it can be conducted entirely within the boundaries of the state.

NECESSARY AND PROPER CLAUSE, ART. I, § 8 OF THE CONSTITUTION Enables Congress to make all laws that may be "necessary and proper" to execute its other, enumerated powers.

NLRB v. Jones & Laughlin Steel Corp.

Labor board (P) v. Steel company (D)

301 U.S. 1 (1937).

NATURE OF CASE: Action alleging unfair labor practice under the National Labor Relations Act.

FACT SUMMARY: Jones & Laughlin Steel Corp. (Jones & Laughlin) (D), a manufacturing company with subsidiaries in several states and nationwide sales, was charged with an unfair labor practice under the National Labor Relations Act ("the Act"). In defense, Jones & Laughlin (D) claimed that the Act was an unconstitutional attempt to regulate intrastate production.

🏛 RULE OF LAW
Under the Commerce Clause, Congress has the power to regulate any activity, even intrastate production, if the activity has an appreciable effect, either direct or indirect, on interstate commerce.

FACTS: Pursuant to a complaint filed by a labor union, the National Labor Relations Board (NLRB or "the Board") (P) found that Jones & Laughlin Steel Corp. (Jones & Laughlin) (D) had engaged in "unfair labor practices." The Board (P) issued a cease and desist order to Jones & Laughlin (D) to stop using discriminatory and coercive practices to prevent union organization at two steel plants in and around Pittsburgh. The company refused to comply and the Board (P) went to court for judicial enforcement of its order under the authority of the National Labor Relations Act of 1935 ("the Act"). Jones and Laughlin (D) contended that the order was an unconstitutional exercise of the Board's (P) authority since the plants were not engaged in interstate commerce, being totally manufacturing facilities. The court of appeals upheld the company's position and refused enforcement of the order on the ground the order "lay beyond the range of federal power."

ISSUE: Does Congress have the power to regulate any activity, even intrastate production, under the Commerce Clause if the activity has an appreciable effect, either directly or indirectly, on interstate commerce?

HOLDING AND DECISION: (Hughes, C.J.) Yes. Under the Commerce Clause, Congress has the power to regulate any activity, even intrastate production, if the activity has an appreciable effect, either direct or indirect, on interstate commerce. The Board (P) ordering Jones & Laughlin (D) to cease interfering with its employees' rights of self-organization and collective bargaining is an exercise of the congressional power to regulate interstate commerce. The definitions in the National Labor Relations Act restrict the Board's (P) actions to protecting interstate commerce in the constitutional sense, and the Board (P) is given the power to determine if the practice in question affects com-

merce in such a way as to be subject to federal control. Congress has the power to protect interstate commerce by all appropriate types of legislation, and the controlling question is the effect on interstate commerce, not the source of the interference. Although such legislation may result in the regulation of acts that are intrastate in character, Congress still has the power to regulate if the intrastate acts bear such a close and substantial relation to interstate commerce that control is appropriate for the protection of commerce. Congress is forbidden only from regulating acts that have a remote and indirect effect on interstate commerce. Here, even though the application of the National Labor Relations Act results in the regulation of labor practices at Jones & Laughlin's (D) manufacturing plants, the circumstances indicate the required substantial effect on interstate commerce. If production were interrupted at one of the plants due to a labor dispute, the extensive nationwide operations of Jones & Laughlin (D) indicate there would necessarily be an immediate effect on interstate commerce. Therefore, the National Labor Relations Act as applied to the facts of this case is a proper exercise of Congress's power to regulate interstate commerce. Reversed.

▶ ANALYSIS

With this case the Supreme Court retreated from its strict geographical definition of interstate commerce and the direct/indirect approach that it used in *A.L.A. Schechter Poultry Corp. v. United States*, 295 U.S. 495 (1935), and *Carter v. Carter Coal Co.*, 298 U.S. 238 (1936). *Jones & Laughlin* states that under the Commerce Clause Congress has the power to regulate any activity that has a significant effect on interstate commerce, regardless of whether that effect is direct or indirect. This new concept is often called the "affectation doctrine." Although the court cited prior cases in its opinion and said it was not creating new law, *Jones & Laughlin* is, in effect, a reversal of the *Schechter* line of cases. The Court now bases its opinions on a combination of the Commerce Clause and the Necessary and Proper Clause—power to regulate interstate commerce extends to control over intrastate activities when necessary and appropriate to make regulation of interstate commerce effective.

■=■

Continued on next page.

Quicknotes

COLLECTIVE BARGAINING Negotiations between an employer and employee that are mediated by a specified third party.

COMMERCE CLAUSE Article 1, section 8, clause 3 of the United States Constitution, granting Congress the power to regulate commerce with foreign countries and between the states.

NATIONAL LABOR RELATIONS ACT Guarantees employees the right to engage in collective bargaining and regulates labor unions.

United States v. Lopez

Federal government (P) v. Handgun possessor (D)

514 U.S. 549 (1995).

NATURE OF CASE: Certiorari from reversal of conviction for violation of the Gun-Free School Zones Act.

FACT SUMMARY: Lopez (D) was arrested for carrying a handgun in school in violation of state and federal law.

🏛 RULE OF LAW
Congress has the authority to regulate through its commerce power only those activities that have a substantial effect upon interstate commerce.

FACTS: Lopez (D) was a twelfth-grade student at Edison High School in San Antonio, Texas. He arrived at school with a .38 caliber handgun and five bullets. He was arrested and charged under Texas law for firearm possession on school premises. State charges were dropped after federal agents charged Lopez (D) with violating the Gun-Free School Zones Act of 1990 ("the Act"). The district court convicted Lopez (D). The Fifth Circuit Court of Appeals reversed because it held that the Act was beyond the power of Congress under the Commerce Clause.

ISSUE: Does the Gun-Free School Zones Act exceed the powers of Congress under the Commerce Clause?

HOLDING AND DECISION: (Rehnquist, C.J.) Yes. Congress has the authority to regulate through its commerce power only those activities that have a substantial effect upon interstate commerce. The Constitution creates a federal government of enumerated powers that are listed in Article 1, § 8. That power expanded dramatically under later court decisions but has always retained some outer limits. There are three broad categories of activity that Congress may regulate under its commerce power: (1) Congress may regulate the use of the channels of interstate commerce; (2) Congress may regulate and protect the instrumentalities of interstate commerce even if the threat is only from intrastate activities; and (3) Congress may regulate those activities having a substantial relation to interstate commerce. The activities addressed by the Gun-Free School Zones Act definitely do not fall into either of the first two categories. Moreover, there is nothing in the statute itself or in its legislative history that expresses congressional findings regarding the effects upon interstate commerce of gun possession in a school zone. It would be imprudent to convert congressional authority under the Commerce Clause into a general police power of the sort retained by the states. Affirmed.

CONCURRENCE: (Kennedy, J.) There are two lessons to be learned from reviewing prior decisions about the Commerce Clause. The first is that there is imprecision of

content-based boundaries involved, such as distinction between "commerce" and "manufacture." The second is that there is an immense stake in the stability of the Commerce Clause jurisprudence. Stare decisis counsels not to call into question the essential principles of Commerce Clause analysis. That does not mean, however, that courts lack the authority and responsibility to review congressional attempts to alter the federal balance. Therefore, the political branches must not forget their sworn obligation to preserve and protect the Constitution. The Gun-Free School Zones Act upsets the federal balance and is an unconstitutional assertion of the commerce power.

CONCURRENCE: (Thomas, J.) The power that we have accorded to Congress through the Commerce Clause has swallowed Article I, § 8. The "substantial effects" test has eviscerated any notion of federalism. Without boundaries that limit use of the Commerce Clause to truly commercial activity, we give the federal government a blank check to regulate anything under the guise of the Commerce Clause.

DISSENT: (Stevens, J.) Guns are articles of commerce and can be used to restrain commerce. The national interest justifies prohibiting the possession of guns by school-age children.

DISSENT: (Souter, J.) The Court should only look into whether the legislative judgment is within the realm of reason. Congress should have plenary power to legislate under the Commerce Clause as long as the law passes the rational basis test.

DISSENT: (Breyer, J.) Violence in the schools interferes with the quality of education. Education is inextricably tied to the economy. Therefore, Congress could have rationally concluded that the possession of guns in school zones is related to interstate commerce. Furthermore, the majority decision contradicts well-settled precedent that allows Congress to regulate non-commercial activity that affects interstate commerce.

▶ ANALYSIS

The *Lopez* decision generated some discussion about whether there was going to be a serious modification of the "1937 Revolution" and therefore a major restriction on the powers of Congress through the Commerce Clause. Immediately after the *Lopez* decision came down, the Supreme Court decided *United States v. Robertson*, 514 U.S. 669 (1995), a per curiam reversal of the Ninth Circuit's

Continued on next page.

reversal of a RICO (Racketeer Influenced and Corrupt Organizations Act) conviction because the defendant's investment in an Alaskan gold mine may not have been engaged in or affecting interstate commerce. The Supreme Court noted that the defendant purchased $100,000 of equipment and supplies, some of which were purchased in California. Similarly, the defendant also sought workers from out of state and took some of the profits out of state.

Quicknotes

CERTIORARI A discretionary writ issued by a superior court to an inferior court in order to review the lower court's decisions; the Supreme Court's writ ordering such review.

STARE DECISIS Doctrine whereby courts follow legal precedent unless there is good cause for departure.

National Federation of Independent Business v. Sebelius

Business group (P) v. Government official (D)

567 U.S. 519 (2012).

NATURE OF CASE: Appeal from judgment in action challenging the constitutionality of the "individual mandate" provision of the 2010 Patient Protection and Affordable Care Act. [The procedural posture of the case is not presented in the casebook extract.]

FACT SUMMARY: A coalition of plaintiffs (P) challenged the constitutionality of the "individual mandate" provision of the 2010 Patient Protection and Affordable Care Act (Act). The Government (D) contended that the individual mandate was a valid exercise of Congress's authority under the Commerce Clause and the Necessary and Proper Clause.

RULE OF LAW

(1) The "individual mandate" provision of the Patient Protection and Affordable Care Act, which requires individuals to purchase health-care insurance under certain circumstances, is not a valid exercise of Congress's power under the Commerce Clause.

(2) The "individual mandate" provision of the Patient Protection and Affordable Care Act, which requires individuals to purchase health-care insurance under certain circumstances, is not a valid exercise of Congress's power under the Necessary and Proper Clause.

FACTS: In 2010, Congress enacted the Patient Protection and Affordable Care Act ("the Act") to increase the number of Americans covered by health insurance and decrease the cost of health care. A key provision of the Act is the individual mandate, which requires most Americans to maintain "minimum essential" health-insurance coverage. For individuals who are not exempt, and who do not receive health insurance through an employer or government program, the means of satisfying the requirement is to purchase insurance from a private company. Those who do not comply with the mandate must make a "shared responsibility payment" to the federal government based on income and subject to a statutory cap. A coalition of plaintiffs (P) challenged the individual mandate as unconstitutional. The Government (D) contended the individual mandate was a valid exercise of Congress's authority under the Commerce Clause and the Necessary and Proper Clause. The Government (D) asserted the health-care market is characterized by a significant cost-shifting problem. This problem arises because, according to the Government (D), everyone will eventually need health care at a time and to an extent they cannot predict, but if they do not have insurance, they often will not be able to pay for it. Because

state and federal laws nonetheless require hospitals to provide a certain degree of care to individuals without regard to their ability to pay, hospitals end up receiving compensation for only a portion of the services they provide. To recoup the losses, hospitals pass on the cost to insurers through higher rates, and insurers, in turn, pass on the cost to policyholders in the form of higher premiums. Congress estimated that the cost of uncompensated care raises family health-insurance premiums, on average, by over $1,000 per year. To address this problem, at least in part, Congress included "guaranteed-issue" and "community-rating" provisions in the Act. These provisions together prohibit insurance companies from denying coverage to those with preexisting conditions or charging unhealthy individuals higher premiums than healthy individuals. The guaranteed-issue and community-rating reforms do not, however, address the issue of healthy individuals who choose not to purchase insurance to cover potential health-care needs. In fact, the reforms sharply exacerbate that problem, by providing an incentive for individuals to delay purchasing health insurance until they become sick, relying on the promise of guaranteed and affordable coverage. The reforms also threaten to impose massive new costs on insurers, who are required to accept unhealthy individuals but prohibited from charging them rates necessary to pay for their coverage. This will lead insurers to significantly increase premiums on everyone. The individual mandate was Congress's solution to these problems. By requiring that individuals purchase health insurance, the mandate prevents cost-shifting by those who would otherwise go without it. In addition, the mandate forces into the insurance risk pool more healthy individuals, whose premiums on average will be higher than their health care expenses. This allows insurers to subsidize the costs of covering the unhealthy individuals the reforms require them to accept. The Government (D) contended the individual mandate is within Congress's power because the failure to purchase insurance "has a substantial and deleterious effect on interstate commerce" by creating the cost-shifting problem. The Government (D) also contended the mandate is an "integral part of a comprehensive scheme of economic regulation"—the guaranteed-issue and community-rating insurance reforms—so Congress has the authority to enact the individual mandate under the Necessary and Proper Clause. The Supreme Court granted certiorari. [The procedural posture of the case is not presented in the casebook extract.]

Continued on next page.

ISSUE:

(1) Is the "individual mandate" provision of the Patient Protection and Affordable Care Act, which requires individuals to purchase health-care insurance under certain circumstances, a valid exercise of Congress's power under the Commerce Clause?

(2) Is the "individual mandate" provision of the Patient Protection and Affordable Care Act, which requires individuals to purchase health-care insurance under certain circumstances, a valid exercise of Congress's power under the Necessary and Proper Clause?

HOLDING AND DECISION: (Roberts, C.J.)

(1) No. The "individual mandate" provision of the Patient Protection and Affordable Care Act ("the Act"), which requires individuals to purchase health-care insurance under certain circumstances, is not a valid exercise of Congress's power under the Commerce Clause. Congress has never attempted to rely on the commerce power to compel individuals not engaged in commerce to purchase an unwanted product—and with good reason. Congress is empowered to regulate commerce, which presupposes the existence of commercial activity to be regulated. If the power to "regulate" something included the power to create it, many of the provisions in the Constitution would be superfluous. The Constitution's language supports such a conclusion, as does the Court's precedent, which uniformly describes the commerce power as reaching "activity." The individual mandate, however, does not regulate existing commercial activity. It instead compels individuals to become active in commerce by purchasing a product, on the ground their failure to do so affects interstate commerce. Construing the Commerce Clause to permit Congress to regulate individuals precisely because they are doing nothing would open a new and potentially vast domain to congressional authority, as the Government's (D) logic would justify a mandatory purchase to solve almost any problem. People, for reasons of their own, often fail to do things that would be good for them or good for society. Those failures—joined with the similar failures of others—can readily have a substantial effect on interstate commerce. Under the Government's (D) logic, that authorizes Congress to use its commerce power to compel citizens to act as the Government (D) would have them act. Congress already possesses expansive power to regulate what people do. Upholding the Act under the Commerce Clause would give Congress the same license to regulate what people do not do. The Framers knew the difference between doing something and doing nothing. They gave Congress the power to regulate commerce, not to compel it. Ignoring that distinction would undermine the principle the federal government is a government of limited and enumerated powers. Contrary to the Government's (D) contention, the uninsured to be affected by the individual mandate are not "active in the market for health care." In fact, the individual mandate's regulation of the uninsured as a class is particularly divorced from any link to existing commercial activity. The mandate primarily affects healthy, often young adults who are less likely to need significant health care and have other priorities for spending their money. It is precisely because these individuals, as an actuarial class, incur relatively low health-care costs that the mandate helps counter the effect of forcing insurance companies to cover others who impose greater costs than their premiums are allowed to reflect. If the individual mandate is targeted at a class, it is a class whose commercial inactivity rather than activity is its defining feature. The Commerce Clause is not a general license to regulate an individual from cradle to grave, simply because he will predictably engage in particular transactions. Any police power to regulate individuals as such, as opposed to their activities, remains vested in the states. The individual mandate thus cannot be sustained under Congress's power to "regulate Commerce."

(2) No. The "individual mandate" provision of the Patient Protection and Affordable Care Act ("the Act"), which requires individuals to purchase health-care insurance under certain circumstances, is not a valid exercise of Congress's power under the Necessary and Proper Clause. Each of this Court's prior cases upholding laws under that Clause involved exercises of authority derivative of, and in service to, a granted power. The individual mandate, by contrast, vests Congress with the extraordinary ability to create the necessary predicate to the exercise of an enumerated power and draw within its regulatory scope those who would otherwise be outside of it. This is in no way an authority that is "narrow in scope," or "incidental" to the exercise of the commerce power, as required by precedent. Rather, the Government's (D) conception of the Necessary and Proper Clause would work a substantial expansion of federal authority. No longer would Congress be limited to regulating under the Commerce Clause those who by some preexisting activity bring themselves within the sphere of federal regulation. Instead, Congress could reach beyond the natural limit of its authority and draw within its regulatory scope those who otherwise would be outside of it. Thus, even if the individual mandate is "necessary" to the Act's other reforms, such an expansion of federal power is not a "proper" means for making those reforms effective. Accordingly, the individual mandate cannot be upheld as a "necessary and proper" component of the insurance reforms. Affirmed in part and reversed in part. [The procedural posture of the case is not presented in the casebook extract.]

Continued on next page.

CONCURRENCE AND DISSENT: (Ginsburg, J.) Beyond question, Congress could have provided a single-payer federal health-care scheme similar to Social Security, whereby the federal government would be the only health-care insurer. However, it chose to preserve a central role for private insurers and state governments. According to the majority opinion on this issue, authored by the Chief Justice, the Commerce Clause does not permit that preservation. This rigid reading of the Clause makes scant sense and is stunningly retrogressive. The problem the Act seeks to remedy with the individual mandate is that the uninsured heavily burden the national health-care market. Those with health insurance subsidize the medical care of those without it, or, in the words of economists, the uninsured "free ride" on those who pay for health insurance. States cannot resolve the problem of the uninsured on their own. A state offering universal health care would place itself in a position of economic disadvantage as compared with neighbors or competitors, because it would have to raise taxes, private health-insurance companies would have to increase premiums, and higher taxes and increased insurance costs would, in turn, encourage businesses and healthy individuals to leave the state. Because the states cannot resolve this problem on their own, Congress stepped in with the Act to provide a national solution. However, Congress comprehended guaranteed-issue and community-rating laws alone will not work. When insurance companies are required to insure the sick at affordable prices, individuals can wait until they become ill to buy insurance. The result is those in need of immediate medical care—i.e., those who cost insurers the most—become the insurance companies' main customers. This "adverse selection" problem leaves insurers with two choices: They can either raise premiums dramatically to cover their ever-increasing costs or they can exit the market. This, in fact, is what happened in those states that implemented guaranteed-issue and community-rating laws without requiring universal acquisition of insurance coverage, and the results were disastrous. In the one state—Massachusetts—that succeeded, almost all residents were required to obtain a minimum level of health insurance. Congress passed the minimum coverage provision as a key component of the Act to address an economic and social problem that has plagued the country for decades: the large number of U.S. residents who are unable or unwilling to obtain health insurance. Congress had the prerogative to make this policy decision, which passes muster under the Commerce Clause and the Necessary and Proper Clause. As to the Commerce Clause, precedent holds Congress's authority under the Commerce Clause is dependent upon "practical" considerations, including "actual experience," and Congress is afforded the leeway "to undertake to solve national problems directly and realistically." When appraising Congress's social and economic legislation, the Court asks only (1) whether Congress had a "rational basis" for concluding the regulated activity substantially affects interstate commerce, and (2) whether there is a "reasonable connec-

tion between the regulatory means selected and the asserted ends." In answering these questions, it is presumed the statute under review is constitutional, and the Court may strike it down only on a "plain showing" Congress acted irrationally. Here, Congress had a rational basis for concluding the uninsured, as a class, substantially affect interstate commerce. The individual mandate, furthermore, bears a "reasonable connection" to Congress's goal of protecting the health-care market from the disruption caused by individuals who fail to obtain insurance. By requiring those who do not carry insurance to pay a toll, the minimum coverage provision gives individuals a strong incentive to insure. This incentive, Congress had good reason to believe, would reduce the number of uninsured and, correspondingly, mitigate the adverse impact the uninsured have on the national health-care market. Further, Congress also acted reasonably in requiring uninsured individuals, whether sick or healthy, either to obtain insurance or to pay the specified penalty. Because it is not disputed all U.S. residents participate in the market for health services over the course of their lives, contrary to the Chief Justice's position, Congress is not compelling individuals not engaged in commerce to purchase an unwanted product, even assuming the Chief Justice is correct that it is beyond Congress's power to compel individuals that way. Also contrary to the Chief Justice's position, the facts show an uninsured's consumption of health care is thus quite proximate: It is virtually certain to occur in the next five years and more likely than not to occur this year. It is Congress's role, not the Court's, to delineate the boundaries of the market Congress seeks to regulate. The Chief Justice defines the health-care market as including only those transactions that will occur either in the next instant or within some (unspecified) proximity to the next instant. However, Congress could reasonably have viewed the market from a long-term perspective, encompassing all transactions virtually certain to occur over the next decade, not just those occurring here and now. Moreover, precedent directs that Congress may dictate the conduct of an individual today because of prophesied future activity. Congress's actions in this case are rational, where the future activity (the consumption of medical care) is certain to occur, the sole uncertainty being the time the activity will take place. Thus, upholding the individual mandate on the ground that all are participants or will be participants in the health-care market does not imply that Congress may use its commerce power to mandate individuals to buy products and services other than the ones they do or will buy at some point. Further, it is inaccurate to say, as does the Chief Justice, that the individual mandate compels individuals to purchase an unwanted product, given that virtually everyone will at some point or another seek medical care. In requiring individuals to obtain health insurance, Congress is therefore not mandating the

Continued on next page.

purchase of a discrete, unwanted product. Rather, Congress is merely defining the terms on which individuals pay for an interstate good they consume. Additionally, contrary to the Chief Justice's view, the individual mandate is not an effort to have the young and healthy subsidize the health care of the unhealthy or infirm. Under the current health-care system, healthy persons who lack insurance receive a benefit for which they do not pay: They are assured that, if they need it, emergency medical care will be available, although they cannot afford it. Those who have insurance bear the cost of this guarantee. By requiring the healthy uninsured to obtain insurance or pay a penalty structured as a tax, the minimum coverage provision ends the free ride these individuals currently enjoy. Viewed over a life-span, the costs and benefits may even out, and everyone will be covered for catastrophic loss, even if not everyone will need to use that coverage; that is the nature of insurance. The Constitution's language and precedent also do not support the Chief Justice's interpretation that by enacting the individual mandate, Congress is not regulating something already in existence, but rather is bringing the subject of the regulation into existence. Requiring individuals to obtain insurance unquestionably regulates the interstate health-insurance and health-care markets, both in existence well before the Act's enactment. Thus, the "something to be regulated" was surely there when Congress created the minimum coverage provision. A long line of precedent also rejects the Chief Justice's formalistic distinction between activity and inactivity as a measure of the subject of Congress's commerce power. The fear the commerce power would be unlimited unless limited to regulating active participants in a commercial market is unfounded. Given the unique attributes of the health-care market, upholding the individual mandate would not give Congress carte blanche to enact any and all purchase mandates. Nor would the commerce power be unbridled, absent an "activity" limitation, as Congress would remain unable to regulate noneconomic conduct that has only an attenuated effect on interstate commerce and is tradition-ally left to state law. The choice to self-insure, however, does not have an attenuated effect on commerce, but is an economic act with the requisite connection to interstate commerce. Also, the democratic process serves as another check on Congress's purchase-mandating behavior. Finally, merely because the individual mandate is a novelty is not a reason to override it. To the contrary, and as the Court has recognized for decades, Congress must be permitted to adapt to the changing "economic and financial realities." The individual mandate is also a valid exercise of Congress's commerce power under the Necessary and Proper Clause. That Clause empowers Congress to enact laws in effectuation of its commerce power that are not within its authority to enact in isolation. It is undisputed the Congress has the power to eliminate the insurance industry's practice of charging higher prices or denying coverage to individuals with preexisting medical conditions. Without the individual mandate, however, this goal would be un-

dercut and would lead to an adverse-selection death-spiral in the health-insurance market. Therefore, the individual mandate is an essential part of a larger regulation of eco-nomic activity that may be upheld under the Necessary and Proper Clause. Additionally, it is spurious to suggest, as does the Chief Justice, that the individual mandate improp-erly intrudes on "essential attributes of state sovereignty." First, the Act does not operate in an area such as criminal law enforcement or education where states historically have been sovereign. Second, and more importantly, the mini-mum coverage provision, along with the Act's other provisions, addresses the very sort of interstate problem that made the commerce power essential in our federal system. Instead of intruding on state's rights, the Act is an attempt to solve a problem the states cannot solve separately, on their own; the Act serves the general welfare of the people of the United States while retaining a promi-nent role for the states.

DISSENT: (Scalia, J.) It is manifestly clear there are structural limitations on the commerce power and on what Congress can prescribe with respect to private conduct, and upon what it can impose upon the states. To say Congress's commerce power reaches inactivity would be to permit Congress to regulate virtually every aspect of human activ-ity and inactivity. If the individual mandate regulates anything it is the failure to maintain minimum essential coverage. That failure is abstention from commerce, not commerce. One does not regulate commerce that does not exist by compelling its existence. The meaning of "regulate" at the time the Constitution was written was "[t]o adjust by rule, method or established mode." It can mean to direct the manner of something but it has never been understood to mean to direct that something come into being. When Congress provides citizens must buy an insurance contract, it goes beyond "adjust[ing] by rule or method," or "direct[ing] according to rule;" it directs the creation of commerce. The fact the proposed regulations will impose great costs on the health-insurance industry does not justi-fy pressing into service healthy individuals who could be but are not customers of the relevant industry, to offset the undesirable consequences of the regulation. Congress's de-sire to force these individuals to purchase insurance is motivated by the fact they are further removed from the market than unhealthy individuals with preexisting condi-tions, because they are less likely to need extensive care in the near future. If Congress can reach out and command even those furthest removed from an interstate market to participate in the market, then the Commerce Clause becomes a font of unlimited power. Precedent makes clear the Commerce Clause, even when supplemented by the Necessary and Proper Clause, is not carte blanche for doing whatever will help achieve the ends Congress seeks by the regulation of commerce. The precedent on which the Government (D) relies to support the individual

Continued on next page.

mandate is also distinguishable, as that precedent did not represent the expansion of the federal power to direct into a broad new field. The mandating of economic activity does, and since it is a field so limitless that it converts the Commerce Clause into a general authority to direct the economy, that mandating is inconsistent with the letter and spirit of the Constitution. Moreover, in that precedent, the prohibition was the only practicable way of achieving the desired outcome. Here, in contrast, there are many ways other than the individual mandate by which the regulatory scheme's goals of reducing insurance premiums and ensuring the profitability of insurers could be achieved. For example, those who did not purchase insurance could be subjected to a surcharge when they do enter the health-insurance system, or they could be denied a full income tax credit given to those who do purchase the insurance. Also, the Government's (D) argument the individual mandate regulates activities having a substantial relation to interstate commerce must be rejected. The Government (D) argues the provision directs the manner in which individuals purchase health-care services and related goods, but the primary problem with this argument is it does not apply only to persons who purchase all, or most, or even any, of the health-care services or goods the mandated insurance covers. Those persons—generally healthy and young—are not participants in the health-care market the individual mandate purports to regulate. Because the decision to forgo participation in an interstate market is not itself commercial activity within Congress's power to regulate, the individual mandate cannot be justified by claiming it regulates such decisions because they have a substantial and deleterious effect on interstate commerce. If the Government (D) is permitted to regulate everyone who may at some point engage in commerce, there no longer will be any limits on the Government's (D) powers. Although Justice Ginsburg is correct in pointing out that Congress needs only a rational basis for concluding regulated activity substantially affects interstate commerce, she disregards the premise this test contains, which is that what is regulated is activity, not merely the failure to engage in commerce. If all inactivity affecting commerce is commerce, commerce is everything. The constitutional order is threatened by such an expansive reading of the commerce power, by which all private conduct (including failure to act) becomes subject to federal control, effectively destroying the Constitution's division of governmental powers. Contrary to Justice Ginsburg's treatment of the Constitution as an enumeration of problems Congress can address, the Constitution is not an enumeration of federally soluble problems, but federally available powers. Accordingly, the individual mandate is unconstitutional, and because it is not severable from the Act's other provisions, the Act in its entirety must be struck down.

DISSENT: (Thomas, J.) A "substantial effects" test under the Commerce Clause is inconsistent with the origi-

nal understanding of Congress's powers and with the Court's early Commerce Clause cases. The Court's continued use of that test has encouraged the Government (D) to persist in its view the Commerce Clause has virtually no limits. Here, the Government's (D) unprecedented claim that it may regulate not only economic activity but also inactivity that substantially affects interstate commerce is a case in point.

▶ *ANALYSIS*

The Court's former endeavors to impose categorical limits on the commerce power did not fare well. In several pre-New Deal cases, the Court attempted to cabin Congress's Commerce Clause authority by distinguishing "commerce" from activity once conceived to be noncommercial, notably, "production," "mining," and "manufacturing." The Court also sought to distinguish activities having a "direct" effect on interstate commerce, and for that reason, subject to federal regulation, from those having only an "indirect" effect, and therefore not amenable to federal control. These line-drawing exercises were untenable, and the Court long ago abandoned them. Accordingly, Justice Ginsburg opines the Chief Justice has failed to learn from history and instead "plows ahead" with his formalistic distinction between those who are "active in commerce," and those who are not. She also, therefore, warns hindering Congress's ability to address the health-care problem is shortsighted, and predicts that if history is any guide, the Court's constriction of the Commerce Clause will not endure.

■■■

Quicknotes

COMMERCE CLAUSE Article 1, section 8, clause 3 of the Constitution, granting Congress the power to regulate commerce with foreign countries and among the states.

NECESSARY AND PROPER CLAUSE, ART. I, § 8 OF THE CONSTITUTION Enables Congress to make all laws that may be "necessary and proper" to execute its other, enumerated powers.

■■■

City of Philadelphia v. New Jersey

Municipality (P) v. State (D)

437 U.S. 617 (1978).

NATURE OF CASE: Appeal of state court decision upholding state-imposed limitations on waste importation.

FACT SUMMARY: New Jersey (D) enacted a statute banning the importation of waste products for disposal.

RULE OF LAW

A state may not enact bans on articles of commerce absent legitimate public welfare concerns.

FACTS: The State of New Jersey (D) enacted a ban on the importation of refuse into the state for disposal. The law was couched in environmentalist terms. Philadelphia (P) and other entities interested in disposing in New Jersey (D) challenged the constitutionality of the law. The New Jersey Supreme Court upheld the measure, and Philadelphia (P) appealed.

ISSUE: May a state enact bans on articles of commerce absent legitimate public welfare concerns?

HOLDING AND DECISION: (Stewart, J.) No. A state may not enact bans on articles of commerce absent legitimate public welfare concerns. Only when there is something apart from the external status of an article giving the reason for the prohibition of importation may the prohibition be legitimate. When the focus is on the out-of-state character of the article, the measure is protectionist. Whether the article is desirable or undesirable is irrelevant. Here, the only distinction made is between in-state and out-of-state waste. The public health is an issue, but public health cannot be advanced in a way that unnecessarily burdens interstate commerce. While New Jersey (D) could attack this problem by regulating more closely all waste, it cannot do so by enacting protectionist measures. Reversed.

ANALYSIS

Generally speaking, health measures restricting interstate commerce fall into two categories. One is protectionism in health and safety clothing. This is illegitimate. The other is legitimate safety legislation incidentally affecting commerce, which are valid enactments. The law here was something different, a legitimate health measure that was accomplished by protectionist means.

Quicknotes

COMMERCE CLAUSE Article 1, section 8, clause 3 of the United States Constitution, granting Congress the power to regulate commerce with foreign countries and among the states.

C & A Carbone, Inc. v. Clarkstown

Recycling center (D) v. Town (P)

511 U.S. 383 (1994).

NATURE OF CASE: Review of municipal ordinance regulating solid waste disposal.

FACT SUMMARY: The Town of Clarkstown (P) mandated that all solid waste leaving the city be processed through a particular transfer station.

🏛 RULE OF LAW
Discrimination against interstate commerce in favor of local businesses is per se invalid unless the municipality can demonstrate that it has no other means to advance a legitimate local interest.

FACTS: The Town of Clarkstown ("the Town") (P) entered into an arrangement with a local contractor that the latter would build and operate a solid waste transfer station. In order to amortize the cost of the facility, the Town (P), by ordinance, mandated that all solid waste leaving the Town (P) be processed through that station. When C & A Carbone, Inc. (Carbone) (D), a recycling center in town, attempted to ship its nonrecyclable waste to another state in order to save money, the Town (P) sought an injunction to force Carbone (D) to comply with the ordinance. Carbone (D) challenged the ordinance as contrary to the Commerce Clause. The state courts rejected the challenge, and the U.S. Supreme Court granted review.

ISSUE: Is discrimination against interstate commerce per se invalid?

HOLDING AND DECISION: (Kennedy, J.) Yes. Discrimination against interstate commerce is per se invalid unless the municipality can demonstrate that it has no other means to advance a legitimate local interest. Any ordinance that deprives nonlocal businesses from access to local markets discriminates against interstate commerce and is invalid under the dormant Commerce Clause. With respect to waste, the commodity at issue is not the waste itself but rather the service of processing it and/or transporting it. When a city designates a particular commercial entity as the sole provider of such services, nonlocal providers of the service are effectively shut out. Local governments may not use their regulatory power to favor local businesses by prohibiting patronage of out-of-state competitors. Here, the Town (P) has shut out nonlocal solid waste operators, although it has a number of nondiscriminatory alternatives that would satisfy its environmental and fiscal concerns, and thus its ordinance is unconstitutional. Reversed and remanded.

CONCURRENCE: (O'Connor, J.) The proper analysis here is that of benefits versus burdens, not of actual discrimination.

DISSENT: (Souter, J.) The instant ordinance falls outside that class of tariff or protectionist measures the Commerce Clause has traditionally thought to bar states from enacting against each other. By subsuming the ordinance within the class of laws that have been struck down as facially discriminatory, the majority is here in fact greatly extending the Clause's dormant reach.

▶ ANALYSIS

The essential vice in discriminatory ordinances that mandate local processing is that they bar the import of the processing service. These laws hoard a local resource—be it shrimp, milk, or solid waste—for the benefit of local businesses that treat it. Clarkstown's (P) ordinance was even more egregiously protectionist than most such laws since it favored a single local proprietor.

Quicknotes

DORMANT COMMERCE CLAUSE The regulatory effect of the Commerce Clause on state activity affecting interstate commerce, where Congress itself has not acted to control the activity; a provision inferred from, but not expressly present in, the language of the Commerce Clause.

INTERSTATE COMMERCE Commercial dealings between two parties located in different states or located in one state and accomplished through a point in another state or a foreign country; commercial dealings transacted between two states.

West Lynn Creamery, Inc. v. Healy

Milk dealer (P) v. State (D)

512 U.S. 186 (1994).

NATURE OF CASE: Review of judicial rejection of legal challenge to agricultural assessment.

FACT SUMMARY: A law assessing a fee on all milk sold in Massachusetts (D), the funds of which were disbursed solely to local producers, was challenged as unconstitutional.

🏛 RULE OF LAW
An assessment scheme that levies a tax on all distribution of a good but disburses its assets only to local producers is unconstitutional.

FACTS: The legislature of the Commonwealth of Massachusetts (D), perceiving a need to protect local dairy producers, enacted an assessment system wherein a certain levy was placed upon all dairy products sold in Massachusetts, the proceeds of which were disbursed only to Massachusetts producers. The system was challenged by West Lynn Creamery (P), a milk dealer who purchased out-of-state milk, as unconstitutional. The state courts rejected the challenge, and the U.S. Supreme Court granted review.

ISSUE: Is an assessment scheme that levies on all distribution of a good but disburses its assets to local producers unconstitutional?

HOLDING AND DECISION: (Stevens, J.) Yes. An assessment scheme that levies on all distribution of a good but disburses its assets only to local producers of the distributed goods is unconstitutional. A state may not enact a tariff on out-of-state goods; to do so is a clear violation of the Commerce Clause. The system at issue here, although taking two steps to achieve its goal, is a de facto tariff. While all producers pay equally into the fund, the assets go only to local producers. This is, in effect, a tariff. The fact that Massachusetts (D) could validly enact either a local subsidy or a nondiscriminatory tax is irrelevant; coupled, the two measures constitute a tariff and cannot stand, as the assessment is clear discrimination against interstate commerce. Reversed.

CONCURRENCE: (Scalia, J.) The Court's opinion unnecessarily broadens the scope of the dormant Commerce Clause. Unless a law facially discriminates against interstate commerce or falls within a precedent of this Court, it should survive Commerce Clause scrutiny. The Massachusetts law should be invalidated because it is indistinguishable from an otherwise nondiscriminatory tax from which in-state members are exempted, a method of taxation that has been held unconstitutional by this Court.

DISSENT: (Rehnquist, C.J.) The Massachusetts law represents this sort of subsidy of a domestic industry that has heretofore been approved under the Commerce Clause.

▶ ANALYSIS

The Commerce Clause, in its dormant expression, operates on two levels. If a law directly discriminates against commerce from another state, it is per se invalid. If it only incidentally burdens interstate commerce, a court must look to the benefits of the law versus its burdens. The law at issue here was of the former type.

Quicknotes

COMMERCE CLAUSE Article 1, section 8, clause 3 of the United States Constitution, granting Congress the power to regulate commerce with foreign countries and between the states.

DORMANT COMMERCE CLAUSE The regulatory effect of the Commerce Clause on state activity affecting interstate commerce, where Congress itself has not acted to control the activity; a provision inferred from, but not expressly present in, the language of the Commerce Clause.

TARIFF Duty or tax imposed on articles imported into the United States.

Exxon Corp. v. Governor of Maryland

Petroleum producers (P) v. State (D)

437 U.S. 117 (1978).

NATURE OF CASE: Appeal of ruling upholding a petroleum retailing statute.

FACT SUMMARY: Maryland (D) enacted a statute prohibiting petroleum producers from operating at the retail level.

⚖ RULE OF LAW
A state may prohibit the retailing of petroleum products by producers.

FACTS: Maryland (D) enacted a statute prohibiting producers or refiners of gasoline from entering the retail market. The effect of this was to force producers to sell to independent distributors or leave the state. All gasoline sold in Maryland (D) was shipped in interstate commerce. Exxon Corp. (P) and other producers sought to have the statute declared a violation of the Commerce Clause. The lower courts upheld the law.

ISSUE: May a state prohibit the retailing of petroleum products by producers?

HOLDING AND DECISION: (Stevens, J.) Yes. A state may prohibit the retailing of petroleum products by producers. To do this is not protectionism, because out-of-state independent retailers are not prohibited from entering the market. The law in no way affects the interstate flow of petroleum products. The fact the burden of regulations falls on some companies that participate in interstate commerce does not make a law unconstitutional. It is only when the interstate market itself is burdened that a law comes under Commerce Clause scrutiny. This has not happened here. Affirmed.

DISSENT: (Blackmun, J.) Here, no facial inequality exists. The state's ban will preclude the major gasoline companies from enhancing brand recognition and consumer acceptance through retail outlets with company-controlled standards, thus inflicting significant hardship on Maryland's major brand gasoline companies, all of which are out-of-state firms. The protectionist discrimination employed by Maryland (D) is not justified by any legitimate state interest that cannot be vindicated by more evenhanded regulation.

▶ ANALYSIS

A side issue raised by *Exxon* was that due to the inherent interstate nature of the petroleum trade, the Commerce Clause by itself preempted the field of retail gas marketing. This only occurs when national uniformity is necessary, and the Court did not believe this to be the case here.

◼▬◼

Quicknotes

COMMERCE CLAUSE Article 1, section 8, clause 3 of the United States Constitution, granting Congress the power to regulate commerce with foreign countries and among the states.

◼▬◼

Kassel v. Consolidated Freightways Corp.

State (D) v. Common carrier (P)

450 U.S. 662 (1981).

NATURE OF CASE: Appeal from decision holding that an Iowa statute unconstitutionally burdens interstate commerce.

FACT SUMMARY: Consolidated Freightways Corp. (P) challenged the constitutionality of an Iowa statute that prohibited the use of certain large trucks within the state boundaries.

RULE OF LAW

A state safety regulation will be unconstitutional if its asserted safety purpose is outweighed by its degree of interference with interstate commerce.

FACTS: The State of Iowa (D) passed a statute restricting the length of vehicles that may use its highways. The state law sets a general length limit of 55 feet for most vehicles, and 60 feet for trucks pulling two trailers ("doubles"). Iowa (D) was the only state in the western or midwestern United States to outlaw the use of 65-foot doubles. Consolidated Freightways Corp. (P), one of the largest common carriers in the country, alleged that the Iowa statute unconstitutionally burdened interstate commerce. The district court and the court of appeals found the statute unconstitutional and Kassel (D), on behalf of the State, appealed.

ISSUE: Will a state safety regulation be held to be unconstitutional if its asserted safety purpose is outweighed by its degree of interference with interstate commerce?

HOLDING AND DECISION: (Powell, J.) Yes. A state safety regulation will be unconstitutional if its asserted safety purpose is outweighed by its degree of interference with interstate commerce. While bona fide state safety regulations are entitled to a strong presumption of validity, the asserted safety purpose must be weighed against the degree of interference with interstate commerce. Less deference will be given to the findings of state legislators where the local regulation has a disproportionate effect on out-of-state residents and businesses. Here, Iowa (D) failed to present any persuasive evidence that 65-foot doubles were less safe than 55-foot single trailers. Consolidated Freightways (P) demonstrated that Iowa's law substantially burdened interstate commerce by compelling trucking companies either to route 65-foot doubles around Iowa or use the smaller trucks allowed by the state statute. Thus, the Iowa statute was in violation of the Commerce Clause. Affirmed.

CONCURRENCE: (Brennan, J.) In ruling on the constitutionality of state safety regulations, the burdens imposed on commerce must be balanced against the regulatory purposes identified by the state legislators. Protectionist legislation is unconstitutional under the Commerce Clause, even if its purpose is to promote safety, rather than economic purposes.

DISSENT: (Rehnquist, J.) A sensitive consideration must be made when weighing the safety purposes of a statute against the burden on interstate commerce. A state safety regulation is invalid if its asserted safety justification is merely a pretext for discrimination against interstate commerce. The Iowa statute is a valid highway safety regulation and is entitled to the strongest presumption of validity.

ANALYSIS

Traditionally, states have been free to pass public safety regulations restricting the use of highways and railway facilities. However, state safety regulations have been struck down when only a marginal increase in safety causes a substantial burden on interstate commerce. This case simply follows this rationale.

Quicknotes

COMMERCE CLAUSE Article 1, section 8, clause 3 of the United States Constitution, granting Congress the power to regulate commerce with foreign countries and between the states.

DORMANT COMMERCE CLAUSE The regulatory effect of the Commerce Clause on state activity affecting interstate commerce, where Congress itself has not acted to control the activity; a provision inferred from, but not expressly present in, the language of the Commerce Clause.

Arizona v. United States

State (D) v. Federal government (P)

567 U.S. 387 (2012).

NATURE OF CASE: Appeal in action brought by the federal government to preempt a state's laws governing immigration. [The procedural posture of the case is not presented in the casebook extract.]

FACT SUMMARY: The United States (P) sought to enjoin, on preemption grounds, several provisions of Arizona's (D) statute, S.B. 1070, which, inter alia, made failure to comply with federal alien-registration requirements a state misdemeanor (§ 3), and made it a misdemeanor for an unauthorized alien to seek or engage in work in the state (§ 5(C)).

RULE OF LAW

A state law will be preempted by federal law where, even though the state law does not directly conflict with federal law, the state law complements, or is an obstacle to, the regulatory system chosen by Congress in a field completely occupied by Congress.

FACTS: In effort to address an "epidemic of crime, safety risks, serious property damage, and environmental problems" associated with the influx of illegal migration across private land near the Mexican border, Arizona (D) enacted S.B. 1070. One of the statute's provisions made failure to comply with federal alien-registration requirements a state misdemeanor (§ 3), and another made it a misdemeanor for an unauthorized alien to seek or engage in work in the state (§ 5(C)). The United States (P) brought suit to enjoin enforcement of these provisions, contending the provisions were preempted by federal immigration law. As part of its immigration laws, the United States (P) has enacted a comprehensive system for alien registration. In the Immigration Reform and Control Act (IRCA), the United States (P) enacted a comprehensive federal program regulating the employment of unauthorized aliens. However, IRCA, which makes it illegal for employers to knowingly hire, recruit, refer, or continue to employ unauthorized workers, does not impose criminal sanctions on illegal alien employees. Instead, aliens who accept unlawful employment are not eligible to have their status adjusted to that of a lawful permanent resident, and aliens also may be removed from the country for having engaged in unauthorized work. IRCA's express preemption provision, which in most instances bars states from imposing penalties on employers of unauthorized aliens, is silent about whether additional penalties may be imposed against the employees themselves. The U.S. Supreme Court granted certiorari. [The procedural posture of the case is not presented in the casebook extract.]

ISSUE: Will a state law be preempted by federal law where, even though the state law does not directly conflict with federal law, the state law complements, or is an obstacle to, the regulatory system chosen by Congress in a field completely occupied by Congress?

HOLDING AND DECISION: (Kennedy, J.) Yes. A state law will be preempted by federal law where, even though the state law does not directly conflict with federal law, the state law complements, or is an obstacle to, the regulatory system chosen by Congress in a field completely occupied by Congress. The United States (P) has broad, undoubted power over the subject of immigration and the status of aliens, as immigration policy has nationwide impacts on trade, investment, tourism, diplomatic relations, and reciprocal treatment of U.S. citizens by other countries. The United States' (P) immigration policies and programs are extensive and complex and embrace immediate human concerns for aliens as well as concerns that immigration policies are consistent with the nation's foreign policies. However, the pervasiveness of federal regulation does not diminish the importance of immigration policy to the states. Here, for example, Arizona (D) bears many of the consequences of unlawful immigration, as hundreds of thousands of deportable aliens are apprehended in Arizona (D) each year. Under our federalist system, Congress may expressly preempt the states from regulating a certain area. Additionally, the states are precluded from regulating conduct in a field Congress, acting within its proper authority, has determined must be regulated by its exclusive governance; and state laws that conflict with federal law are also preempted. This includes cases where compliance with both federal and state regulations is a physical impossibility and those instances where the challenged state law stands as an obstacle to the accomplishment and execution of the full purposes and objectives of Congress. As to § 3, which effectively adds a state-law penalty for conduct proscribed by federal law, the federal government has occupied the field of alien registration through its comprehensive alien registration regime. Where Congress occupies an entire field, as it has in the field of alien registration, even complementary or parallel state regulation is impermissible. Accordingly, § 3 is preempted. As to § 5(C), Arizona (D) enacts a criminal prohibition where no federal counterpart exists. IRCA's express preemption provision, which in most instances bars states from imposing penalties on employers of unauthorized aliens, is silent about whether additional penalties

Continued on next page.

may be imposed against the employees themselves. However, the existence of this express preemption provision does not bar the ordinary working of conflict preemption principles. One of these principles is the well-settled proposition a state law is preempted where it "stands as an obstacle to the accomplishment and execution of the full purposes and objectives of Congress." Section 5(C) would interfere with the careful balance struck by Congress with respect to unauthorized employment of aliens. Although § 5(C) attempts to achieve one of the same goals as federal law—the deterrence of unlawful employment—it involves a conflict in the method of enforcement. Such a conflict in technique can be fully as disruptive to the system Congress enacted as conflict in overt policy. Because it is clear Congress determined it would be inappropriate to impose criminal penalties on aliens who seek or engage in unauthorized employment, a state law to the contrary is an obstacle to the regulatory system Congress chose. Accordingly, § 5(C) is preempted. Affirmed in part and reversed in part. [The procedural posture of the case is not presented in the casebook extract.]

CONCURRENCE AND DISSENT: (Scalia, J.) The majority decision deprives states of what most would consider the defining characteristic of sovereignty: the power to exclude from the sovereign's territory people who have no right to be there. Such a result is not supported by the Constitution or any laws passed by Congress. Merely because the federal government acts in the immigration area is not justification to preempt a core sovereign power of the states. Moreover, federal power over immigration cannot be deemed exclusive merely out of regard for foreign countries' concerns about the status, safety, and security of their nationals in the U.S; even in its international relations, the federal government must live with the inconvenient fact it is a union of independent states, which have their own sovereign powers and which have the independent right to exclude foreign nationals.

CONCURRENCE AND DISSENT: (Thomas, J.) Here, none of Arizona's (D) statutory provisions directly conflict with federal law. The "purposes and objectives" theory of implied preemption (whereby a state law is preempted where it stands as an obstacle to Congress's purposes and objectives), which primarily guides the majority's holding, is inconsistent with the Constitution because it invites courts to engage in freewheeling speculation about congressional purpose that roams well beyond statutory text; preemption should not be based on judicially divined legislative purposes.

CONCURRENCE AND DISSENT: (Alito, J.) There is some evidence that, contrary to the conclusion reached by the majority, Congress did not intend to preempt state laws like § 5(C). Given that Congress expressly preempted certain state and local laws pertaining to employers but remained silent about laws pertaining to employees, one could infer Congress intended to preserve

state and local authority to regulate the employee side of the equation. At the very least, it raises serious doubts about whether Congress intended to preempt such authority. The absence of Congress's express preemption as to employees is probative of congressional intent. Congress's decision not to extend its express preemption provision to state or local laws like § 5(C) is more probative of its intent on the subject of preemption than its decision not to impose federal criminal penalties for unauthorized work. In any event, the inferences can be drawn either way, and there are no necessary inferences that point decisively for or against preemption. Because state employment regulation is a traditional state concern and can be preempted only on a showing of "clear and manifest" congressional intent to preempt, § 5(C) must be allowed to stand.

▶ **ANALYSIS**

The three types of preemption recognized by the Court in this case, and in the Court's precedents, are: (1) express preemption, where the federal statute expressly refers to preemption and identifies the state laws supplanted by the federal statute. This form of preemption was not at issue in this case. (2) Field preemption, where federal regulation in the area is so extensive it gives rise to the inference Congress left no room for the states to supplement federal law. The Court relied on this type of preemption to rule § 3 was preempted. (3) Conflict preemption, where compliance with both federal and state regulations is a physical impossibility, and those instances where the challenged state law stands as an obstacle to the accomplishment and execution of the full purposes and objectives of Congress. The Court relied on this type of preemption to rule that § 5(C) was preempted.

■—■

Quicknotes

FEDERALISM A scheme of government whereby the power to govern is among central and localized governments.

PREEMPTION Doctrine holding that matters of national interest take precedence over matters of local interest; the federal law takes precedence over state law.

■—■

The Scope of Congress's Powers: Taxing and Spending, War Powers, Individual Rights, and State Autonomy

Quick Reference Rules of Law

National Federation of Independent Business v. Sebelius

Business group (P) v. Government official (D)

567 U.S. 519 (2012).

NATURE OF CASE: Appeal from judgment in action challenging the constitutionality of the "individual mandate" provision of the 2010 Patient Protection and Affordable Care Act. [The procedural posture of the case is not presented in the casebook extract.]

FACT SUMMARY: A coalition of plaintiffs (P) challenged the constitutionality of the "individual mandate" provision of the 2010 Patient Protection and Affordable Care Act ("the Act"). The Government (D) contended, inter alia, that the individual mandate was a valid exercise of Congress's taxing power, since it provided that individuals who did not purchase health-care insurance would pay a penalty in the form of a tax.

> 🏛 **RULE OF LAW**
> The "individual mandate" provision of the Patient Protection and Affordable Care Act, which requires that individuals who do not purchase health-care insurance under certain circumstances must pay a penalty in the form of a tax, is a valid exercise of Congress's taxing power.

FACTS: In 2010, Congress enacted the Patient Protection and Affordable Care Act ("the Act") to increase the number of Americans covered by health insurance and decrease the cost of health care. A key provision of the Act is the individual mandate, which requires most Americans to maintain "minimum essential" health-insurance coverage. For individuals who are not exempt, and who do not receive health insurance through an employer or government program, the means of satisfying the requirement is to purchase insurance from a private company. Those who do not comply with the mandate must make a "shared responsibility payment" to the Internal Revenue Service (IRS) based on factors such as income, number of dependents, and joint filing status, and is subject to a statutory cap. A coalition of plaintiffs (P) challenged the individual mandate as unconstitutional. The Government (D) contended, inter alia, the individual mandate was a valid exercise of Congress's taxing power, since the Act provided the penalty would be paid to the IRS with an individual's taxes, and "shall be assessed and collected in the same manner" as tax penalties. The imposition of the individual mandate was expected to raise $4 billion per year by its third year. The Supreme Court granted certiorari. [The procedural posture of the case is not presented in the casebook extract.]

ISSUE: Is the "individual mandate" provision of the Patient Protection and Affordable Care Act, which requires that individuals who do not purchase health-care insurance

under certain circumstances must pay a penalty in the form of a tax, a valid exercise of Congress's taxing power?

HOLDING AND DECISION: (Roberts, C.J.) Yes. The "individual mandate" provision of the Patient Protection and Affordable Care Act, which requires that individuals who do not purchase health-care insurance under certain circumstances must pay a penalty in the form of a tax, is a valid exercise of Congress's taxing power. The individual mandate must be construed as imposing a tax on those who do not have health insurance, if such a construction is reasonable. The most straightforward reading of the individual mandate is it commands individuals to purchase insurance. However, the Government's (D) alternative argument is that the mandate may be upheld as within Congress's power to "lay and collect [t]axes." In pressing its taxing power argument, the Government (D) asks the Court to view the mandate as imposing a tax on those who do not buy a health insurance product. Granting the Act the full measure of deference owed to federal statutes, it can be so read, for the following reasons. First, the exaction imposed by the Act has many of the features of a tax, and is functionally like a tax, and it has the essential feature of a tax insofar as it raises revenue for the Government (D). Taking such a functional approach is confirmed by precedent. Second, taking such an approach, the exaction functions more like a tax than a penalty. For most Americans, the amount due will be far less than the price of insurance, and, by statute, it can never be more. Also, the individual mandate contains no scienter requirement. Further, the payment is collected solely by the IRS through the normal means of taxation—except the IRS is not allowed to use those means most suggestive of a punitive sanction, such as criminal prosecution. For these reasons, the exaction may be viewed as a tax and not as a penalty. Additionally, merely because the individual mandate is designed to regulate individual conduct and encourage the purchasing of health insurance does not mean it cannot be a valid exercise of the taxing power. To some extent, all taxes are regulatory in nature. Because it is estimated four million people each year will choose to pay the IRS rather than buy insurance, and because Congress apparently regards such extensive failure to comply with the mandate as tolerable, it seems Congress did not think it was creating four million outlaws. It suggests instead the shared responsibility payment merely imposes a tax citizens may lawfully choose to pay in lieu of buying health insurance. Contrary to the joint dissenters' opinion, the individual mandate may be upheld as a tax

Continued on next page.

notwithstanding Congress did not frame it as a tax. The mandate's substance is in the form of a tax, and that conclusion should not change simply because Congress used the word "penalty" to describe the payment. Thus, interpreting such a law to be a tax would not impose a tax through judicial legislation, but instead would give practical effect to Congress's enactment. The individual mandate also complies with the other requirements for taxes under the Constitution, as it is not a capitation, and is not a direct tax that is required to be apportioned among the states. A more fundamental objection to a tax on those who lack health insurance—similar to the objection to the individual mandate as exceeding the commerce power—is that it should be troubling to permit Congress to impose a tax for not doing something. There are three reasons why such a tax passes constitutional scrutiny. First, the Constitution does not guarantee that individuals may avoid taxation through inactivity, so that upholding the individual mandate under the Taxing Clause does not recognize any new federal power but is a determination that Congress has used an existing one. Second, while Congress's taxing power has limits, so exactions cannot become punitive, it has already been explained that the individual mandate passes muster as a tax and not as a punitive penalty. Accordingly, it comes within the strict limits within which Congress can tax. Third, Congress's authority under the taxing power is limited to requiring an individual to pay money to the federal government; the individual retains the choice whether to do or not do a certain act, so long as he is willing to pay a tax levied on that choice. The individual mandate also imposes a cost on the choice not to obtain health care insurance. Accordingly, the individual mandate comes within the Constitution's requirements. [The procedural outcome of the case is not presented in the casebook extract.]

DISSENT: (Scalia, J.) The individual mandate cannot be characterized as a tax. Therefore, there is no need to reach the issue of whether it comes within Congress's permissible taxing power.

▶ *ANALYSIS*

The issue of whether the individual mandate comes within Congress's taxing power was reached only because the majority determined the Commerce Clause did not authorize the individual mandate's command to purchase insurance. Because the statute reads more naturally as a command to buy insurance than as a tax, and because the Court held the statute was unconstitutional as a command, the Court exercised its duty to construe the statute to save it, if fairly possible, if it could be interpreted as a tax. Without deciding the Commerce Clause question, the Court would have found no basis to adopt such a saving construction. Through the exercise of its duty of statutory construction, the Court upheld the individual mandate's

constitutionality, but only because the Court determined the statute could reasonably be read as a tax.

■■■■■

Quicknotes

SCIENTER Knowledge of certain facts; often refers to "guilty knowledge," which implicates liability.

TAXING POWER The authority delegated to Congress by the Constitution to impose taxes.

■■■■■

United States v. Butler

Federal government (P) v. Taxpayers (D)

297 U.S. 1 (1936).

NATURE OF CASE: Appeal of decision invalidating portions of the Agricultural Adjustment Act of 1933.

FACT SUMMARY: Congress instituted a tax on certain agricultural processors to subsidize farmers in order to reduce acreage and stabilize farm prices.

 RULE OF LAW
Congress may not tax in an area of local concern.

FACTS: In response to collapsed farm prices, Congress passed the Agricultural Adjustment Act of 1933 in which a tax was levied on certain agricultural processors to pay for a subsidy of farmers who voluntarily reduced their crop output, the goal being acreage reduction. The power invoked for this Act was the taxing and spending power. The tax was challenged in court, and the lower court held the tax unconstitutional.

ISSUE: May Congress tax in an area of local concern?

HOLDING AND DECISION: (Roberts, J.) No. Congress may not tax in an area of local concern. The federal government is one of limited, enumerated powers, and can only act on those enumerated powers. While Congress does have the power to tax and spend for the general welfare, it only has this right in areas within the sphere of federal power. Just as Congress cannot regulate a local business, it may not tax it, as the power to tax is a form of regulation. Here, the businesses taxed are local. Congress may neither regulate nor tax them; to do so would usurp the power of the states. Also, to try to induce certain practices by farmers via subsidies infringes on state powers. Affirmed.

DISSENT: (Stone, J.) Attempting to influence behavior by offering subsidies is not the same as regulation and is a proper exercise of the taxing and spending power.

▌ANALYSIS

The opinion was internally inconsistent. On the one hand, it rejected the view that "general welfare" spending included only specifically enumerated areas (the so-called Madisonian view). On the other hand, the Court held Congress could not tax and spend on areas of "local" concern. It seems the Court both broadened and narrowed the spending power at once.

Quicknotes

TAXING POWER The authority delegated to Congress by the Constitution to impose taxes.

National Federation of Independent Business v. Sebelius

Business group (P) v. Government official (D)

567 U.S. 519 (2012).

NATURE OF CASE: Appeal from judgment in action challenging the constitutionality of the "Medicaid expansion" provision of the 2010 Patient Protection and Affordable Care Act. [The procedural posture of the case is not presented in the casebook extract.]

FACT SUMMARY: A coalition of plaintiffs (P) challenged the constitutionality of the "Medicaid expansion" provision of the 2010 Patient Protection and Affordable Care Act, which expanded certain Medicaid benefits, but also threatened the states, which administer Medicaid, with the loss not only of funding for the increased coverage, but also the loss of all federal Medicaid funds.

🏛 RULE OF LAW

That part of the "Medicaid expansion" provision of the Patient Protection and Affordable Care Act ("the Act") that threatens the states with a loss of all federal Medicaid funding for failing to comply with the Act's expansion of Medicaid benefits and coverage, is not a valid exercise of Congress's power under the Spending Clause.

FACTS: In 2010, Congress enacted the Patient Protection and Affordable Care Act ("the Act") to increase the number of Americans covered by health insurance and decrease the cost of health care. A key provision of the Act is the "Medicaid expansion." The current Medicaid program offers federal funding to states to assist pregnant women, children, needy families, the blind, the elderly, and the disabled in obtaining medical care. The Act would expand the scope of the Medicaid program and increase the number of individuals the states must cover. For example, the Act requires state programs to provide Medicaid coverage by 2014 to adults with incomes up to 133 percent of the federal poverty level, whereas many states now cover adults with children only if their income is considerably lower, and do not cover childless adults at all. The Act increases federal funding to cover the states' costs in expanding Medicaid coverage, but if a state does not comply with the Act's new coverage requirements, it may lose not only the federal funding for those requirements, but all its federal Medicaid funds. A coalition of plaintiffs (P), including some states, challenged the Medicaid expansion as unconstitutionally exceeding Congress's spending power under the Spending Clause by coercing the states to enact the statute. The Supreme Court granted certiorari. [The procedural posture of the case is not presented in the casebook extract.]

ISSUE: Is that part of the "Medicaid expansion" provision of the Patient Protection and Affordable Care Act ("the Act") that threatens the states with a loss of all federal Medicaid funding for failing to comply with the Act's expansion of Medicaid benefits and coverage, a valid exercise of Congress's power under the Spending Clause?

HOLDING AND DECISION: (Roberts, C.J.) No. That part of the "Medicaid expansion" provision of the Patient Protection and Affordable Care Act ("the Act") that threatens the states with a loss of all federal Medicaid funding for failing to comply with the Act's expansion of Medicaid benefits and coverage, is not a valid exercise of Congress's power under the Spending Clause. There is no doubt the Act dramatically increases state obligations under Medicaid. In light of the expansion in coverage mandated by the Act, the Government (D) estimates its Medicaid spending will increase by approximately $100 billion per year, nearly 40 percent above current levels. To be constitutional, Congress's power under the Spending Clause to secure state compliance with federal objectives rests on whether the state voluntarily and knowingly accepts the terms of the "contract" offered by the federal Government (D). The Constitution has never been understood to confer upon Congress the ability to require the states to govern according to Congress's instructions. Otherwise the two-government system established by the Framers would give way to a system that vests power in one central government, and individual liberty would suffer. Thus, Congress may use its spending power to create incentives for states to act in accordance with federal policies, but when pressure turns into compulsion, the legislation runs contrary to our system of federalism. That is true whether Congress directly commands a state to regulate or indirectly coerces a state to adopt a federal regulatory system as its own. Here, the plaintiffs (P) claim Congress has crossed the line from encouragement to coercion by structuring the Medicaid expansion so states that refuse the new conditions not only will not receive new funding, but will lose all existing funding. The plaintiffs (P) claim this threat serves no purpose other than to force unwilling states to sign up for the dramatic expansion in health care coverage effected by the Act. Under the circumstances presented by the case, the plaintiffs (P) are correct—the Government's (D) "inducement" to participate is tantamount to a gun to the head. Respecting some states, the loss of all Medicaid funding represents a loss of

Continued on next page.

as much as 10 percent of the state's entire budget. This is economic coercion that leaves the states with no real option but to acquiesce in the Medicaid expansion. The states contend the expansion is in reality a new program and Congress is forcing them to accept it by threatening the funds for the existing Medicaid program. The Government (D) counters the Medicaid expansion is properly viewed merely as a modification of the existing program, and emphasizes the states agreed Congress could change the terms of Medicaid when they signed on in the first place. The issue is one of substance, not merely what Congress has labeled the program. Here, the Medicaid expansion accomplishes a shift in kind, not merely degree. The original program was designed to cover medical services for four particular categories of the needy. Previous amendments to Medicaid eligibility merely altered and expanded the boundaries of these categories. Under the Act, however, Medicaid is transformed into a program to meet the health-care needs of the entire nonelderly population with income below 133 percent of the poverty level. It is no longer a program to care for the neediest among us, but rather an element of a comprehensive national plan to provide universal health-insurance coverage. A state could hardly have anticipated when it signed on to the Medicaid program that Congress's reservation of the right to "alter" or "amend" the Medicaid program included the power to transform it so dramatically. The constitutional violation is fully remedied by precluding the Government (D) from withdrawing existing Medicaid funds for failure to comply with the requirements set out in the expansion. The other provisions of the Act are not affected. Congress would have wanted the rest of the Act to stand, had it known that states would have a genuine choice whether to participate in the Medicaid expansion. [The procedural outcome of the case is not presented in the casebook extract.]

DISSENT: (Scalia, J.) Contrary to the Government's (D) argument, it is not enough to meet the anticoercion rule if states are free as a matter of law to turn down federal funds. This argument ignores the reality that when a heavy federal tax is levied to support a federal program that offers large grants to the states, states may, as a practical matter, be unable to refuse to participate in the federal program and to substitute a state alternative. This is because, as a practical matter, states would have to impose a huge tax on top of the heavy tax imposed by the federal government. Acceptance of the Government's (D) interpretation of the anticoercion rule would permit Congress to dictate policy in areas traditionally governed primarily at the state or local level. Further, the record shows Congress anticipated 100 percent state participation. The Government (D) asserts this expectation arose because the Act's offer to the states was a generous gift. If, however, that was true, why did more than half the states file this suit claiming the Medicaid expansion was coercive? Also, if the "gift" was so generous, Congress could have made just the new funding provided under the Act contingent on acceptance of the

terms of the Medicaid expansion. Accordingly, the Medicaid expansion must fall, as it is not severable from the Medicaid extension.

CONCURRENCE AND DISSENT: (Ginsburg, J.) Congress could have recalled the existing Medicaid legislation and replaced it with a new law, making Medicaid as embracive of the poor as Congress chose. Congress should not have to take that route. Instead, Congress may expand by amendment the classes of needy persons entitled to Medicaid benefits. A ritualistic requirement that Congress repeals and reenacts spending legislation in order to enlarge the population served by a federally funded program would advance no constitutional principle and would scarcely serve the interests of federalism. Here, Medicaid, and Medicaid as amended by the Act, are not two separate programs, but just one with a constant aim—to enable poor persons to receive basic health care when they need it. Moreover, the states are not entitled to Medicaid funding, and if they accept such funding, they must do so on Congress's terms. Here, there are no coercion concerns, because the expansion relates solely to the federally funded Medicaid program; if states choose not to comply, Congress has not threatened to withhold funds earmarked for any other program. Nor does the Act use Medicaid funding to induce states to take action Congress itself could not undertake. The Government (D) undoubtedly could operate its own health-care program for poor persons, just as it operates Medicare for seniors' health care. Contrary to the Chief Justice's opinion, the Act does not effect a new program; it merely expands the number of people covered by the existing program. The aspects of the expansion cited by the Chief Justice as supporting his premise that the expansion creates a new program do not, in fact, support his premise. The Chief Justice's finding the expansion took states by surprise is also unfounded. The precedent on which he relies merely requires conditions on federal funds be unambiguously clear at the time a state receives and uses the money—not at the time, perhaps years earlier, when Congress passed the law establishing the program. In any event, from the start, the Medicaid Act put states on notice the program could be changed, or even repealed. Thus, the states were on notice of the Act's proposed changes. Further, the Chief Justice does not announce a workable judicial standard for determining when a state is being coerced by the federal government. The coercion inquiry appears to involve political judgments that defy judicial calculation, and conceptions of when a state has been "coerced" are too amorphous to be judicially administrable. In sum, the Chief Justice and the joint-dissenters position is that the states' reliance on federal funds limits Congress's authority to alter its spending programs. This gets things backwards: Congress, not the states, is tasked with spending federal money in service of the general

Continued on next page.

welfare, and each successive Congress is empowered to appropriate funds as it sees fit. For all these reasons, the Medicaid expansion is within Congress's spending power.

▶ *ANALYSIS*

It should be noted that the Court's decision does not strike down any provision of the Act. It prohibits only the "application" of the Secretary of Health and Human Service's authority to withhold Medicaid funds from states that decline to conform their Medicaid plans to the Act's requirements. Thus, the Act's authorization of funds to finance the expansion remains intact, and the Secretary's authority to withhold funds for reasons other than non-compliance with the expansion remains unaffected. The joint dissenters would have held the expansion was not severable from the Medicaid extension, and would have consequently held the entire expansion was invalid. Justice Ginsburg agreed with the Chief Justice the Medicaid Act's severability clause determined the appropriate remedy. That clause provides that "[i]f any provision of [the Medicaid Act], or the application thereof to any person or circumstance, is held invalid, the remainder of the chapter, and the application of such provision to other persons or circumstances shall not be affected thereby." 42 U.S.C. § 1303.

Quicknotes

FEDERALISM A scheme of government whereby the power to govern is among central and localized governments.

SPENDING CLAUSE The power delegated to Congress by the Constitution to spend money in providing for the nation's welfare.

SPENDING POWER The power delegated to Congress by the Constitution to spend money in providing for the nation's welfare.

City of Boerne v. Flores

Zoning authority (D) v. Church (P)

521 U.S. 507 (1997).

NATURE OF CASE: Review of judgment sustaining the constitutionality of the Religious Freedom Restoration Act of 1993.

FACT SUMMARY: A decision by zoning authorities in Boerne (D) to deny a church (P) a building permit was challenged under the Religious Freedom Restoration Act.

🏛 RULE OF LAW
The Religious Freedom Restoration Act (RFRA) unconstitutionally exceeds Congress's enforcement power under the Due Process Clause of the Fourteenth Amendment.

FACTS: The Religious Freedom Restoration Act (RFRA) prohibited the government from substantially burdening a person's exercise of religion, even if the burden is the result of a generally applicable law, unless the government has a compelling interest and is using the least restrictive means. Flores (P) sought a building permit to expand his church, a historic landmark. The City of Boerne (D) denied the permit and Flores (P) sued, invoking RFRA. The district court determined that RFRA exceeded congressional power, but the Fifth Circuit reversed, holding RFRA constitutional. Boerne (D) appealed.

ISSUE: Does the Religious Freedom Restoration Act (RFRA) unconstitutionally exceed Congress's enforcement power under the Due Process Clause of the Fourteenth Amendment?

HOLDING AND DECISION: (Kennedy, J.) Yes. The Religious Freedom Restoration Act (RFRA) unconstitutionally exceeds Congress's enforcement power under the Due Process Clause of the Fourteenth Amendment. Here, Congress, with RFRA, attempts to replace, with the compelling interest test, this Court's decision in *Employment Div., Dept. of Human Resources of Ore. v. Smith*, 494 U.S. 872 (1990). *Smith* held that the compelling interest test is inappropriate in cases where general prohibitions are opposed by free exercise challenges. But RFRA violates the long tradition of separation of powers established by the Constitution. The judiciary is to determine the constitutionality of laws, and the powers of the legislature are defined and limited. While Congress can enact remedial, preventive legislation that deters violations, RFRA is not a preventive law. Instead, RFRA redefines the scope of the Free Exercise Clause and nothing in our history extends to Congress the ability to take such action. RFRA is so out of proportion to a supposed remedial or preventive object that it cannot be regarded as a response to unconstitutional behavior. Reversed.

▶ ANALYSIS

The Religious Freedom Restoration Act (RFRA) was one of the four federal laws overturned by the Supreme Court during its 1997 term. Although the Court has endorsed judicial restraint in recent years, it has not hesitated to quash improper intrusions on its authority to set unconstitutional standards. The Court, however, chose not to revisit the religious freedom issue in its *Boerne* decision, leaving intact the ruling in *Smith* that inspired Congress to pass RFRA. In *Smith*, the Court approved Oregon's use of its ban on peyote to prohibit the drug's use in Native American religious rituals. RFRA was intended to guarantee religious observance a higher-degree of statutory protection than the *Smith* court thought necessary.

Quicknotes

FREE EXERCISE CLAUSE The guarantee of the First Amendment to the United States Constitution prohibiting Congress from enacting laws regarding the establishment of religion or prohibiting the free exercise thereof.

Missouri v. Holland

State (P) v. Federal game warden (D)

252 U.S. 416 (1920).

NATURE OF CASE: An action in equity to enjoin the enforcement of the Migratory Bird Treaty Act.

FACT SUMMARY: Missouri (P) claims that the Bird Treaty Act was an unconstitutional interference with the rights reserved to the states by the Tenth Amendment.

🏛 RULE OF LAW

Congress can constitutionally enact a statute under Article I, section 8 to enforce a treaty created under Article II, section 2, even if the statute by itself is unconstitutional.

FACTS: On December 8, 1916, the United States entered into a treaty with Great Britain to protect birds that migrated between Canada and the United States. Congress passed a statute to enforce the Migratory Bird Treaty that allowed the Secretary of Agriculture to formulate regulations to enforce the treaty. The State of Missouri (P) filed a bill in equity to prevent Holland (D), the game warden of the United States, from enforcing the treaty. Missouri (P) claimed that the statute was an unconstitutional interference with the rights reserved to the states by the Tenth Amendment and that it had a pecuniary interest as owner of the wild birds being affected. Before the treaty had been entered into, Congress had attempted to regulate the killing of migratory birds within the states and that statute, standing by itself, had been declared unconstitutional. The United States contended that Congress had the power to enact the statute to enforce the treaty and that the statute and treaty were the supreme law of the land.

ISSUE: Can Congress validly enact a statute to enforce a treaty if the statute standing by itself would be unconstitutional because it interfered with the rights reserved to the states by the Tenth Amendment?

HOLDING AND DECISION: (Holmes, J.) Yes. Congress can constitutionally enact a statute under Article I, section 8 to enforce a treaty created under Article II, section 2, even if the statute by itself is unconstitutional. Article II, section 2 grants the President the power to make treaties and Article VI, section 2 declares that treaties shall be part of the supreme law of the land. If a treaty is a valid one, Article I, section 8 gives Congress the power to enact legislation that is a necessary and proper means to enforce the treaty. While acts of Congress are the supreme law of the land only when they are made in pursuance of the Constitution, treaties are valid when made under the authority of the United States. The Court stated that there were qualifications to the treaty-making power but felt that

the qualifications must be determined by looking at the facts of each case. There are situations that require national action that an act of Congress could not deal with, but that a treaty enforced with a congressional act could. Because Missouri (P) did not have the power to adequately control the problem connected with the migratory birds (nor did any other state acting alone), this was a situation that required national action. Therefore, even though Missouri (P) would have been able to establish regulations pertaining to the birds if Congress had not already done so, Congress could establish regulations in conjunction with the treaty without infringing on the rights reserved to the states by the Tenth Amendment. The court rejected Missouri's (P) claim that it had a pecuniary interest as an owner when the birds were in the state. There is no ownership until there is possession and the birds never came into the possession of the State of Missouri (P). Congress can, therefore, constitutionally enact a statute under Article I, section 8 to enforce a treaty even if the statute by itself would be unconstitutional. Affirmed.

▶ ANALYSIS

Many people were upset with the decision in this case because they feared that the Court had interpreted the treaty power so broadly that all constitutional limitations could be overridden by use of treaties and accompanying congressional legislation. In 1954, the Bricker Amendment, which was narrowly defeated, required that a treaty could only become effective as internal law in the United States through legislation which would be valid in the absence of the treaty. This would have, in effect, overruled the decision in this case, because the congressional act was not valid when standing by itself. Several other similar proposals were made during the following three years, which also failed.

━━━

Quicknotes

PECUNIARY INTEREST A monetary interest.

TENTH AMENDMENT Amendment to the United States Constitution reserving those powers therein, not expressly delegated to the federal government or prohibited to the states, to the states or to the people.

TREATY POWER The power delegated to the President by the Constitution to enter into treaties upon the approval of two-thirds of the Senate that is present.

━━━

The Distribution of National Powers

Quick Reference Rules of Law

Youngstown Sheet & Tube Co. v. Sawyer (The Steel Seizure Case)

Steel company (P) v. Federal government (D)

343 U.S. 579 (1952).

NATURE OF CASE: Appeal of decision upholding presidentially ordered seizure of steel mills.

FACT SUMMARY: President Truman ordered the seizure of the nation's strike-plagued steel mills absent congressional approval.

🏛 RULE OF LAW
The President may not effect the seizure of private property absent congressional approval.

FACTS: A strike in the steel industry was called by labor leaders. Fearful of the effect a steel shortage might have on national defense and facing nonaction by Congress, President Truman ordered the nation's mills seized so that they would resume production. Youngstown Sheet & Tube Co. (P) complied with the order, but filed suit to have the action enjoined. The district court held the order unconstitutional, but the court of appeals reversed.

ISSUE: May the President effect the seizure of private property absent congressional approval?

HOLDING AND DECISION: (Black, J.) No. The President may not effect the seizure of private property absent congressional approval. Without such approval, such a power could only stem from the Constitution. No such power is expressly granted. The power to do this cannot be implied either. The President's duty to see that the laws are faithfully executed is inapplicable, as no law exists that is being executed. The President's role as Commander-in-Chief does not grant the power, for the theater of war is not so broad as to encompass domestic private property. As only Congress can pass a law taking private property, the President's action was in excess of his powers. Reversed.

CONCURRENCE: (Frankfurter, J.) By not granting the President power to seize the steel mills, Congress has withheld from him authority to do so.

CONCURRENCE: (Jackson, J.) The President's powers are at a maximum when his acts are authorized by Congress. In the absence of congressional input, the President has some areas of action independent of Congress. When Congress specifically disapproves of the President's action, he can rely on only his powers as enumerated in the Constitution. This action falls into the second category, and the President has overstepped his ability to move independent of Congress.

CONCURRENCE: (Douglas, J.) The Fifth Amendment can only be read to give condemnation power to Congress.

DISSENT: (Vinson, C.J.) A work stoppage in the steel mills would put the nation's defense in such jeopardy that the President's military authority legitimized his actions.

▶ ANALYSIS
Of all the opinions here, the most influential was that of Justice Jackson. While only a concurring opinion, it has taken the status as an important authority on the extent and source of presidential power. It is often cited when such power is under debate.

Quicknotes
FIFTH AMENDMENT Provides that no person shall be compelled to serve as a witness against himself, be subject to trial for the same offense twice, or be deprived of life, liberty, or property without due process of law.

United States v. Curtiss-Wright Corp.

Federal government (P) v. Arms dealer (D)

299 U.S. 304 (1936).

NATURE OF CASE: Indictment charging a conspiracy to sell guns illegally.

FACT SUMMARY: Curtiss-Wright Corp. (D) planned to sell machine guns to Bolivia contrary to a presidential proclamation that declared such sales to be illegal.

🏛 RULE OF LAW
Presidential proclamations that pertain to foreign affairs are valid and enforceable.

FACTS: A joint resolution of Congress expressly authorized the President to declare it illegal to sell weaponry in the United States (P) to countries engaged in armed conflict in the Chaco region. Violators of any presidential proclamation to that effect were to be subject to a fine of $10,000 or less and/or a prison sentence of up to two years. Pursuant to the joint resolution, the President did issue a proclamation declaring it illegal to sell weapons to countries at war in the Chaco. Curtiss-Wright Corp. (D) was indicted for allegedly conspiring to sell 15 machine guns to Bolivia, which was then involved in the conflict in the Chaco. Curtiss-Wright (D) demurred to the indictment, contending that the joint resolution was an unconstitutional delegation of legislative powers from Congress to the President. The trial court sustained the demurrer, but on appeal the United States (P) argued that the proclamation was effective and enjoyed the force of law.

ISSUE: Does the President have the power to issue proclamations relating to international affairs?

HOLDING AND DECISION: (Sutherland, J.) Yes. Presidential proclamations that pertain to foreign affairs are valid and enforceable. It is unnecessary to consider whether a proclamation issued under these circumstances would have been valid had it related to domestic matters. The federal government has always had exclusive authority in the area of foreign affairs. This power does not derive from the states but has instead always belonged to the national government. It is exercisable by the President, not always with the aid of Congress. The President alone possesses complete knowledge of often sensitive information concerning foreign governments, and it would be unwise to require him to share his knowledge with Congress so that it might participate in the decision-making process. In fact, information pertaining to foreign affairs is much more jealously protected from disclosure than is domestic information. The President's unique knowledge concerning confidential information makes it appropriate for him to issue occasional proclamations concerning foreign affairs, with or without congressional approval. Clearly, the proclamation in dispute was not the result of an improper delegation of power. Thus, the lower court should not have sustained Curtiss-Wright's (D) demurrer. Reversed.

▶ ANALYSIS

In colonial times, states occasionally enacted laws that frustrated or were inconsistent with treaties entered into by the national government. As a result, the Framers of the Constitution took some care to clarify the respective roles of the state and federal governments in matters relating to foreign affairs. Their simple solution was to confer all powers relating to international relations upon the federal government. It was assumed that individual states had never had any powers with respect to foreign matters, and the Constitution invested them with no such powers. By granting to the President the power to enter into treaties with foreign nations, subject only to the counsel and assent of the Congress, the Framers virtually guaranteed that primary responsibility for foreign affairs would devolve upon the nation's highest-ranking executive officer.

Quicknotes

EXECUTIVE ORDER An order issued by the President, or on behalf of the President, which has the force of law.

Dames & Moore v. Regan

Creditor (P) v. Federal government (D)

453 U.S. 654 (1981).

NATURE OF CASE: Appeal of court order upholding an executive agreement barring claims against Iran or its citizens.

FACT SUMMARY: President Carter, in exchange for release of U.S. hostages, issued an order barring court action against Iran or its citizens.

> **RULE OF LAW**
> A President may issue an order settling legal claims when the order is ancillary to major foreign policy issues and Congress acquiesces.

FACTS: President Carter worked out the following deal in exchange for release of U.S. hostages held in Iran: all existing legal claims against Iran or its citizens were to be dismissed from court and referred to a special claims tribunal. All Iranian assets held in the United States were to be unfrozen. Dames & Moore (P), asserting a contractual claim against several Iranian banks, brought an action to have the executive order declared unconstitutional. Congress had neither approved nor disapproved of the action. The lower courts upheld the order.

ISSUE: May a President issue an order settling legal claims when the order is ancillary to major foreign policy issues and Congress acquiesces?

HOLDING AND DECISION: (Rehnquist, J.) Yes. A President may issue an order settling claims when the order is ancillary to major foreign policy issues and Congress acquiesces. Congress has passed the International Emergency Economic Powers Act, which, while not covering the exact issue at hand, gives the President similar powers for similar situations. Congress cannot be expected to legislate for every contingency, and it can be inferred that if Congress authorizes certain presidential actions, similar action is also authorized. Since the President acted with congressional approval, his powers were at high tide. While extinguishing claims by presidential order is an extreme exercise of power, the fact that Congress had at least tacitly approved it and the President was exercising his constitutional foreign policy role, the action was legitimate. Affirmed.

ANALYSIS

Supreme Court cases cannot be considered in a vacuum. Political reality has a way of intruding on legal niceties. The present decision was made in a political climate that would have been very adverse to a contrary decision and would have left the United States looking foolish to the international community. What precedential effect this decision will have only time will tell. The Court itself, in the opinion, underscored the narrowness of the decision.

Quicknotes

EXECUTIVE ORDER An order issued by the President, or or on behalf of the President, which has the force of law.

Hamdi v. Rumsfeld

Alleged enemy combatant (P) v. Secretary of Defense (D)

542 U.S. 507 (2004).

NATURE OF CASE: Appeal from the denial of right to challenge enemy-combatant status.

FACT SUMMARY: Hamdi (P), an American citizen designated as an enemy-combatant, argued that he was entitled to contest such designation in court.

🏛 RULE OF LAW

Due process requires that a citizen held in the United States as an enemy combatant be given a meaningful opportunity to contest the factual basis for that detention before a neutral decisionmaker.

FACTS: Hamdi (P), an American citizen, was designated by the Government (D) an "enemy combatant" and placed into indefinite detainment. The Federal Court of Appeals held the detention to be legally authorized and that Hamdi (P) was entitled to no further opportunity to challenge his enemy-combatant label. Hamdi (P) appealed to the Supreme Court.

ISSUE: Does due process require that a citizen held in the United States as an enemy combatant be given a meaningful opportunity to contest the factual basis for that detention before a neutral decisionmaker?

HOLDING AND DECISION: (O'Connor, J.) Yes. Due process requires that a citizen held in the United States as an enemy combatant be given a meaningful opportunity to contest the factual basis for that detention before a neutral decisionmaker. It is vital not to give short shrift to the values that this country holds dear or to the privilege that is American citizenship. At the same time, the exigencies of the circumstances may demand that, as here, aside from certain core elements, enemy combatant proceedings may be tailored to alleviate their uncommon potential to burden the executive branch at a time of ongoing military conflict. Hearsay, for example, may need to be accepted as the most reliable available evidence from the government in such a proceeding. Furthermore, even a burden-shifting scheme in which credible government evidence is presumed true would not offend the Constitution so long as such presumption remains a rebuttable one and fair opportunity for rebuttal is provided. The parties agree that initial captures on the battlefield need not receive the full range of constitutional guarantees. While the Court accords the greatest respect and consideration to the judgments of military authorities in matters relating to the actual prosecution of a war and recognizes that the scope of that discretion is necessarily wide, it does not infringe on the core role of the military for the courts to exercise their own time-honored and constitutionally mandated roles of reviewing and resolving claims such as those present here. A state of war is not a blank check for the President when it comes to the rights of the Nation's citizens. Reversed and remanded.

CONCURRENCE AND DISSENT: (Souter, J.) The Government (D) has failed to demonstrate that the Force Resolution authorizes the detention complained of here, even on the facts the Government (D) claims. If the Government (D) raises nothing further than the record now shows, the Non-Detention Act entitles Hamdi (P) to be released. The branch of government asked to counter a serious threat is not the branch on which to rest the nation's entire reliance in striking the balance between the will to win and "the cost in liberty on the way to victory."

DISSENT: (Scalia, J.) If civil rights are to be curtailed during wartime, it must be done openly and democratically, as the Constitution requires, rather than by silent erosion through an opinion of the Court. Whatever the merits of the view that war silences law or modulates its voice, such view has no place in the interpretation and application of a Constitution designed precisely to confront war and, in a manner that accords with democratic principles, to accommodate it.

DISSENT: (Thomas, J.) The executive branch, acting pursuant to powers vested in the President by the Constitution and by explicit congressional approval, has determined that Hamdi (P) is an enemy combatant and should be detained. This detention falls squarely within the war powers of the federal government, and the Court lacks the expertise and capacity to second-guess such decision. Accordingly, Hamdi's (P) habeas challenge should fail, and there is no reason to remand the case.

▶ ANALYSIS

As made clear in the *Hamdi* decision, in cases of this type the court must balance two vital yet competing interests: on the one hand, respect for separation of powers and the fundamental importance of the Nation to be able to protect itself during time of war; on the other hand, the critical and deep-seated individual constitutional interests at stake.

■=■

Quicknotes

DUE PROCESS CLAUSE Clauses found in the Fifth and Fourteenth Amendments to the United States

Continued on next page.

Constitution providing that no person shall be deprived of "life, liberty, or property, without due process of law."

SEPARATION OF POWERS The system of checks and balances preventing one branch of government from infringing upon exercising the powers of another branch of government.

United States v. Nixon

Federal government (P) v. President (D)

418 U.S. 683 (1974).

NATURE OF CASE: Certiorari granted after denial of a motion to quash a third-party subpoena duces tecum.

FACT SUMMARY: Nixon (D) challenges a subpoena served on him as a third party requiring the production of tapes and documents for use in a criminal prosecution.

RULE OF LAW
Absent a claim of need to protect military, diplomatic, or sensitive national security secrets, an absolute, unqualified presidential privilege of immunity from judicial process under all circumstances does not exist.

FACTS: After the grand jury returned an indictment charging seven defendants with various offenses relating to Watergate, Special Prosecutor Jaworski moved for the issuance of a subpoena duces tecum to obtain Watergate-related tapes and documents from Nixon (D). Jaworski claimed that the materials were important to the government's proof at the criminal proceeding against the seven defendants. The subpoena was issued, and Nixon (D) turned over some materials. His lawyer then moved to quash the subpoena. Nixon (D) contended that the separation of powers doctrine precludes judicial review of a presidential claim of privilege and that the need for confidentiality of high-level communication requires an absolute privilege as against a subpoena.

ISSUE: Does the President possess an absolute executive privilege that is immune from judicial review?

HOLDING AND DECISION: (Burger, C.J.) No. Absent a claim of need to protect military, diplomatic, or sensitive national security secrets, an absolute, unqualified presidential privilege of immunity from judicial process under all circumstances does not exist. First of all Nixon (D) claimed the court lacks jurisdiction to issue the subpoena because the matter was an intrabranch dispute within the executive branch. However, courts must look behind names that symbolize the parties to determine whether a justiciable case or controversy exists. Here, the Special Prosecutor, with his asserted need for the subpoenaed material, was opposed by the President with his assertion of privilege against disclosure. This setting assures that there is the necessary concreteness and adversity to sharpen the presentation of the issues. Against Nixon's (D) claim of absolute privilege immune from judicial review, this Court reaffirms the holding of *Marbury v. Madison*, 5 U.S. (1 Cranch) 137 (1803), that "it is emphatically the province of the Judicial Department to say what the law is," and this is true with respect to a claim of executive privilege. Absent a claim of need to protect military, diplomatic, or sensitive national security secrets, neither the doctrine of the separation of powers nor the generalized need for the confidentiality of high-level communications, without more, can sustain an absolute unqualified presidential privilege. Now that the court has decided that legitimate needs of judicial process may outweigh presidential privilege, it is necessary to resolve those competing interests in this case. It is true that the need for confidentiality justifies a presumptive privilege for presidential communications. However, our criminal justice system depends on a complete presentation of all relevant facts. To ensure this presentation, compulsory process must be available. Here, Jaworski has demonstrated a specific need at a criminal trial for the material sought. Nixon (D) has not based his claim of privilege on the military or diplomatic content of the materials but rather on a generalized interest in confidentiality. The allowance of this privilege based on only a generalized interest in confidentiality to withhold relevant evidence in a criminal trial would cut deeply into the guarantee of due process and cannot prevail. Affirmed.

▌*ANALYSIS*

On July 16, 1973, Alexander Butterfield testified before the Senate Select Committee on presidential campaign activities that conversations in President Nixon's offices had been recorded automatically at Nixon's direction. Nixon declined to comply with requests for the tapes from Special Prosecutor Cox and the Senate Select Committee. Nixon maintained that the tapes would remain under his personal control. When a subpoena for the tapes was issued, Nixon replied that he asserted executive privilege and that the President is not subject to compulsory process from the courts. The grand jury then instructed the Special Prosecutor to seek an order for production of the tapes. It was that enforcement proceeding that produced the first ruling in the case. Judge Sirica ordered the President to produce the items for in-camera inspection. The D.C. Circuit Court of Appeals affirmed. *Nixon v. Sirica*, 487 F.2d 700 (1973).

■■■

Quicknotes

ABSOLUTE PRIVILEGE Unconditional or unqualified immunity enjoyed by a person.

SUBPOENA DUCES TECUM A court mandate compelling the production of documents under a witness's control.

■■■

INS v. Chadha

Federal agency (D) v. Illegal immigrant (P)

462 U.S. 919 (1983).

NATURE OF CASE: Consolidated actions challenging the constitutionality of a federal statute.

FACT SUMMARY: Chadha (P) and others challenged the constitutionality of a federal statute that purported to authorize one House of Congress, by resolution, to invalidate the decision of the Attorney General (made under authority delegated by Congress) to allow a particular deportable alien to remain in the United States.

RULE OF LAW
Because it constitutes an exercise of legislative power and is thus subject to the bicameralism and presentment requirements of Article I of the Constitution, the federal statute purporting to authorize a one-house veto of the Attorney General's decision to allow a particular deportable alien to remain in the United States is unconstitutional.

FACTS: Three cases consolidated on appeal all presented the question of the constitutionality of a federal statute that authorized either House of Congress, by resolution, to invalidate the decision of the Attorney General (made pursuant to authority delegated by Congress) to allow a particular deportable alien (P) to remain in the United States. After such a one-house veto effectively overturned the Attorney General's decision to let Chadha (P) and certain other individuals remain in the United States, each instituted action challenging the constitutionality of the aforesaid statute. Chadha (P) filed a petition for a review of his deportation order, with the Immigration and Naturalization Service (INS) (D) actually agreeing with his contention that the statute was unconstitutional. The court of appeals held the statute violated the doctrine of separation of powers.

ISSUE: Is it constitutional for Congress to statutorily authorize a one-house veto of a decision the Attorney General makes, under authority delegated to him by Congress, to allow a particular deportable alien to remain in the United States?

HOLDING AND DECISION: (Burger, C.J.) No. The Constitution does not permit Congress to statutorily authorize a one-house veto of a decision the Attorney General makes, pursuant to authority delegated to him by Congress, to allow a particular deportable alien to remain in the United States. Such an action is clearly an exercise of legislative power, which makes it subject to the bicameralism and presentment requirements of Article I of the Constitution unless one of the express constitutional exceptions authorizing one House to act alone applies here. None of them applies here. Thus, to accomplish what has been attempted by one House of Congress in this case, requires action in conformity with the express procedures of the Constitution's prescription for legislative action: passage by a majority of both Houses and presentment to the President (for his signing or his veto). Such requirements were built into the Constitution to act as enduring checks on each branch and to protect the people from the improvident exercise of power by mandating certain prescribed steps. In attempting to bypass those steps, Congress has acted unconstitutionally. Affirmed.

CONCURRENCE: (Powell, J.) This case should be decided on the narrower ground that Congress assumes a judicial function in violation of the principle of separation of powers when it finds a particular person does not satisfy the statutory criteria for permanent residence in this country. The Court's broader decision will apparently invalidate every use of the legislative veto, which is a procedure that has been much used by Congress and one it clearly views as essential to controlling the delegation of power to administrative agencies. While one may reasonably disagree with Congress's assessment of the veto's utility, the respect due its judgment as a coordinate branch of government cautions that our holding should be no more extensive than necessary to decide this case.

DISSENT: (White, J.) Today's decision sounds the death knell for nearly two hundred statutory provisions in which Congress has reserved a "legislative veto," which has become a central means by which Congress secures the accountability of executive and independent agencies. Without this particular tool, Congress faces a Hobson's choice: either to refrain from delegating the necessary authority, leaving itself with a hopeless task of writing laws with the requisite specificity to cover endless special circumstances across the entire policy landscape, or in the alternative, to abdicate its lawmaking function to the executive branch and independent agencies. Thus, the apparent sweep of the Court's decision today, which appears to invalidate all legislative vetoes irrespective of form or subject, is regrettable. Furthermore, the Court's decision fails to recognize that the legislative veto is not the type of action subject to the bicameralism and presentment requirements of Article 1. Only bills and their equivalent are subject to such requirements. The initial legislation delegating to the Attorney General the power to make a decision on the deportation of a particular alien complied

Continued on next page.

with the Article I requirements. Congress's power to exercise a legislative veto over that decision cannot be viewed, then, as the power to write new law without bicameral approval or presidential consideration. If Congress can delegate lawmaking power to executive agencies, it is most difficult to understand Article I as forbidding Congress from simply reserving a check on legislative power for itself. Without the veto, agencies to whom power has been delegated may issue regulations having the force of law without bicameral approval and without the President's signature. It is thus not apparent why the reservation of a veto over the exercise of that legislative power must be subject to a more exacting test. In both cases, it is enough that the initial statutory authorizations comply with the Article I requirements.

▶ ANALYSIS

It is only within the last 50 years that the legislative veto has come into widespread use. When the federal government began its massive growth in response to the Depression, the legislative veto was "invented" as one means of keeping a check on the sprawling new structure. While many commentators, upon the Court's announcement of this decision, opined that the result was a major shift of power from the legislative branch to the executive branch, Congress through more restrictive draftsmanship should actually see minimal diminishment of its control of those areas over which it desires to retain control.

■≡■

Quicknotes

BICAMERALISM The necessity of approval by a majority of both houses of Congress in ratifying legislation or approving other legislative action.

■≡■

Bowsher v. Synar

Comptroller General (D) v. Union (P)

478 U.S. 714 (1986).

NATURE OF CASE: Appeal from decision that the Gramm-Rudman-Hollings Act violated the doctrine of separation of powers.

FACT SUMMARY: In Synar's (P) action against Bowsher (D), the Comptroller General of the United States, who was assigned by Congress, under the Gramm-Rudman-Hollings Balanced Budget Emergency Deficit Control Act of 1985 ("the Act"), the duty of effectuating across-the-board spending reductions in the federal government, Synar (P) contended that the Act was unconstitutional because Bowsher (D) was authorized, under the Act, to exercise executive functions, violating the doctrine of separation of powers.

RULE OF LAW
When Congress elects to exercise its legislative power, it may not authorize a lesser representative of the legislative branch to act on its behalf.

FACTS: Under the Gramm-Rudman-Hollings Balanced Budget and Emergency Deficit Control Act of 1985 ("the Act"), Bowsher (D), Comptroller General of the United States, was assigned the duty of effectuating across-the-board spending reductions in the federal government. Synar (P) sued Bowsher (D) on behalf of the National Treasury Employees Union, which claimed that its members were injured because Bowsher's (D) spending reductions suspended certain cost-of-living benefit increases. Synar (P) contended that the Act was unconstitutional because the Comptroller General (D) was authorized, under the Act, to exercise executive functions, violating the doctrine of separation of powers. A three-judge district court held the Act unconstitutional on the grounds alleged by Synar (P), and Bowsher (D) appealed.

ISSUE: When Congress elects to exercise its legislative power, may it authorize a lesser representative of the legislative branch to act on its behalf?

HOLDING AND DECISION: (Burger, C.J.) No. When Congress elects to exercise its legislative power, it may not authorize a lesser representative of the legislative branch to act on its behalf. It is clear Congress has consistently viewed the Comptroller General as an officer of the legislative branch. To permit an officer controlled by Congress to execute the law that Congress enacts would be, in essence, to permit a congressional veto. Congress could simply remove, or threaten to remove, an officer for executing the laws in any fashion found to be unsatisfactory to Congress. This kind of congressional control over the execution of the laws is unconstitutionally impermissible.

Here, Congress has retained removal authority over Bowsher (D), as Comptroller General, so that Bowsher (D) may not be entrusted with executive powers. Under the Gramm-Rudman-Hollings Balanced Budget and Emergency Deficit Control Act of 1985 ("the Act"), Bowsher (D) would have the ultimate authority to decide budget cuts to be made. Interpreting a law enacted by Congress to implement the legislative mandate is the very essence of "execution" of the law. Bowsher (D) is, therefore, being given the authority to "execute," under the Act, Congress's mandate. This is unconstitutional.

CONCURRENCE: (Stevens, J.) The Comptroller General (D) must be characterized as an agent of Congress because of his long-standing statutory responsibilities. The powers assigned to the Comptroller General (D) under the Gramm-Rudman-Hollings Act ("the Act") require him to make policy that will bind the nation. Therefore, the Act contains a constitutional infirmity so severe that this flawed provision may not stand.

DISSENT: (White, J.) The Act vesting budget-cutting authority in the Comptroller General (D) represents Congress's judgment that the delegation of such authority to counteract ever-mounting deficits is "necessary and proper" to the exercise of the powers granted the federal government by the Constitution. Under such circumstances, the role of this Court is limited to determining whether the Act so alters the balance of authority among the branches of government as to pose a threat to the basic division between the lawmaking power and the power to execute the law. No such threat was apparent here.

ANALYSIS

The test for validity of a federal act is whether Congress might reasonably find that the act relates to one of the federal powers. If the act bears some reasonable relationship to a grant of power to the federal government, the law must be upheld. If the act relates to such an end, then it is valid so long as it does not violate a specific check on governmental action such as those contained in the Bill of Rights.

■■■

Quicknotes

SEPARATION OF POWERS DOCTRINE Each branch of government is precluded from interfering with the authority of another.

■■■

Morrison v. Olson

Federal government (D) v. Attorney (P)

487 U.S. 654 (1988).

NATURE OF CASE: Appeal of challenge to the independent counsel provisions of the Ethics in Government Act.

FACT SUMMARY: Olson (P) challenged the independent counsel law as violating the Appointments Clause and the separation of powers doctrine.

> **RULE OF LAW**
> The independent counsel provisions of the Ethics in Government Act are constitutional.

FACTS: In 1978, Congress enacted the Ethics in Government Act ("the Act"). Part of the Act created an "independent counsel." The Act provided that when the Attorney General had reasonable grounds to believe that certain federal crimes had been committed by federal officials, he was to report to a specially created court. The court would then appoint a special prosecutor, who would be vested with all the investigative and prosecutorial powers of the Justice Department. The counsel would have certain reporting requirements to the special court and to Congress. The counsel's position could be terminated by the Attorney General, special court, or congressional impeachment. Olson (P), an Environmental Protection Agency (EPA) attorney under investigation by a special counsel, challenged the Act as violative of the Appointments Clause and the separation of powers doctrine. The court of appeals struck down the Act, and the Supreme Court granted review.

ISSUE: Are the independent counsel provisions of the Ethics in Government Act constitutional?

HOLDING AND DECISION: (Rehnquist, C.J.) Yes. The independent counsel provisions of the Ethics in Government Act ("the Act") are constitutional. The Constitution mandates that the President shall appoint what amounts to "principal" executive officers, but permits Congress to delegate to courts the appointment of "inferior" officers. This Court concludes that the independent counsel is an inferior officer. His term is limited, as is his jurisdiction. Also, he must answer to both Congress and the special court. Since Congress may empower courts to appoint inferior officers, the Act does not run afoul of the Appointments Clause. It does not violate Article III's "case or controversy" requirement. While the special court may be participating in a matter insufficient in concreteness to be considered a case or controversy, its role is largely ministerial, and federal courts may play a ministerial role in actions not amounting to a case or controversy. Finally, the Act does not violate the separation of powers doctrine.

The independent counsel, although appointed by a court, is a member of the executive branch, and may be removed by the Attorney General, subject to judicial review. This is not a congressional encroachment upon executive powers, and therefore does not violate separation of powers. Reversed.

DISSENT: (Scalia, J.) The Constitution provides that all, not some, of the executive power shall be vested in the President. The Act places some executive power in the hands of the other branches. Any statute depriving the President of exclusive executive power must fall.

ANALYSIS

This was the third major separation of powers decision of the 1980s. The other two were *INS v. Chadha*, 462 U.S. 919 (1983), and *Bowsher v. Synar*, 478 U.S. 714 (1986). In both cases the Court found the doctrine of separation of powers to be violated. The difference in the present case appears to have been the fact that the independent counsel was found to be an inferior officer, part of the executive branch, and answerable to the President.

Quicknotes

ETHICS IN GOVERNMENT ACT Allows for the appointment of special independent counsel to investigate high ranking government officials.

SEPARATION OF POWERS DOCTRINE Each branch of government is precluded from interfering with the authority of another.

Equality and the Constitution

Quick Reference Rules of Law

State v. Post

State (D) v. Abolitionists (P)

N.J. Sup. Ct., 20 N.J.L. 368 (1845).

NATURE OF CASE: Appeal of constitutional attack on slavery.

FACT SUMMARY: Slavery was challenged as being contrary to the New Jersey State Constitution.

RULE OF LAW
Slavery is not inconsistent with a constitutional declaration that all men are by nature free.

FACTS: The New Jersey Constitution proclaimed that all men were free and independent and endowed with certain rights such as liberty and property. The slave system was challenged as being inconsistent with this.

ISSUE: Is slavery inconsistent with a constitutional declaration that all men are by nature free?

HOLDING AND DECISION: (Nevius, J.) No. Slavery is not inconsistent with a constitutional declaration that all men are by nature free. No one is absolutely free. In a civilized state, all residents give up a portion of their freedoms in exchange for the benefits of civilization. Freedom, then, must be looked at in the context of its society. At the time the New Jersey Constitution was adopted, slavery was an accepted part of society and was not considered incompatible with a free society. This court is not inclined to change that view.

ANALYSIS

Numerous attacks on slavery were mounted in the pre-Civil War era. Some were successful, and others turned out as did this action. The most (in)famous pre-Civil War slavery case was, of course, *Scott v. Sandford*, 60 U.S. 393 (1857).

Dred Scott v. Sandford

Slave (P) v. Owner (D)

60 U.S. (19 How.) 393 (1857).

NATURE OF CASE: Appeal of challenge by slave to slave status.

FACT SUMMARY: Scott (P), a slave, sued for his freedom after having been taken to a free state and returned to a slave state.

🏛 RULE OF LAW
Black individuals are not to be considered "citizens" in the constitutional sense.

FACTS: Scott (P) was born a slave. He had been taken to Illinois, a free state, by his master. Scott (P) was taken to several other free states or territories. Scott (P) was then taken to Missouri, a slave state, and sold to Sandford (D). Scott (P) then sued for his freedom, contending that his having been taken into free states made him free. Jurisdiction was predicated on diversity of citizenship.

ISSUE: Are black individuals considered to be "citizens" in the constitutional sense?

HOLDING AND DECISION: (Taney, C.J.) No. Black individuals are not considered to be "citizens" in the constitutional sense. "Citizens," for constitutional purposes, refers to the sovereign people of the United States as they were understood to be at the time of the Constitution's adoption. At that time, the blacks were considered an inferior class, one having no inherent liberty or property rights. A state may confer rights upon individuals living in it as it sees fit. It cannot, however, confer rights as a U.S. citizen by virtue of state law. The fact that in Illinois Scott (P) could not be a slave does not alter the fact that Illinois' ability to make Scott (P) a free man extends no further than its borders and does not confer upon Scott (P) rights and privileges of U.S. citizenship. Therefore, Scott (P) was not a citizen of a state in U.S. constitutional sense and not entitled to sue in U.S. courts. Affirmed.

▶ ANALYSIS

Dred Scott is, without a doubt, the most vilified decision in Supreme Court history. Under analysis, however, the decision was fairly consistent with the ideals of strict constructionism, a judicial philosophy that was in and out of fashion for much of the twentieth century. The Court basically looked to the intent of the Framers of the Constitution and attempted to be consistent with them.

Quicknotes

CONSTRUCTION The examination and interpretation of statutes.

Plessy v. Ferguson

Railroad passenger (D) v. State (P)

163 U.S. 537 (1896).

NATURE OF CASE: Appeal from criminal prosecution for violating a state railway accommodation segregation law.

FACT SUMMARY: Plessy (D) was arrested for trying to sit in a railroad car that was designated "for whites only."

🏛 RULE OF LAW
Segregation of the races is reasonable if based upon the established custom, usage, and traditions of the people in the state.

FACTS: Plessy (D) who was 7/8 caucasian and whose skin color was white was denied a seat in an all-white railroad car. When he (D) resisted, he was arrested for violating a state law that provided for segregated "separate but equal" railroad accommodations. Plessy (D) appealed the conviction on the basis that separation of the races stigmatized black people and stamped them with the badge of inferiority. He (D) claimed that segregation violated the Thirteenth and Fourteenth Amendments. The trial court found Plessy (D) guilty on the basis the law was a reasonable exercise of the state's police powers based upon custom, usage, and tradition in the state.

ISSUE: Is segregation of the races reasonable if based upon the established custom, usage, and traditions of the people of the state?

HOLDING AND DECISION: (Brown, J.) Yes. Segregation of the races is reasonable if based upon the established custom, usage, and traditions of the people in the state. This is a valid exercise of the state's police power. Where this has been the established custom, usage, or tradition in the state, it may continue to require such segregation as is reasonable to preserve order and the public peace. Such decisions have been continuously upheld. This is not a badge of "slavery" under the Thirteenth Amendment and it violates no provision of the Fourteenth Amendment. The enforced separation of the races is not a badge of servitude or inferiority regardless of how Plessy (D) and other black people deem to treat it. The conviction is sustained.

DISSENT: (Harlan, J.) The statute interferes with the personal freedom of individuals to freely associate with others. The Constitution is color-blind. All citizens should and must be treated alike. Black people are not subordinate or inferior things. They are citizens and are entitled to all the privileges this entails. Enforced separation is an impermissible burden on these privileges and freedoms. The conviction should be overturned.

▶ ANALYSIS

Plessy is of importance only for its historical perspective. Later cases borrowed the "separate but equal" phraseology and turned it around 180 degrees. In *Brown v. Board of Education*, 347 U.S. 483 (1954), the Court, 58 years after *Plessy*, held that separate could never be considered equal. It thus expressly overruled *Plessy*.

◼▬◼

Quicknotes

SEGREGATION The use of separate institutions and facilities for persons of different races, nationalities, religions, etc.

◼▬◼

Brown v. Board of Education of Topeka (Brown I)

Students (P) v. School board (D)

347 U.S. 483 (1954).

NATURE OF CASE: Action seeking order to desegregate public schools.

FACT SUMMARY: Black children were denied admission to public schools attended by white children.

🏛 RULE OF LAW
The "separate but equal" doctrine has no application in the field of education and the segregation of children in public schools based solely on their race violates the Equal Protection Clause.

FACTS: Black children had been denied admission to public schools attended by white children, under laws requiring or permitting segregation according to race. It was found that the black children's schools and the white children's schools had been or were being equalized with respect to buildings, curricula, qualifications, and salaries of teachers.

ISSUE: Does segregation of children in public schools solely on the basis of race, even though the physical facilities are equal, deprive the children of the minority group of equal protection of the law?

HOLDING AND DECISION: (Warren, C.J.) Yes. The "separate but equal" doctrine has no application in the field of education and the segregation of children in public schools based solely on their race violates the Equal Protection Clause. First, intangible as well as tangible factors may be considered. Hence, the fact that the facilities and other tangible factors in the schools have been equalized is not controlling. Segregation of white and black children in public schools has a detrimental effect on the black children because the policy of separating the races is usually interpreted as denoting the inferiority of the black children. A sense of inferiority affects children's motivation to learn. Segregation tends to deprive black children of some of the benefits they would receive in an integrated school. Any language in *Plessy v. Ferguson*, 163 U.S. 537 (1896), contrary to this is rejected. The "separate but equal" doctrine has no place in the field of education. Separate facilities are inherently unequal. Such facilities deprive black children of their right to equal protection of the laws.

▌ *ANALYSIS*

In *Plessy v. Ferguson*, the Court sustained a Louisiana statute requiring "equal, but separate, accommodations" for black and white railway passengers. The separate but equal doctrine was born and under it a long line of statutes providing separate but equal facilities was upheld. Justice Harlan was the only dissenter in *Plessy*. He stated, "The arbitrary separation of citizens, on the basis of race, while they are on a public highway ... cannot be justified upon any legal grounds. The thin disguise of equal accommodations for passengers in railway cars will not mislead anyone, nor atone for the wrong done this day." After the 1954 decision in *Brown v. Board of Education*, the Court found segregation unconstitutional in other public facilities as well. Despite the emphasis on the school context in *Brown*, the later cases resulted in per curiam orders simply citing *Brown*. Facilities that were desegregated included beaches, buses, golf courses, and parks.

Quicknotes

EQUAL PROTECTION CLAUSE A constitutional provision that each person be guaranteed the same protection of the laws enjoyed by other persons in like circumstances.

SEGREGATION The use of separate institutions and facilities for persons of different races, nationalities, religions, etc.

Brown v. Board of Education of Topeka (Brown II)

[Implementation Decision]

349 U.S. 294 (1955).

NATURE OF CASE: Decision to determine the manner in which relief from segregation in public schools is to be accorded.

FACT SUMMARY: In May 1954, the Court decided that racial discrimination in public education is unconstitutional. It requested further arguments on the question of relief.

🏛 RULE OF LAW
School authorities have the primary responsibility for assessing and solving the problem of achieving racial integration in the public schools.

FACTS: These cases were decided in May 1954. The opinions declared that racial discrimination in public education is unconstitutional. They are incorporated here. Because the cases arose under various local conditions and their disposition will involve a variety of local problems, the Court requested additional arguments on the question of relief. All provisions of federal, state, and local laws that permit segregation in public schools must be modified.

ISSUE: Do school authorities have the primary responsibility for assessing and solving the problem of achieving racial integration in the public schools?

HOLDING AND DECISION: (Warren, C.J.) Yes. School authorities have the primary responsibility for assessing and solving the problem of achieving racial integration in the public schools. It will be for courts to consider whether the school authorities' actions are good-faith implementations of the governing constitutional principles. Because of their proximity to local conditions and the possible need for further hearings, the courts that originally heard these cases can best perform this judicial appraisal. In doing so, the courts will be guided by the equitable principles of practical flexibility in shaping remedies and the facility for adjusting and reconciling public and private needs. The courts will require that the defendants make a prompt and reasonable start toward full racial integration in the public schools. Once such a start is made, the courts may determine that additional time is required to carry out the May 1954 ruling. However, the burden rests upon the defendant to determine that such time is necessary and consistent with good-faith compliance with the Constitution. The courts may consider problems related to administration, the facilities, school transportation systems, and revision of school districts and local laws. They will also consider the adequacy of any plans proposed by the defendants and will retain jurisdiction during the transition period. The cases are remanded to the lower courts to enter orders consistent with this opinion as necessary to insure the parties to these cases are admitted to public schools on a racially nondiscriminatory basis with all deliberate speed.

▶ ANALYSIS

After its promulgation of general guidelines in *Brown II* in 1955, the Court maintained silence about implementation for several years. Enforcement of the desegregation requirement was left largely to lower court litigation. In 1958, the Court broke its silence in *Cooper v. Aaron*, 358 U.S. 1 (1958), where it reaffirmed the *Brown* principles in the face of official resistance in Little Rock, Arkansas. It was not until the early sixties, however, that the Court began to consider the details of desegregation plans. During the late 1960s, Court rulings on implementation came with greater frequency, specificity, and urgency. Finally, in *Alexander v. Holmes County Board of Education*, 369 U.S. 19 (1969), the Court called for an immediate end to dual school systems.

Quicknotes

SEGREGATION The use of separate institutions and facilities for persons of different races, nationalities, religions, etc.

New York City Transit Authority v. Beazer

Public authority (D) v. Methadone users (P)

440 U.S. 568 (1979).

NATURE OF CASE: Appeal of court order invalidating certain employment policies.

FACT SUMMARY: A N.Y. Transit Authority (D) policy of not hiring methadone users was challenged as unconstitutional.

RULE OF LAW

A public authority may deny employment to methadone users as a class.

FACTS: The N.Y. Transit Authority (D) had a rule denying employment to anyone using methadone, a synthetic narcotic used in treating heroin addiction. Beazer (P) brought a class action suit alleging that this rule denied equal protection. The evidence showed that at least half of all methadone users were employable. The district court issued an injunction barring enforcement of the rule. The court of appeals affirmed.

ISSUE: May a public authority deny employment to methadone users as a class?

HOLDING AND DECISION: (Stevens, J.) Yes. A public authority may deny employment to methadone users as a class. Methadone users do not have the characteristics of a suspect class, these being distinguishing immutable characteristics. For this reason all that must be shown is a rational relationship between the end, here safety and efficiency, and the means, here denial of employment. The record does not show that the means do not rationally achieve the ends, so the rule is valid. Reversed.

DISSENT: (White, J.) A rule lumping successful methadone patients with unsuccessful ones is overinclusive. Such an arbitrary rule is unconstitutional.

ANALYSIS

For most of the history of civil rights jurisprudence, the "two-tier" system employed here has been the norm. If a classification is suspect, that is, one involving a group that either has immutable distinguishing characteristics or a history of discrimination, strict review of classifications will be made. If, as here, the classification is not suspect, a much more lax standard will be used.

Quicknotes

RATIONAL BASIS REVIEW A test employed by the court to determine the validity of a statute in "equal protection" actions, whereby the court determines whether the challenged statute is rationally related to the achievement of a legitimate state interest.

SUSPECT CLASSIFICATION A class of persons that have historically been subject to discriminatory treatment; statutes drawing a distinction between persons based on a suspect classification, i.e., race, nationality or alienage, are subject to a strict scrutiny standard of review.

Strauder v. West Virginia

Criminal defendant (D) v. State (P)

100 U.S. (10 Otto) 303 (1880).

NATURE OF CASE: Appeal from murder conviction.

FACT SUMMARY: [Strauder (D), a black man, was convicted of murder by a jury from which blacks were excluded.]

RULE OF LAW
A state may not prevent one from serving on a jury because of race or color.

FACTS: [Strauder (D), a black man, was indicted for murder and after a trial was convicted of the charge. On appeal, Strauder (D) argued that at the trial he was denied rights to which he was entitled under the Constitution and laws of the United States because under state law blacks were ineligible to serve on the grand or petit jury.]

ISSUE: May a state prevent one from serving on a jury because of race or color?

HOLDING AND DECISION: (Strong, J.) No. A state may not prevent one from serving on a jury because of race or color. The Fourteenth Amendment was designed to assure to the race recently emancipated the enjoyment of all the civil rights that are under the law enjoyed by white persons, and to give that race the protection of the general government in that enjoyment, whenever it is attempted to be denied by the states. The Fourteenth Amendment not only provided citizenship and its privileges to blacks, but denies to any state the power to withhold from them the equal protection of the laws, and authorized Congress to enforce its provisions by legislation appropriate to that objective. Although the words of the Amendment are prohibitory, they contain a necessary implication of a positive immunity and valuable right to blacks: the right to exemption from unfriendly legislation against them because of their color, exemption from legal discrimination, implying inferiority in civil society, and discriminations that constitute steps towards reducing them to the condition of a subject race. Legislation preventing blacks from serving on juries clearly constitutes a prohibited discrimination. It is well known that prejudices often exist against particular classes in the community. These prejudices may sway juror judgment, and, thus, might operate to deny to persons of those classes the full enjoyment of the protections that others enjoy. Reversed.

ANALYSIS

This case, one of the earliest decisions interpreting the Fourteenth Amendment, discusses two themes that later became significant in determining whether a group constituted a suspect classification, and whether the legislation in question violates constitutional prohibitions. The first is whether the class, as in the case of blacks, is one that has historically been the victim of societal discrimination. The second is whether the legislation in question tends to stigmatize that class in the eyes of society.

Quicknotes

FOURTEENTH AMENDMENT Declares that no state shall make or enforce any law that shall abridge the privileges and immunities of citizens of the United States. No state shall deny to any person within its jurisdiction the equal protection of the laws.

Korematsu v. United States

Japanese American citizen (D) v. Federal government (P)

323 U.S. 214 (1944).

NATURE OF CASE: Appeal from a conviction for violation of exclusion order No. 34.

FACT SUMMARY: Korematsu (D), an American citizen of Japanese ancestry, was convicted of violating exclusion order No. 34, a World War II decree that ordered all persons of Japanese ancestry to leave the military area of the western United States.

🏛 RULE OF LAW
Apprehension by the proper military authorities of the gravest imminent danger to the public safety can justify the curtailment of the civil rights of a single racial group.

FACTS: Korematsu (D), an American citizen of Japanese ancestry, was convicted in federal district court for remaining in San Leandro, California, a "military area," contrary to civilian exclusion order No. 34 of the commanding general of the western command. The order directed that after May 9, 1942, all persons of Japanese ancestry should be excluded from the area to protect against acts of sabotage and espionage during World War II. Those of Japanese ancestry were to report to and temporarily remain in an assembly center and go under military control to a relocation center for an indeterminate period. Korematsu (P) appealed on grounds that the order denied equal protection.

ISSUE: Can apprehension by the proper military authorities of the gravest imminent danger to the public safety justify the curtailment of the civil rights of a single racial group?

HOLDING AND DECISION: (Black, J.) Yes. Apprehension by the proper military authorities of the gravest imminent danger to the public safety can justify the curtailment of the civil rights of a single racial group. While such a classification is immediately suspect and is subject to the most rigid scrutiny, pressing public necessity may sometimes justify such exclusions. When under conditions of modern warfare the country is threatened, "the power to protect must be commensurate with the threatened danger." Korematsu (D) was excluded because the United States was at war with the Empire of Japan, because the proper military authorities feared invasion of the West Coast and believed security required exclusion, and because Congress, placing its confidence in the military, determined that the military should have that power. Affirmed.

DISSENT: (Murphy, J.) It cannot be reasonably assumed that all persons of Japanese ancestry may have a dangerous tendency to commit enemy acts.

DISSENT: (Jackson, J.) A civil court should not be made to enforce an order that violates constitutional limitations even if it is a reasonable exercise of military authority.

▶ ANALYSIS

This case has received severe and growing criticism over the years. However, Chief Justice Warren has expressed the view that in some circumstances the Court will simply not be in a position to reject descriptions by the executive of the degree of military necessity. Where time is of the essence, the court could only reject the necessity not on grounds of factual unassailability, but for insufficiency. Justice Douglas, 30 years later, wrote, "the decisions were extreme and went to the verge of wartime power . . . It is easy in retrospect to denounce what was done, as there actually was no attempted Japanese invasion of our country . . . but those making plans for the defense of the nation had no such knowledge and were planning for the worst." *De Funis v. Odegaard*, 416 U.S. 312 (1974).

■■■

Quicknotes

SUSPECT CLASSIFICATION A class of persons that have historically been subject to discriminatory treatment; statutes drawing a distinction between persons based on a suspect classification, i.e., race, nationality or alienage, are subject to a strict scrutiny standard of review.

■■■

Loving v. Virginia

Interracial couple (D) v. State (P)

388 U.S. 1 (1967).

NATURE OF CASE: Appeal after conviction for violation of state law barring interracial marriage.

FACT SUMMARY: Loving (D), a white man, and Jeter (D), a black woman, both Virginia residents, were married in the District of Columbia. When they returned to Virginia, they were indicted for violating the state's ban on interracial marriage.

RULE OF LAW

A state law restricting the freedom to marry solely because of racial classification violates the Equal Protection Clause.

FACTS: In June 1958, Loving (D) a white man, and Jeter (D), a black woman, both Virginia residents, were married in the District of Columbia, pursuant to its laws. Shortly after their marriage, the Lovings (D) returned to Virginia and were indicted for violating the state's law barring interracial marriage. They pleaded guilty and were sentenced to one year in jail. The trial judge suspended the sentence for 25 years on the condition the Lovings (D) leave the state and not return for 25 years. In 1963, they filed a motion to have the judgment vacated and set aside.

ISSUE: Does a state law restricting the freedom to marry solely because of racial classification violate the Equal Protection Clause?

HOLDING AND DECISION: (Warren, C.J.) Yes. A state law restricting the freedom to marry solely because of racial classification violates the Equal Protection Clause. The Clause demands that racial classifications, especially suspect in criminal statutes, be subjected to the most rigid scrutiny. The clear and central purpose of the Fourteenth Amendment was to eliminate all official state sources of invidious discrimination. There can be no question but that Virginia's (P) miscegenation statutes rest solely upon distinctions drawn according to race. The statutes proscribe generally accepted conduct if engaged in by members of different races. Here, there is patently no legitimate overriding purpose of this legislation independent of invidious racial discrimination. The fact that Virginia (P) prohibits only interracial marriages involving white persons demonstrates that the racial classifications could qualify only as a measure designed to maintain White Supremacy. In fact, the very title of the legislation is "An Act to Preserve Racial Integrity." The Court has consistently denied the constitutionality of measures that restrict the rights of citizens on account of race. Reversed.

CONCURRENCE: (Stewart, J.) It is simply not possible for a state law to be valid under the Constitution, which makes the criminality of an act depend upon the race of the actor.

▶ ANALYSIS

In *McLaughlin v. Florida*, 379 U.S. 184 (1964), a state law banning habitual nighttime cohabitation between whites and blacks not married to each other was held to violate the Equal Protection Clause, since other nonmarried couples were not subject to prosecution for the same acts. Ordinances establishing ghettos in which blacks must reside were found to violate the clause (*Buchanan v. Warley*, 245 U.S. 60 (1917)), as was judicial enforcement of covenants restricting ownership of land to whites (*Shelley v. Kramer*, 334 U.S. 1 (1948)). Racial discrimination in the selection of jurors (*Patton v. Mississippi*, 332 U.S. 463 (1947)), hiring blacks for certain occupations, and establishing racial qualifications for public offices (*Anderson v. Martin*, 375 U.S. 399 (1964)) have all been held to violate equal protection.

■══■

Quicknotes

EQUAL PROTECTION CLAUSE A constitutional provision that each person be guaranteed the same protection of the laws enjoyed by other persons in like circumstances.

■══■

Washington v. Davis

Federal district (D) v. Employment applicant (P)

426 U.S. 229 (1976).

NATURE OF CASE: Appeal from reversal of order sustaining validity of employment qualification test.

FACT SUMMARY: Washington (D) administered a written test of verbal skills, vocabulary, and reading comprehension to applicants for jobs in the Police Department, and since four times as many blacks failed the test as whites, Davis (P) brought suit alleging the invalidity of the test due to its discriminatory impact.

RULE OF LAW

The administration of a race-neutral test on relevant criteria to employment applicants does not violate the Equal Protection Clause where the test results in the elimination of a disproportionate number of racial minorities as opposed to whites.

FACTS: Applicants for jobs as police officers with the District of Columbia Metropolitan Police Department were required by Washington (D) to take a qualifying test that was developed by the Civil Service Commission for use throughout the federal employment system, known as "Test 21." Four times as many black applicants failed this test as white applicants. Davis (P) brought this suit alleging that the disproportionate effect on racial minorities of the test rendered it a denial of equal protection, despite the facts that there was no proof of discriminatory intent, the test was race-neutral, and the test tested verbal skills, vocabulary, and reading comprehension, all of which are relevant to the performance of a police officer's duties. The district court upheld the test due to the absence of proof of intent, but the court of appeals reversed, holding that the discriminatory impact alone was sufficient to show the constitutional violation alleged. The Supreme Court granted certiorari.

ISSUE: Does the administration of a race-neutral test on relevant criteria to employment applicants violate the Equal Protection Clause where the test results in the elimination of a disproportionate number of racial minorities as opposed to whites?

HOLDING AND DECISION: (White, J.) No. The administration of a race-neutral test on relevant criteria to employment applicants does not violate the Equal Protection Clause where the test results in the elimination of a disproportionate number of racial minorities as opposed to whites. The central purpose of the Equal Protection Clause of the Fourteenth Amendment is the prevention of official conduct that discriminates on the basis of race. It has never been held that a law or other official action is unconstitutional solely because it has a racially disproportionate impact. The school desegregation cases have held that a racially discriminatory purpose must be behind law if it is to be found invidiously discriminatory. The Constitution does not prevent the government from seeking to upgrade the communicative skills of its employees by employing a test of those skills that is racially neutral. The administration of a race-neutral test on relevant criteria to employment applicants does not violate the Equal Protection Clause where the tests result in the elimination of a disproportionate number of racial minorities. Some discriminatory intent or purpose must be shown. Reversed.

CONCURRENCE: (Stevens, J.) The line between discriminatory purpose and discriminatory impact is not nearly as bright, and perhaps not quite as critical, as the reader of the Court's opinion might assume. However, "Test 21" survives the challenge of Davis (P) because it serves a neutral and legitimate purpose and is used on all applicants for the job in question, in addition to many others. The evidence of discrimination in this case is therefore insufficient.

ANALYSIS

It is possible to conceive of a test that is race-neutral on its face, but which nonetheless is part of a plan—or purpose—to discriminate. If such a showing is made, the neutrality on the face of the test will not save it, as de jure discrimination will be found if the evidence shows the plan, purpose, or intent. It is only held here that discriminatory effect standing alone is insufficient to invoke the Equal Protection Clause.

Quicknotes

EQUAL PROTECTION CLAUSE A constitutional provision that each person be guaranteed the same protection of the laws enjoyed by other persons in like circumstances.

McCleskey v. Kemp

Inmate (D) v. State (P)

481 U.S. 279 (1987).

NATURE OF CASE: Appeal from denial of writ of habeas corpus.

FACT SUMMARY: McCleskey (D) contended he was denied equal protection when sentenced to death because blacks were statistically more likely to be so sentenced, and such was racially based.

RULE OF LAW

Capital cases require an evaluation of the motivations of individual jurors in sentencing; thus, raw abstract statistical data are not dispositive of a lack of equal protection.

FACTS: McCleskey (D), an African American, was sentenced to death for killing a white. He petitioned for a writ of habeas corpus presenting a statistical study indicating blacks were more likely to be sentenced to death, and that such was racially motivated. The district court and the court of appeals rejected the statistical data as irrelevant to the disposition, and the Supreme Court granted certiorari.

ISSUE: May statistical data be used in a capital case to determine an absence of equal protection?

HOLDING AND DECISION: (Powell, J.) No. Capital cases require an evaluation of the motivations of individual jurors in sentencing; thus, raw abstract statistical studies are irrelevant and not dispositive of a lack of equal protection. Each jury is unique in its composition, rendering statistical studies useless. Each case must be evaluated on its own merits. Thus, these data were properly excluded. Affirmed.

DISSENT: (Brennan, J.) Georgia's (P) legacy of a race-conscious criminal justice system, as well as the Court's own recognition of the persistent danger that racial attitudes may affect criminal proceedings, indicate that McCleskey's (D) claim is not a fanciful product of mere statistical artifice. The fact that one must always act without the illumination of complete knowledge cannot induce paralysis when confronted with what is literally an issue of life and death.

▶ ANALYSIS

The Court appeared reluctant to rely upon statistical data in overturning a jury verdict. The statistical manipulations and fact-gathering methodology in such studies may give a false conclusion regarding the result. Extrapolation and mathematical interpretation was felt to unreasonably impact upon the ultimate conclusion. Any individual jury, after voir dire, can be as independent as necessary, according to the Court, and thus such statistics merely cloud the issue.

■=■

Quicknotes

VOIR DIRE Examination of potential jurors on a case.

■=■

Adarand Constructors, Inc. v. Pena

Contractor (P) v. Administrative agency (D)

515 U.S. 200 (1995).

NATURE OF CASE: Appeal from judgment rejecting, through the application of an intermediate level of review, equal protection challenges to a federal program encouraging the awarding of federal contracts to businesses controlled by socially and economically disadvantaged individuals. [The complete procedural posture of the case is not presented in the casebook extract.]

FACT SUMMARY: Adarand Constructors, Inc. (Adarand) (P) challenged as violating equal protection principles a federal program giving preferences in federal contracting to businesses controlled by socially and economically disadvantaged individuals, who were presumed to include minorities, and contended that the appropriate level of judicial review for such preferences was strict scrutiny, rather than a lower level of review.

RULE OF LAW

All racial classifications, imposed by whatever federal, state, or local governmental actor, must be analyzed by a reviewing court under strict scrutiny.

FACTS: The U.S. Department of Transportation (D) awarded a construction contract. The contractor (Mountain Gravel) solicited subcontracts. Adarand Constructors, Inc. (Adarand) (P) submitted the low bid, but because of federal incentives favoring businesses controlled by socially and economically disadvantaged individuals, who were presumed to include minorities, Adarand (P) was rejected in favor of a minority-owned business (Gonzales). Adarand (P) brought an action, contending that the incentive program was a violation of the equal protection strand of the Due Process Clause. The court of appeals, applying an intermediate level of judicial review, rejected the challenge, and the Supreme Court granted certiorari. [The complete procedural posture of the case is not presented in the casebook extract.]

ISSUE: Must all racial classifications, imposed by whatever federal, state, or local governmental actor, be analyzed by a reviewing court under strict scrutiny?

HOLDING AND DECISION: (O'Connor, J.) Yes. All racial classifications, imposed by whatever federal, state, or local governmental actor, must be analyzed by a reviewing court under strict scrutiny. The Government (D) asserts that program at issue is based on disadvantage, not on race, and thus is subject only to the most relaxed judicial scrutiny. To the extent that the statutes and regulations involved in this case are race neutral, the Government (D) is correct. The Government (D) concedes, however,

that the race-based rebuttable presumption used in some certification determinations under the program is subject to some heightened level of scrutiny, but the parties disagree as to what that level should be. There is no equal protection provision in the Fifth Amendment, such as is found in the Fourteenth, which applies to the states. In *Richmond v. J.A. Croson Co.,* 488 U.S. 469 (1989), the Court held that the Fourteenth Amendment requires strict scrutiny of all race-based action by state and local governments. While *Croson* did not consider what standard of review the Fifth Amendment requires for such action taken by the federal government, the Court's cases through *Croson* had established three general propositions with respect to governmental racial classifications. First, skepticism: "any preference based on racial or ethnic criteria must necessarily receive a most searching examination;" second, consistency: "the standard of review under the Equal Protection Clause is not dependent on the race of those burdened or benefited by a particular classification;" and third, congruence: "equal protection analysis in the Fifth Amendment area is the same as that under the Fourteenth Amendment." Taken together, these propositions lead to the conclusion that any person, of whatever race, has the right to demand that any governmental actor subject to the Constitution justify any racial classification subjecting that person to unequal treatment under the strictest judicial scrutiny. Thus, it is clear the federal government's obligations under the Due Process Clause require it to treat similarly situated individuals in a similar fashion, much as states must do. To the extent that prior authority that held that "benign" racial discrimination by Congress is subject to less rigorous scrutiny than traditional discrimination, such authority is overruled. Good intentions alone are not enough to sustain a supposedly "benign" racial classification: Even though it is not the actual predicate for this legislation, a statute of this kind inevitably is perceived by many as resting on an assumption that those who are granted this special preference are less qualified in some respect that is identified purely by their race. Because that perception—especially when fostered by Congress—can only exacerbate rather than reduce racial prejudice, it will delay the time when race will become a truly irrelevant, or at least insignificant, factor. Accordingly, racial classification of any sort is subject to the highest level of judicial review: the classification must be narrowly tailored to serve a compelling state interest. The eradication of racism in contracting is such an interest, but the means to achieve it must be carefully drawn. When race-based action is

Continued on next page.

necessary to further a compelling interest, such action is within constitutional constraints if it satisfies the Court's "narrow tailoring" test. Vacated and remanded.

CONCURRENCE: (Scalia, J.) Government can never "make up" for past discrimination by present discrimination. In our constitutional system, there can never be a debtor race or a creditor race. The Constitution protects persons, not races. To pursue the concept of racial entitlement—even for the most admirable and benign of purposes—is to reinforce and preserve for future mischief the way of thinking that produced race slavery, race privilege, and race hatred.

CONCURRENCE: (Thomas, J.) There is no racial paternalism exception to the principle of equal protection: government cannot make us equal; it can only recognize, respect, and protect us as equal before the law. The government may not make distinctions on the basis of race, regardless of the impetus for such distinctions, since there is no doubt that racial paternalism and its unintended consequences can be as poisonous and pernicious as any other form of discrimination. Even if the intent behind such discrimination is "benign" and motivated by a desire to redress past inequalities, its effect is to teach many that because of chronic and apparently immutable handicaps, minorities cannot compete with them without their patronizing indulgence. Government-sponsored racial discrimination based on benign prejudice is just as noxious as discrimination inspired by malicious prejudice. In each instance, it is simply racial discrimination.

DISSENT: (Stevens, J.) There is a distinction at the constitutional level between a policy that is designed to subjugate a minority group and a policy that seeks to foster equality in society. The majority's ignoring such a distinction in the name of "consistency" is akin to ignoring the difference between a "No Trespassing" sign and a welcome mat. People understand the difference between good intentions and bad, notwithstanding that it sometimes is difficult to distinguish between "benign" and "invidious" discrimination. Moreover, the majority's approach risks producing anomalous results regarding different classes of people. For example, government will more easily be able to enact affirmative-action programs to remedy discrimination against women (reviewed under intermediate scrutiny) than it will to remedy discrimination against African Americans (reviewed under strict scrutiny)—even though the primary purpose of the Equal Protection Clause was to end discrimination against the former slaves. Further, the majority's reliance on principles of congruence to conclude that there is no significant difference between a decision by Congress to adopt an affirmative-action program and such a decision by a state or a municipality is untenable, since it ignores important practical and legal differences between federal and state or local decision-makers. Federal affirmative-action programs represent the will of the Nation's elected representatives, whereas a state

or local program may have an impact on nonresident entities that played no part in the decision to enact it. Thus, in the state or local context, individuals who were unable to vote for the local representatives who enacted a race-conscious program may nonetheless feel the effects of that program. This difference is similar to the goals of the Commerce Clause, which permits Congress to legislate on certain matters of national importance while denying power to the states in this area for fear of undue impact on out-of-state residents.

▶ *ANALYSIS*

The Court remanded the case because the court of appeals, which had applied only an intermediate level of scrutiny, had not decided whether the interests served by use of subcontractor compensation clauses were properly described as "compelling," and had not addressed the question of narrow tailoring in terms of the Court's strict scrutiny cases. Unresolved questions also remained concerning the details of the complex regulatory regimes implicated by use of such clauses. By remanding, the Court left these unresolved issues for the lower courts to consider under strict scrutiny.

■▬■

Quicknotes

DUE PROCESS CLAUSE Clauses found in the Fifth and Fourteenth Amendments to the United States Constitution providing that no person shall be deprived of "life, liberty, or property, without due process of law."

INTERMEDIATE SCRUTINY A standard of reviewing the propriety of classifications pertaining to gender or legitimacy under the Equal Protection Clause of the United States Constitution which requires a court to ascertain whether the classification furthers an important state interest and is substantially related to the attainment of that interest.

STRICT SCRUTINY Method by which courts determine the constitutionality of a law when a law affects a fundamental right. Under the test, the legislature must have had a compelling interest to enact the law and measures prescribed by the law must be the least restrictive means possible to accomplish its goal.

■▬■

Grutter v. Bollinger

Law school applicant (P) v. Law school (D)

539 U.S. 306 (2003).

NATURE OF CASE: Appeal in racial discrimination case.

FACT SUMMARY: When Grutter (P), a white Michigan resident, was denied admission to the University of Michigan Law School (D), she sued the latter in federal district court, alleging racial discrimination against her in violation of the Equal Protection Clause on basis of the law school's (D) express consideration of race as a factor in the admissions process.

RULE OF LAW

Student body diversity is a compelling state interest that can justify the use of race in university admissions.

FACTS: To attempt to achieve student body diversity, the University of Michigan Law School (D) admissions committee required admissions officials to evaluate each applicant based on all the information in the file, including a personal statement, letters of recommendation, a student's essay, grades, LSAT score, as well as so-called "soft variables." The admissions policy, furthermore, specifically stressed the law school's (D) long-standing commitment to racial and ethnic diversity. When Grutter (P), a white Michigan resident, applied for admission but was denied, she sued the law school (D) in federal district court, alleging racial discrimination against her in violation of the Equal Protection Clause. [The district court upheld Grutter's (P) claim. The court of appeals reversed, and Grutter (P) appealed.]

ISSUE: Is student body diversity a compelling state interest that can justify the use of race in university admissions?

HOLDING AND DECISION: (O'Connor, J.) Yes. Student body diversity is a compelling state interest that can justify the use of race in university admissions. Here, the law school's (D) admissions program bears the hallmarks of a narrowly tailored plan. Truly individualized consideration demands that race be used in a flexible, nonmechanical way. It follows from this mandate that universities cannot establish quotas for members of certain racial groups or put members of those groups on separate admissions tracks. Nor can universities insulate applicants who belong to certain racial or ethnic groups from the competition for admission. Universities can, however, as was done here, consider race or ethnicity more flexibly as a plus factor in the context of individualized consideration of each and every applicant. The law school's (D) goal of

attaining a critical mass of underrepresented minority students does not transform its program into a quota. The evidence indicated that the law school (D) engaged in a highly individualized, holistic review of each applicant's file, giving serious consideration to all the ways an applicant might contribute to a "diverse educational environment." Furthermore, evidence showed that the law school (D) gives substantial weight to diversity factors besides race by frequently accepting nonminority applicants with grades and test scores lower than underrepresented minority applicants. There was no law school (D) policy, either de facto or de jure, of automatic acceptance or rejection based on any single "soft" variable. Narrow tailoring does not require exhaustion of every conceivable race-neutral alternative. Nor does it require a university to choose between maintaining a reputation for excellence or fulfilling a commitment to provide educational opportunities to members of all racial groups. Affirmed.

CONCURRENCE: (Ginsburg, J.) From today's vantage point, one may hope, but not firmly forecast, that over the next generation's span, progress toward nondiscrimination and genuinely equal opportunity will make it safe to sunset affirmative action.

DISSENT: (Rehnquist, C.J.) Although the law school claims it must take the steps it does to achieve a "critical mass" of underrepresented minority students, its actual program bears no relation to this asserted goal. Stripped of its "critical mass" veil, the law school's (D) program is revealed as a naked effort to achieve racial balancing.

DISSENT: (Kennedy, J.) Refusal of the Court to apply strict scrutiny that is meaningful will lead to serious consequences. By deferring to the law school's (D) choice of minority admissions programs, courts will lose the talents and resources of the faculties and administrators in devising new and fairer ways to ensure individual consideration.

CONCURRENCE AND DISSENT: (Scalia, J.) Unlike a clear constitutional holding that racial preferences in state educational institutions are impermissible, or even a clear anticonstitutional holding, today's decision seems perversely designed to prolong the controversy and the litigation. The Constitution proscribes government discrimination on the basis of race, and state-provided education is no exception.

CONCURRENCE AND DISSENT: (Thomas, J.) Blacks can achieve in every avenue of American life

Continued on next page.

without the meddling of university administrators. The majority upholds the law school's (D) racial discrimination not by interpreting the people's Constitution, but by responding to a faddish slogan.

▎ *ANALYSIS*

As seen in *Grutter* and predecessor Supreme Court decisions, not every decision influenced by race is equally objectionable, and "strict scrutiny" is designed to provide a framework for carefully examining the importance and the sincerity of the reasons advanced by the governmental decisionmaker for the use of race in any given context.

Quicknotes

EQUAL PROTECTION CLAUSE A constitutional provision that each person be guaranteed the same protection of the laws enjoyed by other persons in like circumstances.

Parents Involved in Community Schools v. Seattle School District No. 1

Parents of unadmitted students (P) v. Public school district (D)

551 U.S. 701 (2007).

NATURE OF CASE: Suits challenging school-assignment plans under the Equal Protection Clause.

FACT SUMMARY: Two metropolitan school districts sought to assign students to schools to achieve racial balance.

RULE OF LAW
Racial balance between local high school districts is not a compelling government interest under the Equal Protection Clause.

FACTS: The Seattle School District in Seattle, Washington (Seattle) (D) implemented a student assignment plan designed to achieve numerically defined racial balance between Seattle's (D) ten public high schools. Seattle (D), however, had never been found to run racially segregated schools. The Jefferson County Public Schools in Louisville, Kentucky (Louisville) was under a desegregation order from 1975 to 2000; the order was dissolved in 2001 when a federal court ruled that Louisville (D) had reached unitary status by largely eliminating the district's earlier racial segregation. After the decree was dissolved, Louisville (D) voluntarily adopted a student assignment plan that required specific minimum and maximum enrollment percentages for black students. Parents (P) of students who were denied admission in each school district sued their respective district, alleging, in part, violations of the Equal Protection Clause. After the intermediate appellate courts in both cases upheld the assignment plans, the parents (P) petitioned the Supreme Court for further review.

ISSUE: Is racial balance between local high school districts a compelling government interest under the Equal Protection Clause?

HOLDING AND DECISION: (Roberts, C.J.) No. Racial balance between local high school districts is not a compelling government interest under the Equal Protection Clause. Because both school districts (D) have apportioned government benefits on the basis of race, the applicable standard of review in these cases is strict scrutiny: Seattle (D) and Louisville (D) must show that their race-based discrimination (1) advances a compelling government interest through (2) means that are narrowly tailored to achieve the intended purpose. The asserted interests in both Seattle (D) and Louisville (D) reduce to nothing more than the goal of numerical racial balance between each district's (D) schools. This Court has consistently found such a purpose illegitimate. *Grutter v. Bollinger*, 539 U.S. 306 (2003), does not control here because *Grutter*

involved the specific interests of higher education; it is also instructive, though, that *Grutter* upheld the law school admission policy there because racial diversity was only one of a mix of admissions criteria. Here, on the other hand, pure numerical racial balance, by itself, is the government interest, and that interest has never been recognized as valid. The plans at issue here also fail because the school districts (D) have failed to show that they seriously considered other means besides explicit racial classifications. Reversed.

CONCURRENCE: (Thomas, J.) Racial imbalance and racial segregation are not synonymous; it is possible to have racial imbalance through no conscious decision to segregate. Further, forced racial mixing of students may or may not provide educational benefits in general or higher achievement for black students in particular. The color-blind Constitution, then, requires that these student assignment plans be struck down.

CONCURRENCE: (Kennedy, J.) Contrary to the Chief Justice's plurality opinion, race can be considered as one among several factors in examining school enrollments. General, indirect solutions to problems of racial composition of schools are much better than the crude plans in these cases as ways to address those problems. The United States has special obligations to ensure equal opportunity for all children, and government should be permitted to consider race in its attempts to fulfill that mission. As the plurality correctly notes, though, government may not classify students based solely on race without first making a showing that such a step is necessary.

DISSENT: (Stevens, J.) In his demand of strict equality under the Constitution, the Chief Justice forgets that, before *Brown*, only black students were told where they could and could not go to school. Today's plurality decision rewrites the history of our landmark school-desegregation decision.

DISSENT: (Breyer, J.) These voluntary plans bear striking resemblance to plans that this Court has long required, permitted, and encouraged local school districts to formulate and use. Every branch of government has acknowledged that government may voluntarily use race-conscious plans to address race-based problems even when such plans are not constitutionally obligatory. The plurality overlooks the fact that no case has ever decided that all racial classifications should receive precisely the same scrutiny. Actually, our decisions have applied different

Continued on next page.

standards to assess racial classifications depending on whether the government's purpose was to exclude persons from, or to include persons in, government programs. The plurality's interpretation of strict scrutiny, however, would automatically invalidate all race-conscious government action. The school districts' (D) interest here serves remedial, educational, and democratic purposes; such a multiplicity of concerns means that *Grutter*'s rationale controls here and requires upholding these assignment plans. Even under the strictest scrutiny, though, the plans here pass muster under the Equal Protection Clause because they are more narrowly tailored than the plan approved in *Grutter*. Accordingly, these plans are consistent with equal protection of the laws.

▶ *ANALYSIS*

Chief Justice Roberts's plurality opinion in *Parents Involved* focuses on the firm percentages used by Seattle (D) and Louisville (D) in making student-assignment decisions. Despite Justice Breyer's objections in dissent, it is difficult to see how such an overtly numerical approach differs from the quota-based systems the Court consistently has struck down under the Equal Protection Clause. See, e.g., *Regents of the University of California v. Bakke*, 438 U.S. 265, 307 (1978), "If [the University's] purpose is to assure within its student body some specified percentage of a particular group merely because of its race or ethnic origin, such a preferential purpose must be rejected not as insubstantial but as facially invalid."

Quicknotes

EQUAL PROTECTION CLAUSE A constitutional provision that each person be guaranteed the same protection of the laws enjoyed by other persons in like circumstances.

STRICT SCRUTINY The method by which courts determine the constitutionality of a law when a law affects a fundamental right. Under the test, the legislature must have had a compelling interest to enact the law and measures prescribed by the law must be the least restrictive means possible to accomplish its goal.

Craig v. Boren

Males 18–20 years of age (P) v. State (D)

429 U.S. 190 (1976).

NATURE OF CASE: Appeal from an action to have an Oklahoma statute declared unconstitutional.

FACT SUMMARY: Craig (P) appealed after a federal district court upheld two sections of an Oklahoma statute prohibiting the sale of "nonintoxicating" 3.2 percent beer to males under the age of 21 and to females under the age of 18 on the ground such a gender-based differential did not constitute a denial to males 18–20 years of age of equal protection of the laws.

RULE OF LAW

Laws that establish classifications by gender must serve important governmental objectives and must be substantially related to achievement of those objectives to be constitutionally in line with the Equal Protection Clause.

FACTS: Craig (P) brought suit to have two sections of an Oklahoma statute, which prohibited the sale of "nonintoxicating" 3.2 percent beer to males under the age of 21 and to females under the age of 18, declared unconstitutional. Craig (P) contended that such a gender-based differential constituted a denial to males 18–20 years of age of the equal protection of the laws in violation of the Fourteenth Amendment. Boren (D), representing the State of Oklahoma, argued that this law was enacted as a traffic safety measure and that the protection of public health and safety was an important function of state and local governments. Boren (D) introduced statistical data demonstrating that 18–20-year-old male arrests for "driving under the influence" and "drunkenness" substantially exceeded female arrests for the same age range. The district court upheld the ordinance on the ground it served the important governmental objective of traffic safety. Craig (P) appealed.

ISSUE: Are laws that establish classifications by gender constitutional if they do not serve important governmental objectives and are not substantially related to achievement of those objectives?

HOLDING AND DECISION: (Brennan, J.) No. Laws that establish classifications by gender must serve important governmental objectives and must be substantially related to achievement of those objectives to be constitutionally in line with the Equal Protection Clause. It appears that the objective underlying the statute in controversy is the enhancement of traffic safety. Clearly, the protection of public health and safety represents an important function of state and local governments. However, the statistics presented by Boren (D) in this Court's

view cannot support the conclusion that the gender-based distinction closely serves to achieve the objective. The most relevant of the statistical surveys presented as evidence by Boren (D) in support of the statute, arrests of 18–20-year-olds for alcohol-related driving offenses, establish 2 percent more males than females are arrested for that offense. Such a disparity can hardly form the basis for employment of a gender line as a classifying device. Certainly, if maleness is to serve as a proxy for drinking and driving, a correlation of 2 percent must be considered unduly tenuous. Indeed, prior cases have consistently rejected the use of sex as a decision-making factor. Therefore, since the gender-based differential does not serve an important governmental objective, the Oklahoma statute constitutes a denial of the equal protection of the laws to males aged 18–20 and is unconstitutional. The judgment of the district court is reversed.

CONCURRENCE: (Powell, J.) The state legislature, by the classification it has chosen, has not adopted through the enactment of the statute a means that bears a fair and substantial relation to the objective of traffic safety.

CONCURRENCE: (Stevens, J.) It is difficult to believe that the statute in question was actually intended to cope with the problem of traffic safety, since it has only a minimal effect on access to a not-very-intoxicating beverage and does not prohibit its consumption.

DISSENT: (Rehnquist, J.) The Court's disposition of this case is objectionable on two grounds. First, is its conclusion that men challenging a gender-based statute that treats them less favorably than women may invoke a more stringent standard of judicial review than pertains to most other types of classifications. Second, is the court's enunciation of this standard, without citation to any source, as being that "classifications by gender must serve important governmental objectives and must be substantially related to achievement of those objectives." The Equal Protection Clause contains no such language, and none of our previous cases adopts that standard.

ANALYSIS

Cases concerning whether males and females should be considered as reaching a majority age equally has met with some stiff opposition. In *Stanton v. Stanton*, 552 P.2d 112 (1976), Utah Supreme Court Justice Ellett observed: "Regardless of what a judge may think about equality, his thinking cannot change the facts of life. . . . To judicially

Continued on next page.

hold that males and females attain their maturity at the same age is to be blind to the biological facts of life."

Quicknotes

EQUAL PROTECTION CLAUSE A constitutional provision that each person be guaranteed the same protection of the laws enjoyed by other persons in like circumstances.

United States v. Virginia

Federal government (P) v. Public institution (D)

518 U.S. 515 (1996).

NATURE OF CASE: Appeal from final judgment upholding a college's male-only admission policy.

FACT SUMMARY: Virginia Military Institute (D), a state-sponsored university, had a policy of excluding women from attending.

 RULE OF LAW
Public schools may not exclude women.

FACTS: Since 1839, Virginia Military Institute (VMI) (D), a Virginia (D) public institution, had been a male-only college that sought to train "citizen-soldiers." In 1990, the Attorney General (P) sued VMI (D) and Virginia (D), claiming that the admissions-policy violated the Equal Protection Clause. Virginia (D) eventually proposed a remedial plan under which a parallel program would be developed for women. The Virginia Women's Institute for Leadership (VWIL) would be created at Mary Baldwin College. The trial court and an appellate court upheld this remedial plan, but the Attorney General (P) appealed and the Supreme Court granted a writ of certiorari.

ISSUE: May public schools exclude women?

HOLDING AND DECISION: (Ginsburg, J.) No. Public schools may not exclude women. States must show that a sex-based government action serves important governmental objectives and that the discriminatory means employed are substantially related to the achievement of those objectives. There must be an exceedingly persuasive justification for the action. This heightened review standard prevents classifications that perpetuate the legal, social, and economic inferiority of women. While single-sex education may provide benefits to some students, Virginia (D) has not shown it pursued this option as a means to providing a diversity of educational opportunities. On the other hand, the historical record shows Virginia (D) has systematically prevented women from obtaining higher education until relatively recently. The fact women have been successfully integrated into the armed forces and service academies demonstrates Virginia Military Institute's (VMI's) (D) stature will not be downgraded by admitting women. The proposed Virginia Women's Institute for Leadership (VWIL) does not qualify as VMI's (D) equal in terms of faculty, facilities, course offerings, and reputation. Accordingly, since Virginia (D) is unable to provide substantial equal opportunities for women who desire to attend VMI (D), the male-only admission policy is unconstitutional. Reversed.

CONCURRENCE: (Rehnquist, C.J.) The majority decision is correct but there is no basis for stating that states must demonstrate an exceedingly persuasive justification to support sex-based classifications.

DISSENT: (Scalia, J.) The majority sweeps away an institution that has thrived for 150 years and the precedents of this Court to embark on a course of proscribing its own elite opinions on society. Virginia (D) has an important interest in providing education, and single-sex instruction is an approach substantially related to this goal. The proposed Virginia Women's Institute for Leadership was designed for women and not designed to be exactly equal to the Virginia Military Institute (D).

ANALYSIS

Justice Scalia's dissent carries a tone of disgust for the majority opinion. As he did in *Romer v. Evans*, 517 U.S. 620 (1996), Scalia states the majority seeks to satisfy some unidentified group of antimajoritarian elites. This attitude is unusual for a member of the Supreme Court since dissents are usually restricted to attacks on the majority's legal reasoning.

Quicknotes

EQUAL PROTECTION CLAUSE A constitutional provision that each person be guaranteed the same protection of the laws enjoyed by other persons in like circumstances.

Romer v. Evans

Municipality (P) v. State (D)

517 U.S. 620 (1996).

NATURE OF CASE: Review of order striking down state constitutional amendment.

FACT SUMMARY: A Colorado law that preempted local ordinances prohibiting discrimination against homosexuals was challenged as unconstitutional.

🏛 RULE OF LAW
States may not enact laws prohibiting localities from proscribing discrimination against a class of persons.

FACTS: In 1992, Colorado voters adopted a statewide initiative. The law, known as Amendment 2, preempted local ordinances from prohibiting discrimination on the basis of sexual preference. The Colorado Supreme Court struck down the law as contrary to Equal Protection. The U.S. Supreme Court granted review.

ISSUE: May states enact laws prohibiting localities from proscribing discrimination against a class of persons?

HOLDING AND DECISION: (Kennedy, J.) No. States may not enact laws prohibiting localities from proscribing discrimination against a class of persons. Colorado's Amendment 2 has the peculiar property of imposing a broad rule on a singled named group, as it places a particular burden in terms of access to the political process. Groups not affected by this law have greater access to this process. This clearly implicates the Equal Protection Clause of the Fourteenth Amendment. Such a law must bear a rational relationship to a legitimate government purpose. Amendment 2 is a status-based law undertaken for its own sake without serving any legitimate interest. Therefore, it is unconstitutional. Affirmed.

DISSENT: (Scalia, J.) Colorado's Amendment 2 is a modest attempt against assaults on basic morals by a politically powerful interest group. States must be free to disfavor conduct its citizens find reprehensible.

▶ ANALYSIS

Interestingly, the majority opinion here did not mention the last major case involving homosexuality, *Bowers v. Hardwick*, 478 U.S. 18 (1986). That case held it constitutional for a state to criminalize homosexual conduct. Assuming *Bowers* to still be good law, it seems that states can criminalize homosexual conduct, but cannot preempt local laws regarding homosexuals as a class.

Quicknotes

EQUAL PROTECTION CLAUSE A constitutional provision that each person be guaranteed the same protection of the laws enjoyed by other persons in like circumstances.

RATIONAL BASIS REVIEW A test employed by the court to determine the validity of a statute in equal protection actions, whereby the court determines whether the challenged statute is rationally related to the achievement of a legitimate state interest.

SUSPECT CLASSIFICATION A class of persons that have historically been subject to discriminatory treatment; statutes drawing a distinction between persons based on a suspect classification, i.e., race, nationality or alienage, are subject to a strict scrutiny standard of review.

Sugarman v. Dougall

State (D) v. Alien (P)

413 U.S. 634 (1973).

NATURE OF CASE: Appeal of ruling invalidating state law prohibiting aliens from civil service employment.

FACT SUMMARY: New York (D) had a statutory system prohibiting aliens from civil service positions involving competitive examinations.

🏛 RULE OF LAW
A state may not refuse all civil service positions on the basis of alienage alone.

FACTS: New York (D) prohibited aliens from civil service positions requiring competitive examinations. All civil service positions not involving election or appointment were based on examination scores. Dougall (P), an alien, challenged this as a violation of equal protection. The lower court held the system unconstitutional.

ISSUE: May a state refuse all civil service positions on the basis of alienage alone?

HOLDING AND DECISION: (Blackmun, J.) No. A state may not refuse all civil service positions on the basis of alienage alone. Aliens have a history of being a discrete and insular minority, and therefore classifications based on alienage trigger strict scrutiny, which means the classification must advance a compelling interest and be narrowly drawn. New York (D) argues that it has an interest in allowing into the civil service system only those free of competing loyalties. This is an important interest, but the statute excludes from alien employment positions in which this interest is irrelevant, while not including higher-level positions where the interest is greater. As the statute is both under- and over-inclusive, it must fail. Affirmed.

DISSENT: (Rehnquist, J.) Unlike race, alienage should not trigger heightened scrutiny, so all that New York (D) should have been required to show was a rational basis for the classification, something it could have done.

▶ ANALYSIS

Several factors are taken into account in deciding upon whether a class will be suspect. As the Court said in the opinion, a history of being a discrete minority is a factor. Other factors are a history of discrimination and immutable distinguishing characteristics. Obviously, not all factors must be present at all times, as alienage is not an immutable characteristic.

═══

Quicknotes

Implied Fundamental Rights

Quick Reference Rules of Law

The Slaughter-House Cases

Slaughterhouses (P) v. State (D)

83 U.S. (16 Wall.) 36 (1873).

NATURE OF CASE: Appeal of ruling upholding a state-imposed slaughterhouse monopoly.

FACT SUMMARY: The State of Louisiana granted a monopoly to a certain slaughterhouse, and this was challenged as being contrary to the Fourteenth Amendment.

🏛 RULE OF LAW
The Privileges and Immunities Clause of the Fourteenth Amendment only guarantees those federal rights protected as of the time of the Amendment's adoption.

FACTS: The State of Louisiana (D) conferred by statute a monopoly in the slaughterhouse business on a certain slaughterhouse. Competing slaughterhouses (P) challenged this as an abridgment of the right to own and use property, which the plaintiffs contended was a right guaranteed by the Privileges and Immunities Clause of the Fourteenth Amendment. The lower courts upheld the statute.

ISSUE: Does the Privileges and Immunities Clause of the Fourteenth Amendment only guarantee those federal rights protected as of the time of the Amendment's adoption?

HOLDING AND DECISION: (Miller, J.) Yes. The Privileges and Immunities Clause of the Fourteenth Amendment only guarantees those federal rights protected as of the time of the Amendment's adoption. The Amendment must be interpreted in light of its purpose. The first section overrules the *Dred Scott* decision, 60 U.S. (19 How.) 393 (1987), by conferring both national and state citizenship on those born in the United States. It would be a major leap to presume, however, that the Amendment was intended to change the nature of the privileges granted by the United States vis-à-vis the states. Certain federally guaranteed rights do exist, but, by and large, the extent to which individual freedoms and rights have been granted is a matter of state prerogative, and the Court is not inclined to hold that the amendment alters that. Affirmed.

DISSENT: (Field, J.) The Amendment should be construed as guaranteeing basic freedoms for all U.S. citizens. Even holding, as the Court does, that the clause goes no further than the Privileges and Immunities Clause of Article IV, the result should be different. The freedom to engage in one's livelihood is a basic freedom.

DISSENT: (Bradley, J.) The right to follow one's employment of choice is the most basic of rights and should be protected by the clause.

▶ ANALYSIS

The Slaughter-House Cases represents the first major Supreme Court pronouncement on the Fourteenth Amendment. It was argued that the Privileges and Immunities Clause applied the Bill of Rights to the states and this was rejected. The Court has, of course, largely done this by using the Equal Protection and Due Process Clauses. Some have said that the Court would have been more honest in applying the Bill of Rights to the states by overruling the *Slaughter-House Cases*, but it has not seen fit to do this.

Quicknotes

DUE PROCESS CLAUSE Clauses found in the Fifth and Fourteenth Amendments to the United States Constitution providing that no person shall be deprived of "life, liberty, or property, without due process of law."

EQUAL PROTECTION CLAUSE A constitutional provision that each person be guaranteed the same protection of the laws enjoyed by other persons in like circumstances.

FOURTEENTH AMENDMENT Declares that no state shall make or enforce any law that shall abridge the privileges and immunities of citizens of the United States. No state shall deny to any person within its jurisdiction the equal protection of the laws.

McDonald v. City of Chicago

Citizens (P) v. State (D)

561 U.S. 742 (2010).

NATURE OF CASE: Appeal from affirmance of judgment that the Second Amendment does not apply to the states.

FACT SUMMARY: [Several plaintiffs (P) challenged a ban on handguns in Chicago, contending the ban was unconstitutional because the Second Amendment applies to the states.]

RULE OF LAW

The Second Amendment applies to the states by incorporation through the Due Process Clause.

FACTS: [The cities of Chicago (D) and Oak Park (D) in Illinois had gun bans. Several lawsuits were filed against the cities challenging those bans after the Supreme Court decided *District of Columbia v. Heller*, 554 U.S. 570 (2008), where the Court held a District of Columbia handgun ban violated the Second Amendment because the D.C. law was enacted under the authority of the federal government and, therefore, the Second Amendment was applicable. The plaintiffs (P) in this case argued the Second Amendment also applies to the states, and because it does, the Chicago (D) handgun bans were unconstitutional. The district court dismissed the suits and on appeal, the U.S. Court of Appeals for the Seventh Circuit affirmed. The Supreme Court granted certiorari.]

ISSUE: Does the Second Amendment apply to the states by incorporation through the Due Process Clause?

HOLDING AND DECISION: (Alito, J.) Yes. The Second Amendment applies to the states by incorporation through the Due Process Clause. As a threshold matter, the Privileges or Immunities Clause does not incorporate the Second Amendment. Also, under the Court's "selective incorporation" approach, once a right under the Bill of Rights is incorporated, it applies fully to the states. In *Heller,* it was decided the right to self-defense is a right that is "fundamental to the Nation's scheme of ordered liberty" and "deeply rooted in this Nation's history and tradition." Although by the 1850s the threat that had prompted the Second Amendment, that the national government would disarm the universal militia, had passed, Congress nevertheless upheld the right to bear arms as a fundamental right, and arguments to the contrary are not supported by history. Instead, as history shows, after the Civil War, the southern states engaged in systematic efforts to disarm and injure African Americans. These injustices prompted the 39th Congress to pass the Freedmen's Bureau Act of 1866 and the Civil Rights Act of 1866 to protect the right to keep and bear arms. Congress, however, ulti-

mately deemed these legislative remedies insufficient, and approved the Fourteenth Amendment. Today, it is generally accepted that that Amendment was understood to provide a constitutional basis for protecting the rights set out in the Civil Rights Act, and that the right to bear arms for self-defense was viewed as fundamental. Contrary to the municipalities' (D) arguments, Congress did not overwhelmingly view § 1 of the Fourteenth Amendment as purely an antidiscrimination rule. Although § 1 does contain an antidiscrimination rule, i.e., the Equal Protection Clause, it can hardly be said that the section does no more than prohibit discrimination. If what the municipalities (D) mean is that the Second Amendment should be singled out for special—and specially unfavorable—treatment, the Court rejects the suggestion. The right to keep and bear arms must be regarded as a substantive guarantee, not a prohibition that could be ignored so long as the states legislated in an evenhanded manner. If this were not so, for example, many of the criminal protections of the Bill of Rights, which are unique to our country, would not be incorporated against the states. [Reversed and remanded.]

CONCURRENCE: (Scalia, J.) Justice Stevens's dissent is wrong and premised on a subjective standard. Essentially, he advocates disregarding precedent and Due Process principles, and relying exclusively on what judges believe is correct. Under this approach, judges get to pick the rights they want to protect and discard those they don't. Justice Stevens asserts his standard is not subjective because it provides sufficient constraints on judges' subjectivity. The first constraint he offers is that he would avoid attempts to provide any all-purpose, top-down, totalizing theory of liberty. The notion the absence of a coherent theory of the Due Process Clause will somehow curtail judicial subjectivity makes no sense. To the contrary, indeterminacy means opportunity for courts to impose whatever rule they like; it is the problem, not the solution. In other words, if there are no correct answers, there are no wrong answers, either. Another constraint he offers is requiring judges to show respect for the democratic process. While that serves as a constraint on subjectivity, the manner in which Justice Stevens would apply that constraint is extraordinary, as it would give rights the states are considering restricting—such as the right to bear arms—less protection, while giving a privilege the political branches (instruments of the democratic process) have withheld entirely and continue to withhold more protection. This is a topsy-turvy approach that insults rather than respects the democratic process. The next constraint Justice Stevens

Continued on next page.

suggests is more difficult to assess. He advocates judges have "sensitivity to the interaction between the intrinsic aspects of liberty and the practical realities of contemporary society." It is unclear what this means. Is it some sixth sense instilled in judges when they ascend to the bench? Or does it mean judges are more constrained when they agonize about the cosmic conflict between liberty and its potentially harmful consequences? In any event, the historically focused approach is significantly better than the "living Constitution," subjective, approach recommended by Justice Stevens. The historical approach is much less subjective, and intrudes much less upon the democratic process because it depends upon a body of evidence susceptible of reasoned analysis rather than a variety of vague ethicopolitical "First Principles" whose combined conclusion can be found to point in any direction the judges favor. Moreover, the latter approach would not eliminate, but multiply, the hard questions courts must confront, since it would not replace history with moral philosophy, but would have courts consider both.

DISSENT: (Stevens, J.) The core issue to be resolved here is whether the Second Amendment guarantees individuals a fundamental right, enforceable against the states, to possess a functional, personal firearm, including a handgun, within the home. That is a different question than the incorporation question, which was already decided in the late 19th century. This is a substantive due process case. The rights protected by the Due Process Clause are not principally procedural in nature, and substantive due process is fundamentally a matter of personal liberty. Regardless of whether a substantive due process interest is expressly identified in the Constitution, the key inquiry is whether that interest is comprised within the term liberty. Flowing from these principles is the notion that the rights protected against state infringement by the Fourteenth Amendment's Due Process Clause need not be identical in shape or scope to the rights protected against federal government infringement by the various provisions of the Bill of Rights. Substantive due process claims that are based on purely local or particular interests, rather than more universal liberty interests, are not constitutionally protected. Such a liberty test undeniably requires judges to apply their own reasoned judgment, but that does not mean it involves an exercise in abstract philosophy. In addition, historical and empirical data of various kinds ground the analysis. A rigid historical test is inappropriate because the substantive due process doctrine has never evaluated substantive rights in purely, or even predominantly, historical terms. If it were really the case that the Fourteenth Amendment's guarantee of liberty embraces only those rights "so rooted in our history, tradition, and practice as to require special protection," then the guarantee would serve little function, except to ratify those rights that states and municipalities have already been according the most extensive protection. A purely historical approach would be unfaithful to the expansive principles inherent in

the Fourteenth Amendment and to the level of generality in its language. To find otherwise, would mean we would have to countenance the most revolting injustices in the name of continuity, and not be responsive to newly recognized injustices, such as the subjugation of women and other rank forms of discrimination. To adhere to the purely historical approach would in effect be judicial abdication in the guise of judicial modesty. The question then arises how to avoid injecting too much subjectivity when determining substantive due process liberty claims. In addition to grounding the analysis in historical experience and reasoned judgment, there are several constraints that militate against subjectivity. First, the courts must eschew attempts to provide any all-purpose, top-down, totalizing theory of "liberty," which was not defined by the Framers, and which by its very nature cannot be reduced to a formula or otherwise pigeonholed. Nevertheless, the parameters of liberty have been elucidated by a conceptual core that refines and delimits the notion of liberty. The clause safeguards, most basically, "the ability independently to define one's identity," "the individual's right to make certain unusually important decisions that will affect his own, or his family's, destiny," and the right to be respected as a human being. Self-determination, bodily integrity, freedom of conscience, intimate relationships, political equality, dignity and respect—these are the central values implicit in the concept of ordered liberty. A second constraint is respect for the democratic process, so that where the states have already carefully considered a particular liberty interest, judicial intervention may not be appropriate. The real issue here, then, is not whether the Second Amendment applies to the states merely because it has been incorporated by the Fourteenth Amendment—it has not—but whether the Second Amendment applies because of the Fourteenth Amendment's mandate to protect liberty. Understood as a liberty question, the plea of homeowners to keep arms in their home has real force, founded on a desire for self-defense and to protect their liberty and property. While the individual's interest in firearm possession is thus heightened in the home, the state's corresponding interest in regulation is somewhat weaker. However, under a substantive due process analysis, precedent supports Chicago's (D) ban. First, firearms have a fundamentally ambivalent relationship to liberty. Just as they can help homeowners defend their families and property from intruders, they can help thugs and insurrectionists murder innocent victims. Second, owning a handgun or any particular type of firearm is not critical to leading a life of autonomy, dignity, or political equality. Further, the experience of other advanced democracies, including those that share our British heritage, undercuts the notion an expansive right to keep and bear arms is intrinsic to ordered liberty, as those countries place stricter restrictions on firearms than does the U.S. Finally, Justice Scalia's historically focused approach does

Continued on next page.

not lead to an objective approach. To the contrary, numerous threshold questions that frame the analysis arise before one ever gets to the history—and there is no neutral, objective answer to these questions. Even then, it is hardly a novel insight that history is not an objective science, and that its use can therefore "point in any direction the judges favor." His method invites not only bad history, but also bad constitutional law. While history must be a factor in the analysis, it should not be the determinative factor, and the net result of Justice Scalia's approach is to give federal judges unprecedented lawmaking powers in an area in which they have no special qualifications, and where the political process has handled the issue for decades. Moreover, not only can historical views be less than completely clear or informative, but they can also be wrong. Some notions that many Americans deeply believed to be true, at one time, turned out not to be true. The fact that the Nation has a written Constitution does not consign the Nation to a static legal existence.

▶ *ANALYSIS*

Most scholars agree that when the Bill of Rights was adopted, it was intended to limit the federal, not state, government. After the adoption of the Fourteenth Amendment in 1868, the Supreme Court held that rights from the Bill of Rights may be selectively applied, or "incorporated," through the Due Process Clause. In *McDonald*, the Court stated that provisions of the Bill of Rights may be incorporated only if they are "fundamental to *our* scheme of ordered liberty," or "deeply rooted in this Nation's history and tradition." The case therefore represents a restriction on the application of the Due Process Clause.

Quicknotes

DUE PROCESS CLAUSE Clauses found in the Fifth and Fourteenth Amendments to the United States Constitution providing that no person shall be deprived of "life, liberty, or property, without due process of law."

FOURTEENTH AMENDMENT Declares that no state shall make or enforce any law that shall abridge the privileges and immunities of citizens of the United States. No state shall deny to any person within its jurisdiction the equal protection of the laws.

PRIVILEGES AND IMMUNITIES CLAUSE Refers to the guarantee set forth in the Fourteenth Amendment to the United States Constitution recognizing that any individual born in any of the United States is entitled to both state and national citizenship and guaranteeing such citizens the privileges and immunities thereof.

Lochner v. New York

Bakery owner (D) v. State (P)

198 U.S. 45 (1905).

NATURE OF CASE: Appeal from conviction for violation of a labor law.

FACT SUMMARY: A state labor law prohibited employment in bakeries for more than 60 hours a week or more than 10 hours a day. Lochner (D) permitted an employee in his bakery to work over 60 hours in one week.

🏛 RULE OF LAW
To be a fair, reasonable, and appropriate use of a state's police power, an act must have a direct relation, as a means to an end, to an appropriate and legitimate state objective.

FACTS: Lochner (D) was fined for violating a state labor law. The law prohibited employment in bakeries for more than 60 hours a week or more than 10 hours a day. Lochner (D) permitted an employee to work in his bakery for more than 60 hours in one week.

ISSUE: To be a fair, reasonable, and appropriate use of a state's police power, must an act have a direct relation, as a means to an end, to an appropriate and legitimate state objective?

HOLDING AND DECISION: (Peckham, J.) Yes. To be a fair, reasonable, and appropriate use of a state's police power, an act must have a direct relation, as a means to an end, to an appropriate and legitimate state objective. The general right to make a contract in relation to one's business is part of the liberty of the individual protected by the Fourteenth Amendment. The right to purchase or sell labor is part of the liberty protected by this amendment. However, the states do possess certain police powers relating to the safety, health, morals, and general welfare of the public. If the contract is one that the state, in the exercise of its police power, has the right to prohibit, the Fourteenth Amendment will not prevent the state's prohibition. When, as here, the state acts to limit the right to labor or the right to contract, it is necessary to determine whether the rights of the state or the individual shall prevail. The Fourteenth Amendment limits the state's exercise of its police power; otherwise the state would have unbounded power once it stated that legislation was to conserve the health, morals, or safety of its people. It is not sufficient to assert that the act relates to public health. Rather, it must have a more direct relation, as a means to an end, to an appropriate state goal, before an act can interfere with an individual's right to contract in relation to his labor. In this case, there is no reasonable foundation for holding the act to be necessary to the health of the public or of bakery officials. Statutes such as this one are mere meddlesome interferences with the rights of the individual. They are invalid unless there is some fair ground to say that there is material danger to the public health or to the employees' health if the labor hours are not curtailed. It cannot be said that the production of healthy bread depends upon the hours that the employees work. Nor is the trade of a baker an unhealthy one to the degree that would authorize the legislature to interfere with the rights to labor and of free contract. Lochner's (D) conviction is reversed.

DISSENT: (Harlan, J.) Whether or not this would be wise legislation is not a question for this Court. It is impossible to say that there is not substantial or real regulation between the statute and the state's legitimate goals. This decision brings under the court's supervision matters that supposedly belonged exclusively to state legislatures.

DISSENT: (Holmes, J.) The word "liberty" in the Fourteenth Amendment should not invalidate a statute unless it can be said a reasonable person would say the statute infringes fundamental principles of our people and our law. A reasonable person might think this statute valid. Citizens' liberty is regulated by many state laws that have been held to be valid, i.e., the Sunday laws, the lottery laws, and laws requiring vaccination.

▶ ANALYSIS

From the *Lochner* decision in 1905 to the 1930s the Court invalidated a considerable number of laws on substantive due process grounds, such as laws fixing minimum wages, maximum hours, prices, and laws regulating business activities. The modern Court claims to have rejected the *Lochner* doctrine. It has withdrawn careful scrutiny in most economic areas but has maintained and increased intervention with respect to a variety of non-economic liberties. However, not only economic regulations were struck down under *Lochner*. That doctrine formed the basis for absorbing rights such as those in the First Amendment into the Fourteenth Amendment concept of liberty. *Lochner* also helped justify on behalf of other non-economic rights such as the right to teach in a foreign language (*Meyers v. Nebraska*, 262 U.S. 390 (1923)). *Meyers* was to be relied upon in the birth control decision, *Griswold v. Connecticut*, 381 U.S. 479 (1965).

■▬▬■

Quicknotes

DUE PROCESS CLAUSE Clauses found in the Fifth and Fourteenth Amendments to the United States

Continued on next page.

Constitution providing that no person shall be deprived of "life, liberty, or property, without due process of law."

FOURTEENTH AMENDMENT Declares that no state shall make or enforce any law that shall abridge the privileges and immunities of citizens of the United States. No state shall deny to any person within its jurisdiction the equal protection of the laws.

Skinner v. Oklahoma

Criminal (D) v. State (P)

316 U.S. 535 (1942).

NATURE OF CASE: Constitutional challenge to state law.

FACT SUMMARY: Skinner (D) was deemed to be a habitual criminal and was ordered sterilized under a state (P) statute.

🏛 RULE OF LAW
A statute that arbitrarily excludes a class from its purview violates the Equal Protection Clause of the Fourteenth Amendment where fundamental rights are involved.

FACTS: Skinner (D) was convicted of crimes on three separate occasions. Under an Oklahoma (P) statute he could be declared a habitual criminal and could be ordered to be sterilized to prevent the passing on of criminal genetic traits. The statute applied to those convicted of two or more crimes amounting to felonies involving moral turpitude. The Attorney General could maintain a suit to have the convicted party sterilized. A full trial would be held. The issue was confined to whether the party was a habitual criminal and whether he should be sterilized. Offenses arising out of violations of prohibitory laws, revenue acts, embezzlement, or political offenses were not within the purview of the statute. Skinner (D) was adjudged a habitual criminal and was ordered sterilized. Skinner (D) challenged the constitutionality of the statute.

ISSUE: May a state arbitrarily discriminate between like classes where fundamental rights are involved?

HOLDING AND DECISION: (Douglas, J.) No. A statute that arbitrarily excludes a class from its purview violates the Equal Protection Clause of the Fourteenth Amendment where fundamental rights are involved. We do not pass on the constitutionality of sterilization of habitual criminals or the state's procedure. We do find that the State (P) statute is unconstitutional under the Equal Protection Clause of the Fourteenth Amendment. We are dealing herein with a fundamental right, i.e., the right to have children. Statutes dealing with such rights are closely scrutinized. While a state may treat classes unequally based on experience, it may not arbitrarily seek to add or exclude a particular group from treatment. There must be a rational basis for the distinction. The law treats the embezzler in the same manner as other criminals, e.g., those convicted of grand larceny. There is no viable difference between their offenses or gene traits. Failure to treat them equally under the sterilization statute cannot be supported and violates the Equal Protection Clause. The statute is unconstitutional on its face. Reversed.

CONCURRENCE: (Stone, C.J.) There is no scientific proof that criminal tendencies are inherited. I would find that the statute violates personal liberties secured by the Due Process Clause. The law sets up arbitrary standards that cannot be supported by evidence/fact.

▶ ANALYSIS

A law that condemns, without hearing, all the individuals of a class to a harsh measure merely because some or many are deserving of such treatment, lacks the basic attributes of due process. *Morrison v. California*, 291 U.S. 82 (1934). In *Skinner*, the Court expressly left the constitutional issue as to sterilization open even if the equal protection problem was solved. This is based on the Court's concern to decide all cases on the narrowest possible grounds.

Quicknotes

DUE PROCESS CLAUSE Clauses found in the Fifth and Fourteenth Amendments to the United States Constitution providing that no person shall be deprived of "life, liberty, or property, without due process of law."

EQUAL PROTECTION CLAUSE A constitutional provision that each person be guaranteed the same protection of the laws enjoyed by other persons in like circumstances.

FOURTEENTH AMENDMENT Declares that no state shall make or enforce any law that shall abridge the privileges and immunities of citizens of the United States. No state shall deny to any person within its jurisdiction the equal protection of the laws.

Harper v. Virginia State Board of Elections

Taxpayers (P) v. Board of elections (D)

383 U.S. 663 (1966).

NATURE OF CASE: Suits challenging the constitutionality of Virginia's poll tax.

FACT SUMMARY: Harper (P) and other Virginia residents brought this suit to have Virginia's (D) poll tax declared unconstitutional.

> ## 🏛 RULE OF LAW
> The right to vote is a fundamental and basic right, and where such rights are asserted under the Equal Protection Clause, classifications that might restrain those rights must be closely scrutinized and carefully confined. Lines drawn on the basis of wealth or property, like those of race, are traditionally disfavored.

FACTS: Harper (P) and other Virginia residents brought these suits to have Virginia's (D) poll tax declared unconstitutional. The three-judge district court, being bound by the court's decision in *Breedlove v. Suttles*, 302 U.S. 277 (1937), dismissed the complaint. Harper (P) appealed. The law at issue conditions the right to vote in state elections upon the payment of a poll tax.

ISSUE: Is a poll tax, the payment of which is a required prerequisite for voting, constitutional?

HOLDING AND DECISION: (Douglas, J.) No. The right to vote is a fundamental and basic right, and where such rights are asserted under the Equal Protection Clause, classifications that might restrain those rights must be closely scrutinized and carefully confined. Lines drawn on the basis of wealth or property, like those of race, are traditionally disfavored. A state violates the Equal Protection Clause whenever it makes the affluence of the voter or the payment of a fee an electoral standard. The right to vote is a basic and fundamental one, especially since it preserves other rights. Any alleged infringement on the right to vote must be carefully scrutinized. A state's interest, when it comes to voting, is limited to the power to fix qualifications. Wealth, like race or creed or color, is irrelevant to one's ability to participate intelligently in the electoral process. Further lines drawn on the basis of wealth or property, like those of race, are traditionally disfavored. The requirement of the payment of a fee as a condition of obtaining a ballot causes invidious discrimination. *Breedlove* sanctioned this use of the poll tax, and to that extent it is overruled. Reversed.

DISSENT: (Black, J.) So long as a distinction drawn is not irrational, unreasonable, or invidious, it must be upheld. There are certainly rational reasons for Virginia's poll tax, such as the state's desire to collect revenue and its belief that voters who pay a poll tax will be interested in furthering the state's welfare. Hence, the tax must be upheld. If it is to be struck down, it should be done by the legislature, rather than the courts.

DISSENT: (Harlan, J.) The Equal Protection Clause does not impose upon this country an ideology of unrestrained egalitarianism.

> ## ▶ ANALYSIS
> If, as the dissenters in *Harper* argue, the poll tax classification is not wholly "irrational," the case represents a greater intervention than the courts undertook under old equal protection. There is some question as to whether this greater scrutiny was because the "fundamental rights" of voting are affected or because "lines drawn on the basis of wealth" are traditionally disfavored. In *McDonald v. Board of Election Commissioners*, 394 U.S. 802 (1969), the Court sees wealth as an independent ground (apart from impact on fundamental rights) for strict scrutiny. There is a series of cases preceding and following *Harper* (among them *Reynolds v. Sims*, 377 U.S. 533 (1964)) that support the invoking of strict scrutiny when voting rights are affected.

■■■

Quicknotes

STRICT SCRUTINY The method by which courts determine the constitutionality of a law when a law affects a fundamental right. Under the test, the legislature must have had a compelling interest to enact the law and measures prescribed by the law must be the least restrictive means possible to accomplish its goal.

■■■

Kramer v. Union Free School District

Unmarried taxpayer (P) v. School district (D)

395 U.S. 621 (1969).

NATURE OF CASE: Action challenging the constitutionality of a state law.

FACT SUMMARY: A New York law provided that residents who were otherwise eligible to vote in state and federal elections may vote in the school district election only if they owned or leased taxable property in the district or had custody of children enrolled in local public schools.

🏛 RULE OF LAW
A statute that grants the right to vote to some residents of requisite age and citizenship and denies this right to others must be subjected to strict scrutiny by the court.

FACTS: A New York law provided that in certain school districts, residents who were otherwise eligible to vote in state and federal elections may vote in the school district election only if they owned or leased taxable property within the district or had custody of children enrolled in local public schools. Kramer (P) was a childless bachelor who neither owned nor leased taxable property. He claimed the law violated equal protection.

ISSUE: Must a statute that grants the right to vote to some residents of requisite age and citizenship and denies this right to others be subjected to strict scrutiny by the court?

HOLDING AND DECISION: (Warren, C.J.) Yes. The right to vote in a free and unimpaired manner is preservative of other basic and civil rights. Any unjustified discrimination in determining who may vote undermines the legitimacy of representative government. Hence, a statute that grants the right to vote to some residents of requisite age and citizenship while denying the right to others must be subjected to strict scrutiny by the Court. Such statutes are not granted the presumption of constitutionality given other state laws, and they must be supported by a compelling state interest rather than merely a rational basis. Here, assuming arguendo that, as New York argues, a state can limit the right to vote to those primarily interested, close scrutiny demonstrates that this law does not accomplish this purpose with sufficient precision since it denies the right to many who might be so interested.

DISSENT: (Stewart, J.) This law has a rational basis. A stricter standard is not applicable, since neither a racial classification nor any constitutionally protected right is involved. The Constitution does not confer the right of suffrage upon anyone.

▶ ANALYSIS

In *Cipriano v. City of Houma*, 395 U.S. 701 (1969), decided the same day as *Kramer*, the Court was unanimous in invalidating a law granting only property taxpayers the right to vote on the approval of the issuance of revenue bonds by a municipal utility. The Court noted that the revenue bonds would be financed from the operation of the utilities, not from property taxes. In a concurring notation, Justices Black and Stewart stated that this case, unlike *Kramer*, involved a voting classification wholly irrelevant to the achievement of the state's objective.

Quicknotes

STRICT SCRUTINY REVIEW A test, employed by the court to determine the constitutionality of a statute, whereby the proponent of the statute must demonstrate the classifications drawn therein serve a compelling interest and are necessary for the furtherance of a state objective.

Reynolds v. Sims

[Parties not identified.]

377 U.S. 533 (1964).

NATURE OF CASE: Appeal of ruling invalidating state legislative apportionment schemes.

FACT SUMMARY: The apportionment schemes of several states were challenged as not reflecting the states' population distributions.

RULE OF LAW
As nearly as practicable, a state apportionment scheme must reflect a state's population distribution.

FACTS: The apportionment schemes of several states were not based solely on the one-person-one-vote principle but rather took other factors into consideration, with the result being that the various districts had unequal populations. In six companion cases, the constitutionality of this practice was challenged.

ISSUE: As nearly as practicable, must a state apportionment scheme reflect a state's population distribution?

HOLDING AND DECISION: (Warren, C.J.) Yes. As nearly as practicable, a state apportionment scheme must reflect a state's population distribution. The right to vote is the most basic right in a democratic society, and all other rights are derivative of this right. To the extent a citizen's right to vote is diluted, his citizenship is diluted. A state may have an interest in protecting certain segments of society, but the giving of unequal voting power is not the way to accomplish it. A state is free, in keeping with the one-person-one-vote principle, to draw districts roughly approximating political subdivisions, so long as that principle is in fact adhered to. The main consideration, however, is not to dilute the voting power of any portion of the electorate. Affirmed and remanded.

DISSENT: (Harlan, J.) The legislative history of the Fourteenth Amendment shows it was not intended to intrude on the internal workings of a state legislature.

ANALYSIS

An important principle underlying this decision was the protection of majority rule. In some of the states involved in the present action, control was effectively in the hands of political minorities. As the Court made clear, the dilution of the majority's voting power was not the way to protect minority interests.

Quicknotes

FOURTEENTH AMENDMENT Declares that no state shall make or enforce any law that shall abridge the privileges and immunities of citizens of the United States. No state shall deny to any person within its jurisdiction the equal protection of the laws.

City of Mobile v. Bolden

Municipality (D) v. Voters (P)

446 U.S. 55 (1980).

NATURE OF CASE: Appeal in action challenging as unconstitutional an at-large voting system. [The procedural posture of the case is not presented in the casebook extract.]

FACT SUMMARY: The City of Mobile, Alabama, (Mobile) (D) maintained an at-large city commission voting system, rather than one broken into districts, and, although the City had a sizeable African American population, no African American had ever been elected to the commission. On this basis, the at-large system was challenged as violating the Equal Protection Clause.

RULE OF LAW

An at-large voting system, not created specifically to discriminate against a minority's voting power, is not unconstitutional, notwithstanding that such a system has a discriminatory effect on minorities.

FACTS: The City of Mobile, Alabama, (Mobile) (D) was governed by a three-person board of commissioners. Each commissioner was elected by the city at large, not by district. Notwithstanding that Mobile (D) had a large African American population, no African American had ever been elected to the commission. The at-large voting structure was challenged as unconstitutionally submerging the voting power of minorities. The Supreme Court granted certiorari in the case. [The procedural posture of the case is not presented in the casebook extract.]

ISSUE: Is an at-large voting system, not created specifically to discriminate against a minority's voting power, unconstitutional, notwithstanding that such a system has a discriminatory effect on minorities?

HOLDING AND DECISION: (Stewart, J.) No. An at-large voting system, not created specifically to discriminate against a minority's voting power, is not unconstitutional, notwithstanding that such a system has a discriminatory effect on minorities. Only if there is purposeful discrimination by a governmental entity does an equal protection violation occur. Although the Equal Protection Clause confers a substantive right to participate in elections on an equal basis with other qualified voters, this right to equal participation in the electoral process does not protect any "political group," however defined, from electoral defeat. The Constitution does not guarantee an inherent right to proportional representation of any political group, and the dissent errs in finding such a right in the principle of "one person, one vote." Because Mobile (D) is a unitary electoral district and the commission elections are

conducted at large, nobody's vote has been "diluted." Since the evidence also did not prove any intentional invidious discrimination by Mobile (D), no violation of a constitutional right occurred. [Reversed and remanded.]

DISSENT: (Marshall, J.) The equal protection problem attacked by the "one person, one vote" principle is one of vote dilution, and under the Court's precedent, each citizen must have an "equally effective voice" in the election of representatives. Here, the alleged vote dilution, although caused by the combined effects of the electoral structure and social and historical factors rather than by unequal population distribution, is analytically the same concept: the unjustified abridgment of a fundamental right. Contrary to the majority's characterization of this argument, it does not in any way mean that there is a constitutional requirement of proportional representation for groups. Instead, the constitutional protection against vote dilution, which does not extend to those situations in which a group has merely failed to elect representatives in proportion to its share of the population, is triggered when a group is able to demonstrate that it has been effectively fenced out of the political process. Here, it has been proved not only that no African American has been elected to Mobile's (D) Commission, but also that the persistence of severe racial bloc voting makes it highly unlikely that any African American will be elected at large in the foreseeable future. It has also been shown that Mobile (D) African Americans have been unable to use alternative avenues of political influence, and that they still suffer pervasive present effects of massive historical, official and private discrimination. Moreover, it has been shown that the City Commission has been quite unresponsive to the needs of the minority community, which is grossly underrepresented on city boards and committees, and that the city's distribution of public services is racially discriminatory. Notwithstanding such proof, even if proof of discriminatory intent is necessary to support vote-dilution claims in cases such as the one at bar, the issue becomes what evidence will be sufficient to support a finding of such intent. The appropriate evidentiary requirement should be the common-law foreseeability presumption, the application of which in cases such as this one would demonstrate that official action was produced by pervasive bias. Like outright racial hostility, selective racial indifference reflects a belief that the concerns of the minority are not worthy of the same degree of attention paid to problems perceived by the majority. When an interest as fundamental as voting is diminished

Continued on next page.

along racial lines, a requirement that discriminatory purpose must be proved should be satisfied by such a showing.

▶ ANALYSIS

The present decision was a plurality one. It is not clear whether or not a precedent has been set that there is no inherent right to group representation. If one looks at the issue presented here as one of equal protection and not of fundamental rights, as the Court did, the Court's holding would appear consistent with the jurisprudence of equal protection.

Quicknotes

EQUAL PROTECTION CLAUSE A constitutional provision that each person be guaranteed the same protection of the laws enjoyed by other persons in like circumstances.

Shapiro v. Thompson

[Parties not identified.]

394 U.S. 618 (1969).

NATURE OF CASE: Appeal from decisions holding residency requirements for welfare applicants unconstitutional.

FACT SUMMARY: Statutory provisions deny welfare assistance to residents who have not resided within their jurisdiction for at least one year.

🏛 RULE OF LAW
Any classification that serves to penalize the exercise of a constitutional right is unconstitutional unless it is shown to be necessary to promote a compelling governmental interest, rather than merely shown to be rationally related to a legitimate purpose.

FACTS: A three-judge district court held unconstitutional certain state and District of Columbia statutory provisions. The provisions denied welfare assistance to residents of the state or district who have not resided within their jurisdictions for at least one year immediately preceding their applications for such assistance.

ISSUE: Does a statutory prohibition of welfare benefits to residents of less than a year create a classification denying them equal protection of the laws?

HOLDING AND DECISION: (Brennan, J.) Yes. Any classification that serves to penalize the exercise of a constitutional right is unconstitutional unless it is shown to be necessary to promote a compelling governmental interest, rather than merely shown to be rationally related to a legitimate purpose. The states justify the waiting period requirement as a protective device to preserve the fiscal integrity of their public assistance programs, by discouraging needy families from entering their jurisdictions. However, this act of inhibiting migration by needy persons into the state is constitutionally impermissible, since the right to travel from state to state is protected by the Constitution from laws or regulations that would unreasonably burden such movement. If a law has no other purpose than to chill the assertion of constitutional rights by penalizing those who choose to exercise them, it is patently unconstitutional. Further, the statutes create two classes of persons, different only in that one class has been in the area for one year. A state has a valid interest in preserving the fiscal integrity of its programs. But it cannot accomplish this purpose by invidious discrimination between classes of its citizens. The saving of welfare costs cannot be an independent ground for invidious classification. The states also assert that the waiting period serves certain administrative goals. They contend that a mere showing of a rational relationship and these permissible state goals will justify the classification. This is not true. As stated above, the right to travel is a constitutional right. Any classification that serves to penalize the exercise of a constitutional right is unconstitutional unless it is shown to be necessary to promote a compelling governmental interest. All the administrative arguments advanced are either unfounded, irrational, or may be accomplished by a less drastic means. [Affirmed.] [The procedural posture of the case is not presented in the casebook extract.]

CONCURRENCE: (Stewart, J.) Contrary to the view of Justice Harlan in his dissent, this decision does not create a new "fundamental right" but merely gives force to a long-recognized constitutional right, the right to travel.

DISSENT: (Harlan, J.) The particular formulation of the equal protection doctrine accepted by the majority is of recent vintage. Under this formulation, any departure from equal protection requires a compelling governmental interest as justification. However, this doctrine creates an exception that threatens to swallow the standard equal protection rule. Virtually every state statute affects important rights, and when such rights are protected by the Constitution, any infringement can be dealt with under the Due Process Clause. Thus, the new formulation of the doctrine is unnecessary. Moreover, when a statute affects rights not protected by the Constitution, and it is not arbitrary or irrational, there is nothing that entitles the Court to pick out particular human activities, characterize them as "fundamental," and give them added protection under an unusually stringent equal protection test. Accordingly, the residency requirements at issue here should be judged by ordinary equal protection standards, and, under those standards, the requirements, which have valid legislative aims, are not unconstitutional. The next issue under a standard equal protection analysis is whether the requirements unduly burden the right to travel, which is a fundamental right that has its source in the Due Process Clause. On balance, the governmental interests outweigh the requirements' burdens on travel, which are indirect and insubstantial. The residence requirements are well suited to achieving the government's legitimate goals, and to abolish them might discourage highly worthwhile experimentation in the welfare field. The requirements also are presumptively valid, and, although the same objectives arguably could have been achieved by less restrictive means, this is an area in which the judiciary should be especially slow to fetter legislative judgment in the choice of methods. Finally, the residence requirements have advantages, such as

Continued on next page.

administrative simplicity and relative certainty, that are not shared by the proposed alternative solutions.

▶ *ANALYSIS*

Many agreed with Justice Harlan's dissent that the Court was simply resurrecting the judicial intervention of substantive due process under the guise of a new stricter equal protection test. One commentator warned, "Looming down the path is the specter of economic due process, of judges riding to the rescue of Oklahoma's opticians or the Railway Express Agency." Supporters of the new doctrine answered that it was limited to minorities that seem permanently voiceless and invisible and whom the power structure in the political process tends to ignore. Subsequent decisions have shown the Court to be willing to expand the number of suspect classifications to include national origin and sex as well as race.

Quicknotes

EQUAL PROTECTION CLAUSE A constitutional provision that each person be guaranteed the same protection of the laws enjoyed by other persons in like circumstances.

San Antonio Independent School District v. Rodriguez

School district (D) v. Students (P)

411 U.S. 1 (1973).

NATURE OF CASE: Appeal of ruling invalidating a public school system financing scheme.

FACT SUMMARY: The San Antonio School District (D) had a property tax-based financing system whereby schools in the more affluent neighborhoods received higher per-pupil expenditure than those in poorer areas.

🏛 **RULE OF LAW**
A public education financing system that involves substantial disparities in expenditure amounts between the districts is not unconstitutional.

FACTS: The San Antonio School District (D) was largely funded by property taxes, with the taxes of each subdistrict being spent on the school in that district. The result of this was that the per-pupil expenditures in schools in affluent neighborhoods were much higher than those in poorer ones. This disparity was challenged in federal court and the district court, applying strict scrutiny, held the system unconstitutional.

ISSUE: Is a public education financing system that involves substantial disparities in expenditure amounts between the districts unconstitutional?

HOLDING AND DECISION: (Powell, J.) No. A public education financing system that involves substantial disparities in expenditure amounts between the districts is not unconstitutional. Such a system will be subject to strict scrutiny only if it abridges a fundamental right or involves a suspect class. Wealth (or the lack thereof) triggers heightened scrutiny only when that class is completely deprived of some desired benefit. This was not the case here, as it was not contended that the education the plaintiffs received under the system is worthless. Education is, of course, a basic right that might trigger strict scrutiny, but that right was not denied here because, as stated above, it was not contended that the plaintiffs are receiving no education. Since strict scrutiny is not called for, all that must be shown is that the school financing system is rational. Financing public education is a particularly local endeavor, and the Court is reluctant to interfere with it. Reversed.

DISSENT: (White, J.) No showing was made here that the state school financing system was rationally related to any legitimate state interest.

DISSENT: (Marshall, J.) The right to a public education is fundamental. Deprivation of this right need not consist of absolute deprivation. Substandard provision of a right is also deprivation. Also, no legitimate state interest

appears to be served by the financing scheme. Finally, strict adherence to the two-tier system of review is proving insufficient as a standard of constitutional review.

▶ **ANALYSIS**

Despite the protestations of Justice Marshall, the Court declined to declare public education a fundamental right. The Court, which has since been loath to carve out new fundamental rights, has not reversed itself. It does seem odd that something like travel would be considered a fundamental right while education is not, but that is the status of the law.

■▬■

Quicknotes

HEIGHTENED SCRUTINY A purposefully vague judicial description of all levels of scrutiny more exacting than minimal scrutiny.

STRICT SCRUTINY REVIEW A test, employed by the court to determine the constitutionality of a statute, whereby the proponent of the statute must demonstrate the classifications drawn therein serve a compelling interest and are necessary for the furtherance of a state objective.

■▬■

Plyler v. Doe

State (D) v. Children of undocumented aliens (P)

457 U.S. 202 (1982).

NATURE OF CASE: Constitutional challenge to a state educational restriction statute.

FACT SUMMARY: A class action suit challenged a Texas law that prohibited the use of state funds to educate the children of undocumented aliens.

RULE OF LAW
Absent a showing that such a policy furthers a substantial state interest, a state may not deny a public education to the children of undocumented aliens.

FACTS: In a class action suit, a Texas statute [Tex. Educ. Code Ann. § 21.031 (1981)] was sought to be invalidated on the ground it unconstitutionally denied equal protection to the children of undocumented aliens. The statute prohibited the use of state funds for the education of any children not legally admitted to the United States. Both the district court and the Fifth Circuit Court of Appeals held that § 21.031 violated the Equal Protection Clause of the Fourteenth Amendment. Texas (D) appealed, contending the statute was not unduly discriminatory and was, in fact, justified for three reasons: (1) it was designed to protect the state from an influx of illegal immigrants; (2) it would relieve some of the special burdens educating undocumented aliens imposes on the educational system; and (3) it would relieve the state of the burden of educating children who are less likely to remain in the state and contribute than other children.

ISSUE: May a state deny a public education to the children of undocumented aliens, absent a showing that such a policy is justified by a substantial state interest?

HOLDING AND DECISION: (Brennan, J.) No. Absent a showing that such a policy furthers a substantial state interest, a state may not deny a public education to the children of undocumented aliens. To begin with, the proper standard of judicial scrutiny must be identified. As the people involved (undocumented aliens) are not members of a suspect class and as the right to an education, although clearly important, has not been held to constitute a fundamental constitutional right, the statute in question will be upheld if it is found to be rationally related to a substantial state interest. Upon examination, however, none of the three state interests advanced by Texas (D)—protection from an influx of illegal immigrants; relief from special burdens on the educational system; or relief from the burdens of educating children who will be more likely to leave the state—justify the statute in question. The legislative scheme found in § 21.031 cannot in any way be

deemed as advancing the interests asserted by the state (even assuming these interests are "substantial state interests"). Denying children who are not responsible for their status a public education will stigmatize them with the heavy burden of illiteracy for the rest of their lives. They will be unable to participate in our civic institutions. The cost to the nation over their life spans will be greater than the cost of providing them an education now. As such, the statute must fall, as it is in violation of the equal protection clause. Affirmed.

CONCURRENCE: (Marshall, J.) While joining in the Court's opinion, I do so without in any way retreating from my opinion in *San Antonio Independent School District v. Rodriguez*, 411 U.S. 1 (1973).

CONCURRENCE: (Blackmun, J.) Today's decision is consistent with *Rodriguez* since the Court there reserved judgment on the constitutionality of a state system that occasioned an absolute denial of educational opportunities to any of its children.

CONCURRENCE: (Powell, J.) The unique nature of this case must be emphasized. Texas (D) has attempted to "visit the sins of the parents" on their innocent children, and has asserted no substantial state interest justifying doing so. Such a policy cannot be constitutionally upheld.

DISSENT: (Burger, C.J.) The Court oversteps its bounds in striking down the Texas (D) statute. Once it is conceded that neither a suspect class nor a fundamental right is involved only a rational relationship to a legitimate state interest need be found to uphold the law. Despite the fact it may not be the same course the members of the Court would take if they were legislating, it cannot be said that the Texas (D) law is irrational. As such, it is a valid law.

ANALYSIS

As mentioned in Justice Marshall's concurrence, the Court seems to be taking one step closer to the "sliding scale" approach of equal protection analysis that has long been advocated by certain legal theorists. Under this approach, a court would have greater flexibility than merely identifying the analysis required as being either "strict scrutiny" or "rational basis," and, as such, could better tailor the legal analysis to the facts of the case and the interests involved.

Continued on next page.

Quicknotes

DUE PROCESS CLAUSE Clauses found in the Fifth and Fourteenth Amendments to the United States Constitution providing that no person shall be deprived of "life, liberty or property, without due process of law."

Griswold v. Connecticut

Director/Doctor (D) v. State (P)

381 U.S. 479 (1965).

NATURE OF CASE: Appeal from conviction for violating state laws prohibiting the counseling of married persons to take contraceptives.

FACT SUMMARY: Doctor (D) and layman (D) were prosecuted for advising married persons on the means of preventing conception.

🏛 RULE OF LAW

The right to privacy, although not explicitly stated in the Bill of Rights, is a penumbra, formed by certain other explicit guarantees. As such, it is protected against state regulation that sweeps unnecessarily broad.

FACTS: Griswold (D), the Executive Director of the Planned Parenthood League of Connecticut, and Dr. Buxton (D) were convicted under a Connecticut law that made counseling of married persons to take contraceptives a criminal offense.

ISSUE: Is the right to privacy although not explicitly stated in the Bill of Rights, a penumbra, formed by certain other explicit guarantees?

HOLDING AND DECISION: (Douglas, J.) Yes. The right to privacy, although not explicitly stated in the Bill of Rights, is a penumbra, formed by certain other explicit guarantees. As such, it is protected against state regulation that sweeps unnecessarily broad. The various guarantees that create penumbras, or zones, of privacy include the First Amendment's right of association, the Third Amendment's prohibition against the peacetime quartering of soldiers, the Fourth Amendment's prohibition against unreasonable searches and seizures, the Fifth Amendment's self-incrimination clause, and the Ninth Amendment's reservation to the people of unenumerated rights. The Connecticut (P) law by forbidding the use of contraceptives, rather than regulating their manner of sale, seeks to achieve its goals by means having a maximum destructive impact upon that relationship. Reversed.

CONCURRENCE: (Goldberg, J.) The Ninth Amendment, while not constituting an independent source of rights, suggests that the list of rights in the first eight amendments is not exhaustive. This right is a "fundamental" one that cannot be infringed on the state's slender justification in protecting marital fidelity.

CONCURRENCE: (Harlan, J.) To say that the state may not pry into the intimate affairs of a married couple does not, and need not, derive from the Bill of Rights. Rather, the right of marital privacy is implicit in any society

concerned with individual liberty. These rights necessary in a free society derive directly from the Due Process Clause and not from the Bill of Rights by way of the clause.

CONCURRENCE: (White, J.) The Due Process Clause should be the test in determining whether such laws are reasonably necessary for the effectuation of a legitimate and substantial state interest and are not arbitrary or capricious in application. Here, the causal connection between married persons engaging in extramarital sex and contraceptives is too tenuous.

DISSENT: (Black, J.) While the law is offensive, neither the Ninth Amendment nor the Due Process Clause invalidates it. Both lead the Court into imposing its own notions as to what are wise or unwise laws. That which constitutes "fundamental" values this Court is incapable of determining. Keeping the Constitution "in tune with the times" is accomplished only through the amendment process. Similarly, the Due Process Clause is too imprecise and lends itself to subjective interpretation.

DISSENT: (Stewart, J.) The Due Process Clause is not the "guide" because there was no claim here that the statute is unconstitutionally vague, or that the defendants were denied any of the elements of procedural due process at their trial. The Ninth Amendment simply restricts the federal government to a government of express and limited powers. Finally, the Constitution is silent on the "right to privacy."

▶ ANALYSIS

Although the theory of "substantive due process" has declined as a means to review state economic regulation—at least since 1937—the Court, as here, has freely applied strict scrutiny of state laws affecting social areas.

Quicknotes

DUE PROCESS CLAUSE Clauses found in the Fifth and Fourteenth Amendments to the United States Constitution providing that no person shall be deprived of "life, liberty, or property, without due process of law."

NINTH AMENDMENT The Ninth Amendment to the United States Constitution provides that the enumeration of any rights contained therein, are not to be construed as denying or disparaging other rights retained by the people.

Roe v. Wade

Single woman (P) v. State (D)

410 U.S. 113 (1973).

NATURE OF CASE: Challenge to state laws making it a crime to procure an abortion except by medical advice to save the life of the mother.

FACT SUMMARY: [Roe (P), a single woman, wished to have her pregnancy terminated by an abortion.]

🏛 RULE OF LAW
The right of privacy found in the Fourteenth Amendment's concept of personal liberty and restrictions upon state action is broad enough to encompass a woman's decision whether or not to terminate her pregnancy.

FACTS: [The Texas abortion laws challenged here were typical of those adopted by most states. The challengers were Roe (P), a single pregnant woman, a childless couple with the wife not pregnant (J. and M. Doe), and a licensed physician with two criminal charges pending (Halford). Only Roe (P) was found to be entitled to maintain the action. Although her 1970 pregnancy had been terminated, her case was not found moot since pregnancy "truly could be capable of repetition, yet evading review."]

ISSUE: Does the constitutional right of privacy include a woman's right to choose to terminate her pregnancy?

HOLDING AND DECISION: (Blackmun, J.) Yes. The right of privacy found in the Fourteenth Amendment's concept of personal liberty and restrictions upon state action is broad enough to encompass a woman's decision whether or not to terminate her pregnancy. While the Constitution does not explicitly mention any right of privacy, such a right has been recognized. This right of privacy, whether founded in the Fourteenth Amendment's concept of personal liberty and restrictions upon state action, as this Court feels it is, or in the Ninth Amendment's reservation of rights to the people, is broad enough to encompass a woman's decision to terminate her pregnancy. A statute regulating a fundamental right, such as the right to privacy, may be justified only by a compelling state interest and such statutes must be narrowly drawn. Here, Texas (D) argued the fetus is a person within the meaning of the Fourteenth Amendment whose right to life is guaranteed by that amendment. However, there are no decisions indicating such a definition for "fetus." The unborn have never been recognized in the law as persons in the whole sense. Texas (D) may not, by adopting one theory of life, override the rights of the pregnant woman that are at stake. However, neither are the woman's rights to privacy absolute. The state does have a legitimate interest in preserving the health of the pregnant woman and in

protecting the potentiality of life. Each of these interests grows in substantiality as the woman approaches term, and, at a point, each becomes compelling. During the first trimester, mortality in abortion is less than mortality in childbirth. After that point, in promoting its interest in the mother's health, the state may regulate the abortion procedure in ways related to maternal health (i.e., licensing of physicians, facilities, etc.). Prior to viability, the physician, in consultation with the pregnant woman, is free to decide a pregnancy should be terminated without interference by the state. Subsequent to viability, the state, in promoting its interest in the potentiality of life, may regulate, and even proscribe, abortion, except where necessary to save the mother's life. Because the Texas (D) statute makes no distinction between abortions performed in early pregnancy and those performed later, it sweeps too broadly and is, therefore, invalid.

CONCURRENCE: (Stewart, J.) The Texas statute infringed upon the "liberty" protected by the Fourteenth Amendment Due Process Clause. That clause protects liberties not explicitly named in the Bill of Rights, including a right of personal choice in matters of marriage and family life.

CONCURRENCE: (Douglas, J.) While childbirth endangers the lives of some women, voluntary abortion at any time and place regardless of medical standards would impinge on a rightful concern of society. The woman's health is part of that concern, as is the life of the fetus after quickening. These concerns justify the state in treating the procedure as a medical one.

DISSENT: (White, J.) This issue, for the most part, should be left with the people. There is nothing in the language or history of the Constitution to support the Court's opinion.

DISSENT: (Rehnquist, J.) The test to be applied is whether the abortion law has a rational relation to a valid state objective. Here, the Court applies the compelling state interest test. The application of this test requires the Court to examine the legislative policies and pass on the wisdom of those policies, tasks better left to the legislature.

▶ ANALYSIS

Doe v. Bolton, 410 U.S. 179 (1973), was the companion case to *Roe v. Wade*. The Georgia laws attacked in *Doe* were more modern than the Texas laws. They allowed a physician to perform an abortion when the mother's life

Continued on next page.

was in danger, or when the fetus would likely be born with birth defects, or when the pregnancy had resulted from rape. The Court held that a physician could consider all attendant circumstances in deciding whether an abortion should be performed. No longer could only the three situations specified be considered. The Court also struck down the requirements of prior approval for an abortion by the hospital staff committee and of confirmation by two physicians. They concluded that the attending physician's judgment was sufficient. Lastly, the Court struck down the requirement the woman be a Georgia resident.

Quicknotes

FOURTEENTH AMENDMENT DUE PROCESS CLAUSE Provides that protections mandated by the U.S. Constitution and observed by the federal government are equally applicable, and therefore must be observed by the states.

Planned Parenthood of Southeastern Pennsylvania v. Casey

Medical clinics/Doctors (P) v. State (D)

505 U.S. 833 (1992).

NATURE OF CASE: Appeal of order upholding abortion statutes, except a husband-notification provision.

FACT SUMMARY: Planned Parenthood (P) facially challenged the constitutionality of Pennsylvania's (D) abortion law.

▥ RULE OF LAW
A law is unconstitutional as an undue burden on a woman's right to an abortion before fetal viability, if the law places a substantial obstacle in the path of a woman seeking to exercise her right.

FACTS: The Pennsylvania Abortion Control Act required: (a) a doctor to provide a woman seeking an abortion with information designed to persuade her against abortion and imposed a waiting period of at least 24 hours between provision of the information and the abortion; (b) a minor to obtain consent of one parent or a judge's order before having an abortion; (c) a married woman to sign a statement averring that her husband had been notified, her husband was not the father, her husband forcibly had impregnated her, or that she would be physically harmed if she notified her husband; and (d) a public report on every abortion, detailing information on the facility, physician, patient, and steps taken to comply with the Act. The name of the patient was confidential. It provided the first three provisions would not apply in a "medical emergency," i.e., a condition a doctor determines to require immediate abortion to avert death or serious risk of substantial, irreversible impairment of a major bodily function. Five clinics (P), including Planned Parenthood (P), and five doctors (P) sued Pennsylvania (D), including Governor Casey (D), claiming the Act was unconstitutional on its face. The district court held the entire Act invalid under *Roe v. Wade*, 410 U.S. 113 (1973). The court of appeals reversed, upholding the entire Act except the husband-notification requirement. Planned Parenthood et al. (P) appealed.

ISSUE: Is a law unconstitutional as an undue burden on a woman's right to an abortion before fetal viability, if the law places a substantial obstacle in the path of a woman's exercise of her right?

HOLDING AND DECISION: (O'Connor, J.) Yes. A law is unconstitutional as an undue burden on a woman's right to an abortion before fetal viability when it places a substantial obstacle in the path of a woman seeking to exercise her right. For two decades people have organized lives relying on the availability of abortion. The Court rarely resolves a controversy as intensely divisive as in *Roe*. Such a decision should be overturned only if it proves unworkable or if new information arise that renders the decision unjustified in the present. *Roe* is neither unworkable nor based on outdated assumptions. Medical technology has altered the age of viability, but that does not affect the validity of viability as a dividing line. Viability is the point at which a fetus can be said to be an independent life, so that the state's interest in protecting it then outweighs the mother's decision-making interest. The Court and the nation would be seriously damaged if the Court were to overturn *Roe* simply on the basis of a philosophical disagreement with the 1973 Court, or as surrender to political pressure. The liberty rights of women and the personal, intimate nature of child bearing sharply limit state power to insist a woman carry a child to term or accept the state's vision of her role in society. Thus, the integrity of the Court, stare decisis, and substantive due process require the central principle of *Roe* to be reaffirmed: a state may not prevent a woman from making the ultimate decision to terminate her pregnancy before viability. *Roe* also recognized the state interest in maternal health and in protecting potential life. Application of the rigid trimester framework often ignored state interests, leading to striking down abortion regulations that in no real sense deprived women of the ultimate decision. Therefore, the trimester framework must be rejected and undue burden analysis put in its place. Here, the information requirement is not an undue burden. Truthful, nonmisleading information on the nature of abortion procedure, health risks, and consequences to the fetus is reasonable to ensure informed choice, one which might cause a woman to choose childbirth. The 24-hour waiting period does not create a health risk and reasonably furthers the state interest in protecting the unborn. Requiring a period of reflection to make an informed decision is reasonable. A waiting period may increase cost and risk of delay, but on a facial challenge it cannot be called a substantial obstacle. Prior cases establish that a state may require parental consent before abortions by minors, provided there is a judicial bypass procedure. On its face, the statute's definition of "medical emergency" is not too narrow. The reporting requirement is reasonably directed to the preservation of maternal health, providing a vital element of medical research, and the statute protects patient confidentiality. The husband-notification requirement imposes an undue burden on abortion rights of the abused women who fear for their safety and the safety of their children and are likely to be deterred from procuring an abortion as surely as if the state outlawed abortion. A husband has a strong interest in his wife's pregnancy, but before birth it is a biological fact that regulation of the fetus has a far greater impact on the woman.

Continued on next page.

The husband-notification requirement is unconstitutional, and the rest of the statute is valid. Affirmed.

CONCURRENCE AND DISSENT: (Blackmun, J.)

The regulation designed to inform the public about public expenditures does not further the state's interest in maintaining maternal health. Such a regulation, therefore, cannot justify a legally significant burden on a woman's right to obtain an abortion. When the state restricts a woman's right to terminate her pregnancy, it deprives a woman of the right to make her own decision about reproduction and family planning—critical life choices the Court long has deemed central to the right of privacy.

CONCURRENCE AND DISSENT: (Stevens, J.)

A burden is "undue" if it is too severe or lacks legitimate justification. The information and waiting period requirements are invalid. The state interest in protecting potential life is legitimate, but not grounded in the Constitution. A woman has constitutional liberty rights to bodily integrity and to decide personal and private matters. So, the state may promote a preference for childbirth, but decisional autonomy must limit the state's power to interject into a woman's most personal deliberations its own views of what is best. Pennsylvania's law goes too far by requiring a doctor to provide information designed to persuade a woman to opt against abortion, just as she is weighing her personal choice. In contrast, the requirement of informing a woman of the nature and risks of abortion and childbirth enhances decision-making. The 24-hour waiting period illegitimately rests on assumptions that a decision to terminate pregnancy is wrong, and that a woman is unable to make decisions.

CONCURRENCE AND DISSENT: (Rehnquist, C.J.)

Roe was wrongly decided, has led to a confusing body of law, and should be overturned. The Court's decision, replacing *Roe*'s strict scrutiny standard and trimester framework with a new, unworkable undue burden test, cannot be justified by stare decisis. Authentic principles of stare decisis do not require erroneous decisions to be maintained. The Court's integrity is enhanced when it repudiates wrong decisions. Americans have grown accustomed to *Roe*, but that should not prevent the Court from correcting a wrong decision. The Fourteenth Amendment concept of liberty does not incorporate any all-encompassing right of privacy. Unlike marriage, procreation, and contraception, abortion terminates potential life and must be analyzed differently. Historic traditions of the American people, critical to an understanding of fundamental rights, do not support a right to abortion. A woman's interest in having an abortion is liberty protected by due process, but states may regulate abortion in ways rationally related to a legitimate state interest. All provisions of the Pennsylvania law do so and are constitutional. The husband-notification requirement is reasonably related to promoting state interests in protecting the husband's interests, potential life, and the integrity of marriage.

CONCURRENCE AND DISSENT: (Scalia, J.)

The limits on abortion should be decided democratically. The Constitution is silent on abortion, and American traditions have allowed it to be proscribed. Applying the rational basis test, the Pennsylvania law should be upheld in its entirety. *Roe* was wrongly decided. It begged the question by assuming a fetus is merely potential human life. The whole argument of abortion opponents is that the state seeks to protect human life. *Roe* also failed to produce a settled body of law. *Roe* did not resolve the deeply divisive issue of abortion. It made compromise impossible and elevated the issue to a national level where it has proven infinitely more difficult to resolve. Here, the Court claims to rely on stare decisis but throws out *Roe*'s trimester framework. The new undue burden standard is meaningless in application, giving a district judge freedom to strike down almost any abortion restriction he does not like. The Court's suggestion public opposition to an erroneous decision mitigates against overturning it is appalling.

▶ ANALYSIS

The Court also affirmed *Roe*'s holding that after viability the state may regulate, or even proscribe, abortion, except where it is necessary to preserve the life or health of the mother. This was only the second time in modern Supreme Court jurisprudence that an opinion had been jointly authored. Justice Kennedy's portion of the opinion addresses the importance of public faith in and acceptance of the Court's work by opening with the statement: "Liberty finds no refuge in a jurisprudence of doubt." Justice O'Connor expounds on the essential nature of a woman's right to an abortion, while Justice Souter performs the stare decisis analysis, concluding that there is no reason to reverse the essential holding of *Roe*. It appears that the instant case marks the first time the Court had downgraded a fundamental right to a protected liberty and by so doing removed from the usual strict scrutiny standard of review.

■━━■

Quicknotes

FOURTEENTH AMENDMENT Declares that no state shall make or enforce any law that shall abridge the privileges and immunities of citizens of the United States. No state shall deny to any person within its jurisdiction the equal protection of the laws.

STARE DECISIS Doctrine whereby courts follow legal precedent unless there is good cause for departure.

UNDUE BURDEN A burden that is unlawfully oppressive or troublesome.

■━━■

Gonzales v. Carhart

Attorney General (D) v. Abortion doctor (P)

550 U.S. 124 (2007).

NATURE OF CASE: Appeal from judgments invalidating the federal Partial-Birth Abortion Ban Act as facially violating the Due Process Clause.

FACT SUMMARY: The Government (D) contended that the federal Partial-Birth Abortion Ban Act, by which Congress criminalized doctors' performance of partial-birth abortions, was not facially invalid under the Due Process Clause because it was not void for vagueness and did not impose an undue burden on a woman's right to abortion based on overbreadth or lack of a health exception.

RULE OF LAW

The federal Partial-Birth Abortion Ban Act of 2003 is not facially unconstitutional on the grounds it (1) unduly burdens a woman's ability to choose a second-trimester abortion, (2) is too vague, and (3) lacks an exception allowing the prohibited procedure where necessary for the mother's health.

FACTS: In 2003, following the United States Supreme Court's decision in *Stenberg v. Carhart*, 530 U.S. 914 (2000), which held that Nebraska's "partial birth abortion" statute violated the federal Constitution, as interpreted in *Planned Parenthood of Southeastern Pa. v. Casey*, 505 U.S. 833 (1992), Congress passed the Partial–Birth Abortion Ban Act ("the Act") to proscribe a particular method of ending fetal life in the later stages of pregnancy. Nebraska's statute was invalidated on the grounds it contained no exception for the preservation of the health of the mother, as required by *Casey*, and that it imposed an undue burden on the abortion right because it applied not only to an uncommon second-trimester procedure of "dilation and evacuation" (D & E) known as "intact D & E", but also to standard D & E. By contrast, the federal Act did not regulate standard D & E, whereby a doctor dilates the cervix and then inserts surgical instruments into the uterus and maneuvers them to grab the fetus and pull it back through the cervix and vagina. The fetus is usually ripped apart as it is removed, and the doctor may take 10 to 15 passes to remove it in its entirety. In "intact D & E," a doctor extracts the fetus intact or largely intact with only a few passes, pulling out its entire body instead of ripping it apart. In order to allow the head to pass through the cervix, the doctor typically pierces or crushes the skull. The Act responded to *Stenberg* in two ways. First, Congress found that unlike this Court in *Stenberg*, it was not required to accept the district court's factual findings, and that that there was a moral, medical, and ethical consensus that partial-birth abortion is a gruesome and inhumane proce-

dure that is never medically necessary and should be prohibited. Second, the Act's language differs from that of the Nebraska statute struck down in *Stenberg*. Among other things, the Act criminalizes "knowingly perform[ing] a partial-birth abortion . . . that is [not] necessary to save the life of a mother." It defines "partial-birth abortion," as a procedure in which the doctor: "(A) deliberately and intentionally vaginally delivers a living fetus until, in the case of a head-first presentation, the entire fetal head is outside the [mother's] body . . . , or, in the case of breech presentation, any part of the fetal trunk past the navel is outside the [mother's] body . . . , for the purpose of performing an overt act that the person knows will kill the partially delivered living fetus"; and "(B) performs the overt act, other than completion of delivery, that kills the fetus." The lower courts concluded that the Act was facially unconstitutional, and the Government (D) sought further review in the Supreme Court, which granted certiorari.

ISSUE: Is the federal Partial-Birth Abortion Ban Act of 2003 facially unconstitutional on the grounds it (1) unduly burdens a woman's ability to choose a second-trimester abortion, (2) is too vague, and (3) lacks an exception allowing the prohibited procedure where necessary for the mother's health?

HOLDING AND DECISION: (Kennedy, J.) No. The federal Partial-Birth Abortion Ban Act of 2003 ("the Act") is not facially unconstitutional on the grounds it (1) unduly burdens a woman's ability to choose a second-trimester abortion, (2) is too vague, and (3) lacks an exception allowing the prohibited procedure where necessary for the mother's health. *Casey* affirmed that the government has a legitimate and substantial interest in preserving and promoting fetal life. It also set forth the following principles: a woman has the right to choose to have an abortion before fetal viability and to obtain it without undue interference from the state, which may not impose upon this right an undue burden, which exists if a regulation's purpose or effect is to place a substantial obstacle in the path of a woman seeking an abortion before the fetus attains viability. On the other hand, regulations that do no more than create a structural mechanism by which the state, or the parent or guardian of a minor, may express profound respect for the life of the unborn are permitted, if they are not a substantial obstacle to the woman's exercise of the right to choose. The Act's text demonstrates that it regulates and proscribes performing the intact D & E procedure. First, since the doctor must "vaginally delive[r] a living fetus," the Act does not restrict

Continued on next page.

abortions involving delivery of an expired fetus or those not involving vaginal delivery, e.g., hysterotomy or hysterectomy. The Act applies both previability and postviability because, by common understanding and scientific terminology, a fetus is a living organism within the womb, whether or not it is viable outside the womb. Second, because the Act requires the living fetus to be delivered to a specific anatomical landmark depending on the fetus's presentation, an abortion not involving such partial delivery is permitted. Third, because the doctor must perform an "overt act, other than completion of delivery, that kills the partially delivered fetus," the "overt act" must be separate from delivery. It must also occur after delivery to an anatomical landmark, since killing "the partially delivered" fetus, when read in context, refers to a fetus that has been so delivered. Fourth, given the Act's scienter requirements, delivery of a living fetus past an anatomical landmark by accident or inadvertence is not a crime, nor is such a delivery prohibited if the fetus has not been delivered for the purpose of performing an overt act the doctor knows will kill the fetus. The Act, therefore, is not void for vagueness, because it clearly defines the line between potentially criminal conduct on the one hand and lawful abortion on the other; doctors performing D & E will know that if they do not deliver a living fetus to an anatomical landmark they will not face criminal liability. The Act is also not unduly burdensome, because it targets only intact D & Es that are intentionally performed. The Act excludes most standard D & Es in which the doctor intends to remove the fetus in pieces from the outset. Additionally, the identification of specific anatomical landmarks to which the fetus must be partially delivered also differentiates the Act from the statute at issue in *Stenberg*, which only prohibited removal of a "substantial portion" of the fetus, which could be interpreted, for example, to include an arm or a leg. The Act's anatomical landmarks, by contrast, clarify that the removal of a small portion of the fetus is not prohibited. Further, the Act does not on its face impose a substantial obstacle on women seeking an abortion before the fetus is viable. A description of the prohibited abortion procedure demonstrates the rationale for the congressional enactment, which is designed to proscribe a method of abortion in which a fetus is killed just inches before completion of the birth process. Congress through the Act expressed respect for the dignity of human life and was concerned with the effects on the medical community and on its reputation caused by the practice of partial-birth abortion. Where it has a rational basis to act, and it does not impose an undue burden, the state may use its regulatory power to bar certain procedures and substitute others, all in furtherance of its legitimate interests in regulating the medical profession in order to promote respect for life, including life of the unborn. The Act's ban on abortions that involve partial delivery of a living fetus furthers the Government's (D) objectives, since for many, D & E is a procedure itself laden with the power to devalue human life. In a decision so fraught with emotional consequence,

presumably some doctors may prefer not to disclose precise details of the means that will be used, confining themselves to the required statement of risks the procedure entails. It is this lack of information concerning the way in which the fetus will be killed that is of legitimate concern to the state, which has an interest in ensuring so grave a choice is well-informed. The medical profession, furthermore, may find different and less shocking methods to abort the fetus in the second trimester, thereby accommodating legislative demand. The state's interest in respect for life is advanced by the dialogue that better informs the political and legal systems, the medical profession, expectant mothers, and society as a whole of consequences that follow from a decision to elect a late-term abortion. It is objected that the standard D & E is in some respects as brutal, if not more, than the intact D & E, so that the legislation accomplishes little. However, it was reasonable for Congress to think that partial-birth abortion, more than standard D & E, undermines the public's perception of the appropriate role of a physician during the delivery process, and perverts a process during which life is brought into the world. The Court's logic would be flawed if the Court first concluded that a ban on both D & E and intact D & E was overbroad and then ruled that it was irrational to ban only intact D & E because that does not proscribe both procedures.

The Act's failure to allow intact D & E where necessary, in appropriate medical judgment, for the preservation of the mother's health does not have the effect of imposing an unconstitutional burden on the abortion right. The Court assumes the Act's prohibition would be unconstitutional if it subjected women to significant health risks. Whether the Act creates such risks was, however, a contested factual question below: the evidence presented in the trial courts and before Congress demonstrated that both sides have medical support for their positions. The Court's precedents instruct that the Act can survive facial attack in the face of such medical uncertainty, since the state has an interest in promoting respect for human life at all stages in the pregnancy, and abortion doctors should be treated the same as other doctors. Medical uncertainty does not foreclose the exercise of legislative power in the abortion context any more than it does in other contexts. Moreover, safe alternatives to intact D & E, such as standard D & E, are available. In addition, if intact D & E is truly necessary in some circumstances, a prior injection to kill the fetus allows a doctor to perform the procedure, given that the Act's prohibition only applies to the delivery of a living fetus. Where, as here, there is medical disagreement as to the safety of an abortion procedure, and whether it is preferable for a woman's health, an abortion regulation does not necessarily have to contain a health exception merely because substantial medical authority supports the proposition that banning a particular procedure could endanger women's health. In such situations, leaving no

Continued on next page.

margin for legislative error in the face of medical uncertainty is too exacting a standard. Marginal safety considerations, including the balance of risks, are within the legislative competence where, as here, the regulation is rational and pursues legitimate ends, and standard, safe medical options are available. Finally, these considerations tend to indicate that the facial attacks at bar should not have been entertained in the first instance. In these circumstances, the proper means to consider exceptions is by as-applied challenge. This is the proper manner to protect the woman's health if it can be shown that in discrete and well-defined instances a condition has or is likely to occur in which the procedure prohibited by the Act must be used, given that in an as-applied challenge, the nature of the medical risk can be better quantified and balanced than in a facial attack. Reversed.

DISSENT: (Ginsburg, J.) This decision dishonors *Casey*, 505 U.S. 833 (1992), and *Stenberg*, it flies in the face of medical approval of abortion procedures, and it unduly burdens a woman's reproductive choices. All prior abortion cases decided by the Court held that abortion restrictions cannot be imposed absent an exception safeguarding a woman's health, but the majority departs significantly from those precedents. As the majority acknowledges, significant congressional findings supporting the Act were shown in the trial courts to be erroneous. Those courts, conversely, found after close inspection, and on basis of well-respected expert testimony, that intact D & E is safer than alternative procedures and necessary to protect women's health. The majority simply brushes these well-supported findings under the rug. The Act does subject women to significant health risks by forcing them to choose less-safe methods of abortion—and, in the process the statute does not save even one fetus because the Act merely criminalizes a method of abortion, not abortion itself. Thus, the Act in fact does not serve the purported Government (D) interest in promoting fetal life. As the Court suggests, the real basis for today's decision is "moral concerns" for what the majority paternalistically sees as emotionally fragile women. Without support for its beliefs, the majority worries that because of women's fragile emotional state and because of the "bond of love the mother has for her child," doctors may withhold information about the nature of the intact D & E procedure. This solution does not to require doctors to inform women, accurately and adequately, of the different procedures and their attendant risks, but instead deprives women of the right to make an autonomous choice, even at the expense of their safety. This way of thinking reflects ancient notions about women's place in the family and under the Constitution—ideas that have long since been discredited—and it circumvents the concerns for stare decisis that have supported the Court's prior decisions in this area. Instead of drawing the line at viability, the Court refers to Congress's purpose to differentiate "abortion and infanticide" based not on whether a fetus can survive outside the womb, but

on where a fetus is anatomically located when a particular medical procedure is performed. Also perplexing is the majority's holding "facial attacks" are not permissible where medical uncertainty exists, given that, in materially identical circumstances the Court held that a statute lacking a health exception was unconstitutional on its face. Today's decision is, actually, only a veiled attempt to undermine, in a piecemeal fashion, a woman's established right to an abortion.

▌ANALYSIS

The right to an abortion announced in *Roe v. Wade*, 410 U.S. 113 (1973), remains intact after *Gonzales v. Carhart*. That right is now more difficult to exercise, though, and, as Justice Ginsburg suggests in dissent, the federal statute's omission of safeguards for women's health is at best problematic under the Court's prior abortion decisions.

━■━■

Quicknotes

DUE PROCESS The constitutional mandate requiring the courts to protect and enforce individuals' rights and liberties consistent with prevailing principles of fairness and justice and prohibiting the federal and state governments from such activities that deprive its citizens of life, liberty, or property interest.

INJUNCTION A court order requiring a person to do, or prohibiting that person from doing, a specific act.

INJUNCTIVE RELIEF A court order issued as a remedy, requiring a person to do, or prohibiting that person from doing, a specific act.

SCIENTER Knowledge of certain facts; often refers to "guilty knowledge," which implicates liability.

STARE DECISIS Doctrine whereby courts follow legal precedent unless there is good cause for departure.

━■━■

Whole Woman's Health v. Hellerstedt

Abortion providers (P) v. State official (D)

136 S. Ct. 2292 (2016).

NATURE OF CASE: Appeal from reversal of judgment that enjoined the enforcement of abortion regulations on the grounds the regulations unconstitutionally imposed an undue burden on the right to an abortion.

FACT SUMMARY: Abortion providers (P) challenged as unconstitutional two abortion regulations as unduly burdensome on the right to an abortion: (1) an "admitting-privileges requirement" that provided that a physician performing or inducing an abortion had to have admitting privileges at a hospital located not further than 30 miles from the abortion facility, and (2) a "surgical-center requirement" that required an abortion facility to meet the minimum standards for ambulatory surgical centers under state law.

RULE OF LAW
Where evidence in the record and a weighing of benefits against burdens demonstrates that an abortion regulation has the purpose or effect of presenting a substantial obstacle to a woman seeking an abortion and imposes an undue burden on the right to have a previability abortion, the regulation is unconstitutional.

FACTS: Texas (D) enacted House Bill 2 (H.B. 2), which contained two abortion regulations: (1) an "admitting-privileges requirement" that provided that a physician performing or inducing an abortion had to have admitting privileges at a hospital located not further than 30 miles from the abortion facility, and (2), a "surgical-center requirement" that required an abortion facility to meet the minimum standards for ambulatory surgical centers (ASCs) under state law. Abortion providers (P) challenged and sought to enjoin these requirements as unconstitutional, claiming that they had the purpose or effect of presenting a substantial obstacle to a woman seeking an abortion, and imposed an undue burden on the right to have a previability abortion. The district court made extensive findings, including, but not limited to: as the admitting-privileges requirement began to be enforced, the number of facilities providing abortions dropped in half, from about 40 to about 20; this decrease in geographical distribution means that the number of women of reproductive age living more than 50 miles from a clinic has doubled, the number living more than 100 miles away has increased by 150 percent, the number living more than 150 miles away by more than 350 percent, and the number living more than 200 miles away by about 2,800 percent; the number of facilities would drop to seven or eight if the surgical-center provision took effect, and those remaining facilities would see a significant increase in patient traffic; facilities would remain only in five metropolitan areas; before the passage of House Bill 2, abortion was an extremely safe procedure with very low rates of complications and virtually no deaths; it was also safer than many more common procedures not subject to the same level of regulation; and the cost of compliance with the surgical-center requirement would most likely exceed $1.5 million to $3 million per clinic. The district court enjoined enforcement of the provisions, holding that the surgical-center requirement imposed an undue burden on the right of women in Texas (D) to seek previability abortions; that, together with that requirement, the admitting-privileges requirement imposed an undue burden in the Rio Grande Valley, El Paso, and West Texas; and that the provisions together created an "impermissible obstacle as applied to all women seeking a previability abortion." The court of appeals reversed, stating that a law is constitutional if (1) it does not have the purpose or effect of placing a substantial obstacle in the path of a woman seeking an abortion of a nonviable fetus and (2) it is reasonably related to a legitimate state interest. The court of appeals concluded that both requirements were rationally related to a compelling state interest in protecting women's health. The court of appeals also held that the district court erred by substituting its own judgment for that of the legislature when it conducted its undue burden inquiry, in part because medical uncertainty underlying a statute is for resolution by legislatures, not the courts. The Supreme Court granted certiorari.

ISSUE: Where evidence in the record and a weighing of benefits against burdens demonstrates that an abortion regulation has the purpose or effect of presenting a substantial obstacle to a woman seeking an abortion and imposes an undue burden on the right to have a previability abortion, is the regulation unconstitutional?

HOLDING AND DECISION: (Breyer, J.) Yes. Where evidence in the record and a weighing of benefits against burdens demonstrates that an abortion regulation has the purpose or effect of presenting a substantial obstacle to a woman seeking an abortion and imposes an undue burden on the right to have a previability abortion, the regulation is unconstitutional. The court of appeals' standard of review may be read to imply that a district court should not consider the existence or nonexistence of medical benefits when deciding the undue burden question, but precedent requires courts to consider the burdens a law imposes on abortion access together with the benefits those laws confer. The court of appeals' test also mistakenly

Continued on next page.

equates the judicial review applicable to the regulation of a constitutionally protected personal liberty with the less strict review applicable to, e.g., economic legislation. Additionally, the court of appeals' requirement that legislatures resolve questions of medical uncertainty is inconsistent with this Court's case law, which has placed considerable weight upon evidence and argument presented in judicial proceedings when determining the constitutionality of laws regulating abortion procedures. Contrary to the court of appeals' conclusion, the district court applied the correct standard, and correctly considered the evidence in the record—including expert evidence—and then weighed the asserted benefits against the burdens. The record contained adequate legal and factual support for the district court's conclusion that the admitting-privileges requirement imposed an "undue burden" on a woman's right to choose. The requirement's purpose was to help ensure that women had easy access to a hospital should complications arise during an abortion procedure, but the district court, relying on evidence showing extremely low rates of serious complications before the passage of House Bill 2, found no significant health-related problem for the new law to cure. Texas's (D) record evidence, in contrast, did not show how the new law advanced its legitimate interest in protecting women's health when compared to the prior law. At the same time, the record evidence indicated that the requirement placed a "substantial obstacle" in a woman's path to abortion because it led to a dramatic drop in the number of clinics, which meant fewer doctors, longer waiting times, and increased crowding. The surgical-center requirement also provides few, if any, health benefits for women, poses a substantial obstacle to women seeking abortions, and constitutes an "undue burden" on their constitutional right to do so. Before this requirement was enacted, Texas (D) law required abortion facilities to meet a host of health and safety requirements. There was considerable evidence in the record supporting the district court's findings indicating that the statutory provision requiring all abortion facilities to meet all surgical-center standards did not benefit patients and was not necessary. This evidence, along with the absence of any contrary evidence, supported the district court's conclusions, including its ultimate legal conclusion that the requirement was not necessary. At the same time, the record provided adequate evidentiary support for the district court's conclusion that the requirement placed a substantial obstacle in the path of women seeking an abortion. The district court found that it "strained credulity" to think that the seven or eight abortion facilities remaining in the state would be able to meet the demand for abortions. In sum, the challenged provisions had the effect of closing most of the abortion facilities in Texas (D) and placed added stress on those facilities able to remain open. They vastly increased the obstacles confronting women seeking abortions in Texas (D) without providing any benefit to women's health capable of withstanding any meaningful scrutiny. Thus, the provisions are unconstitutional on their face. [Reversed and remanded.]

CONCURRENCE: (Ginsburg, J.) The truth is that complications from an abortion are both rare and rarely dangerous, so that the claimed benefits of the regulations in House Bill 2 are in reality nothing more than impediments to abortion that do little or nothing for women's health. To the contrary, when a state severely limits access to safe and legal procedures, women in desperate circumstances may resort to unlicensed rogue practitioners, at great risk to their health and safety. Statutes that have this effect cannot survive judicial inspection and are unconstitutional.

DISSENT: (Thomas, J.) The Court's abortion jurisprudence is untenable. However, even accepting the Court's precedents in this area, the majority rewrites the undue-burden test. First, the majority requires courts to consider the burdens a law imposes on abortion access together with the benefits those laws confer. Second, the majority tells the courts that, when the law's justifications are medically uncertain, they need not defer to the legislature, and must instead assess medical justifications for abortion restrictions by scrutinizing the record themselves. Finally, even if a law imposes no "substantial obstacle" to women's access to abortions, the law now must have more than a reasonable relation to a legitimate state interest. These precepts are nowhere to be found in the Court's precedents, and they transform the undue-burden test into a test more akin to strict scrutiny. Another problem with the Court's jurisprudence generally is its tiers of scrutiny approach to constitutional adjudication, which, regardless of what tier is purportedly used, is increasingly a meaningless formalism, given that the Court applies whatever standard it likes to any given case. In short, nothing but empty words separate the Court's constitutional decisions from judicial fiat. In practice, the Court tends to relax purportedly higher standards of review for less-preferred rights, so it should abandon the pretense that anything other than policy preferences underlies its balancing of constitutional rights and interests in any given case. Through its use of its tiers of scrutiny jurisprudence, the Court has given preference to rights not found in the Constitution and has simultaneously transformed judicially created rights like the right to abortion into preferred constitutional rights, while disfavoring many of the rights actually enumerated in the Constitution. However, a law either infringes a constitutional right, or not, and the judiciary should not be inventing tolerable degrees of encroachment. Unless the Court abides by one set of rules to adjudicate constitutional rights, it will continue reducing constitutional law to policy-driven value judgments until the last shreds of its legitimacy disappear.

Continued on next page.

DISSENT: (Alito, J.) [Principles of res judicata should have prevented the Court from considering this case in the first place. Even upon consideration of the statute at bar, however, the majority should have severed its provisions, and not struck down the entire statute as unconstitutional. These are settled procedural principles that should apply with even greater force when controversial issues are presented, but the majority has ignored them altogether.] Further, the plaintiffs (P) failed to show that House Bill (H.B.) 2's provisions impose an "undue burden" on women seeking abortions. To do so, they would have to show, at a minimum, that H.B. 2 impacted at least a "large fraction" of Texas (D) women of reproductive age, because the clinics able to comply with the new requirements either lacked the requisite overall capacity or were located too far away to serve a "large fraction" of the women in question. Instead, the plaintiffs (P) merely relied on crude inferences. First, they pointed to the number of abortion clinics that closed after the enactment of H.B. 2 and asked that it be inferred that all these closures resulted from the two challenged provisions. They made little effort to show why particular clinics closed. Second, they pointed to the number of abortions performed annually at ambulatory surgical centers (ASCs) before H.B. 2 took effect and, because this figure was well below the total number of abortions performed each year in Texas (D), they asked that it be inferred that ASC-compliant clinics could not meet the demands of women. But, they failed to provide any evidence of the actual capacity of the facilities that would be available to perform abortions in compliance with the new law. Although H.B. 2 undoubtedly caused the closure of some clinics, such closures may have been a result of the law's proper operation, since its intent, in part, was to close unsafe abortion clinics. The absence of proof regarding the reasons for particular closures is thus problematic. Also problematic is that the plaintiffs (P) provided scant evidence of the capacity of the clinics that were able to comply with the admitting privileges and ASC requirements, or on those clinics' geographic distribution. Reviewing the evidence in the record, it is far from clear that there has been a material impact on access to abortion. For example, it is entirely possible that ASCs could potentially increase the number of abortions performed without prohibitively expensive changes. Additionally, some statistics indicate that if all the H.B. 2-compliant clinics had remained open, 95 percent of women of reproductive age would live within 150 miles of a compliant clinic. The Court previously has held that the need to travel 150 miles to obtain an abortion is not an undue burden on a woman's rights. Because the record did not show why particular facilities closed, the real figure may be even higher than 95 percent. Such scanty evidence should not provide the basis for facially invalidating H.B. 2. If in fact the law caused an undue burden on women's abortion rights in certain situations, such localized problems should have been addressed by narrow as-applied challenges.

▶ *ANALYSIS*

In this landmark abortion rights decision, the Court vindicated the use of record evidence to determine the real-world effects of a challenged statute, rather than deferring to a legislature's characterization of what the statute would achieve. In relying extensively on the district court's assessment of the substantial evidence in the case, the majority essentially found that the Texas (D) legislature's characterization of House Bill 2 as promoting health was, in fact, a pretext for impeding women's access to legal abortion.

Quicknotes

UNDUE BURDEN   A burden that is unlawfully oppressive or troublesome.

Lawrence v. Texas

Sodomy convict (D) v. State (P)

539 U.S. 558 (2003).

NATURE OF CASE: Appeal from a criminal conviction.

FACT SUMMARY: When Lawrence (D) and his male partner, both adults, were prosecuted and convicted for consensual sodomy in their own private dwelling, they argued the unconstitutionality of the statute.

> **RULE OF LAW**
> Legislation that makes consensual sodomy between adults in their own dwelling criminal violates due process.

FACTS: Two Houston, Texas, police officers were dispatched to a private residence, in response to a reported weapons disturbance. They entered an apartment where Lawrence (D) resided. The right of the police to enter was not an issue. The officers observed Lawrence (D) and another man engaging in sodomy. Both men were arrested, charged, and convicted before a justice of the peace of the statutory crime of "deviate sexual intercourse, namely anal sex, with a member of the same sex." Both men were adults at the time of the alleged offense. Their conduct was in private and consensual. Lawrence (D) and his partner appealed to the Supreme Court, arguing the Texas statute to be unconstitutional.

ISSUE: Does legislation that makes consensual sodomy between adults in their own dwelling criminal violate due process?

HOLDING AND DECISION: (Kennedy, J.) Yes. Legislation that makes consensual sodomy between adults in their own dwelling criminal violates due process. Liberty protects the person from unwarranted government intrusions into dwellings or other private places. In our tradition, the state is not omnipresent in the home. Furthermore, freedom extends beyond spatial bounds. Liberty presumes freedom of thought, belief, expression, and certain intimate conduct. The penalties and purposes of the Texas statute in the instant case have far-reaching consequences, touching upon the most private human conduct, sexual behavior, and in the most private of places, the home. The statute seeks to control a personal relationship that, whether or not entitled to formal recognition in the law, is within the liberty of persons to choose without being punished as criminals. This Court acknowledges that adults may choose to enter private relationships in the confines of their own homes and their own private lives and still retain their dignity as free persons. When sexuality finds expression in intimate conduct with another person, the conduct can be but one element in a personal bond that is more enduring. The liberty protected

by the Constitution allows homosexual persons the right to make this choice. Here, two adults who, with full and mutual consent from each other, engaged in sexual practices common to a homosexual lifestyle. They are entitled to respect in their private lives. The state cannot demean their existence or control their destiny by making their private sexual conduct a crime. Reversed.

CONCURRENCE: (O'Connor, J.) Rather than relying on the substantive component of the Fourteenth Amendment's Due Process Clause, as the Court does, I base my conclusion of unconstitutionality on the Fourteenth Amendment's Equal Protection Clause.

DISSENT: (Scalia, J.) Homosexual sodomy is not a right deeply rooted in our nation's history and tradition. Constitutional entitlements do not spring into existence because some states choose to lessen or eliminate sanctions on criminal behavior. Today's opinion is the product of a Court that has largely signed onto the so-called homosexual agenda.

DISSENT: (Thomas, J.) Although I find the instant Texas statute to be "uncommonly silly" and would vote to repeal it if I were a member of the Texas Legislature, I nevertheless find no general constitutional right of privacy violated in this situation.

ANALYSIS

In *Lawrence*, the Supreme Court noted that of the 13 states with laws prohibiting sodomy, only four have enforced their legislation. In those states in which sodomy was still proscribed, whether for same-sex or heterosexual conduct, there was a pattern of nonenforcement with respect to consenting adults acting in private. Even Texas admitted in 1994, that as of that date it had not prosecuted anyone under those circumstances.

Quicknotes

DUE PROCESS CLAUSE Clauses found in the Fifth and Fourteenth Amendments to the United States Constitution providing that no person shall be deprived of "life, liberty, or property, without due process of law."

FOURTEENTH AMENDMENT DUE PROCESS CLAUSE Provides that protections mandated by the U.S. Constitution and observed by the federal government are equally applicable, and therefore must be observed by the states.

Obergefell v. Hodges

[Parties not identified.]

576 U.S.___, 135 S. Ct. 2584 (2015).

NATURE OF CASE: Consolidated actions challenging as unconstitutional a state's denial of the right of same sex couples to marry or to have their marriages, lawfully performed in another state, given full recognition. [The procedural posture of the case is not presented in the casebook extract.]

FACT SUMMARY: Obergefell (P), who had been lawfully married to his same-sex partner, Arthur, in a state that recognized same-sex marriages, contended that it was unconstitutional for their state of residence, which did not recognize such marriages, not to license same-sex marriages, as well as not to recognize such marriages that had been lawfully performed and licensed out-of-state. Other similarly situated same-sex couples (P) made similar claims.

> 🏛 **RULE OF LAW**
> The Fourteenth Amendment requires a state to license a marriage between two people of the same sex and to recognize a marriage between two people of the same sex when their marriage has been lawfully licensed and performed out-of-state.

FACTS: Obergefell (P) and Arthur were a same-sex couple living in Ohio, which did not recognize same-sex marriages. They travelled to Maryland, which does recognize such marriages, and they were married. Three months later, Arthur, who had an incurable disease, died. Following Arthur's death, and in accordance with Ohio law, Arthur's death record failed to record Obergefell as Arthur's "surviving spouse" and listed Arthur as "unmarried" at the time of his death. Obergefell (P) brought suit to be shown as the surviving spouse on Arthur's death certificate. Other similarly situated same-sex couples (P) made similar claims, asserting that state officials violated the Fourteenth Amendment by denying them the right to marry or to have their marriages lawfully performed in another state given full recognition. The Supreme Court granted certiorari, and the actions were consolidated. [The procedural posture of the case is not presented in the casebook extract.]

ISSUE: Does the Fourteenth Amendment require a state to license a marriage between two people of the same sex and to recognize a marriage between two people of the same sex when their marriage has been lawfully licensed and performed out-of-state?

HOLDING AND DECISION: (Kennedy, J.) Yes. The Fourteenth Amendment requires a state to license a marriage between two people of the same sex and to recognize a marriage between two people of the same sex

when their marriage has been lawfully licensed and performed out-of-state. The plaintiffs (P) sought to marry someone of the same sex and have their marriages deemed lawful on the same terms and conditions as marriages between persons of the opposite sex. Marriage as a union between two persons of the opposite sex has been central to the human condition and throughout the annals of human history. The institution of marriage has existed for millennia and across civilizations. This history marks the beginning of this case. To the government defendants (D), it would demean a timeless institution if marriage were extended to same-sex couples. However, the plaintiffs (P), far from seeking to devalue marriage, seek it for themselves because of their respect—and need—for its privileges and responsibilities, as illustrated by the plaintiffs' (P) own experiences. The history of marriage is one of both continuity and change. Changes, such as the decline of arranged marriages and the abandonment of the law of coverture, have worked deep transformations in the structure of marriage, affecting aspects of marriage once viewed as essential. These new insights have strengthened, not weakened, the institution. This dynamic also can be seen in the Nation's experience with gay and lesbian rights. Well into the 20th century, many states condemned same-sex intimacy as immoral, and homosexuality was treated as an illness. Later in the century, cultural and political developments allowed same-sex couples to lead more open and public lives. Extensive public and private dialogue followed, along with shifts in public attitudes. The Court ultimately reflected these changed attitudes in its decisions. The Court has long held the right to marry is protected by the Constitution, and that marriage is "one of the vital personal rights essential to the orderly pursuit of happiness by free men." The Court has reiterated that the right to marry is fundamental under the Due Process Clause. Those prior cases describing the right to marry presumed a relationship involving opposite-sex partners, but it should be kept in mind that the Court, like many institutions, has made assumptions defined by the world and time of which it is a part. Other precedents have expressed broad constitutional principles that go beyond such assumptions. In assessing whether the force and rationale of its cases apply to same-sex couples, the Court must respect the basic reasons why the right to marry has been long protected, and such an analysis compels the conclusion that same-sex couples may exercise the right to marry. Four principles and traditions demonstrate that the reasons marriage is fundamental under the Constitution apply with equal force to same-sex couples. The first premise of this Court's

Continued on next page.

relevant precedents is that the right to personal choice regarding marriage is inherent in the concept of individual autonomy. This abiding connection between marriage and liberty is why the Court invalidated interracial marriage bans under the Due Process Clause. Decisions about marriage are among the most intimate that an individual can make, and this is true for all persons, whatever their sexual orientation. A second principle in this Court's jurisprudence is that the right to marry is fundamental because it supports a two-person union unlike any other in its importance to the committed individuals. Same-sex couples have the same right as opposite-sex couples to enjoy intimate association, a right extending beyond mere freedom from laws making same-sex intimacy a criminal offense. A third basis for protecting the right to marry is that it safeguards children and families and thus draws meaning from related rights of childrearing, procreation, and education. Without the recognition, stability, and predictability marriage offers, children suffer the stigma of knowing their families are somehow lesser. They also suffer the significant material costs of being raised by unmarried parents, relegated to a more difficult and uncertain family life. The marriage laws at issue thus harm and humiliate the children of same-sex couples. Fourth, and finally, this Court's cases and the nation's traditions make clear that marriage is a keystone of the nation's social order. States have contributed to the fundamental character of marriage by placing it at the center of many facets of the legal and social order. There is no difference between same- and opposite-sex couples with respect to this principle, yet same-sex couples are denied the constellation of benefits that the states have linked to marriage and are consigned to an instability many opposite-sex couples would find intolerable. It is demeaning to lock same-sex couples out of a central institution of the nation's society, for they too may aspire to the transcendent purposes of marriage and seek fulfillment in its highest meaning. The government defendants (D) argue that the plaintiffs (P) do not seek to exercise the right to marry but rather a new and nonexistent "right to same-sex marriage." Although liberty under the Due Process Clause must be defined in a most circumscribed manner, with central reference to specific historical practices, such an approach is inconsistent with the approach this Court has used in discussing other fundamental rights, including marriage and intimacy. If rights were defined by who exercised them in the past, then received practices could serve as their own continued justification and new groups could not invoke rights once denied. The right of same-sex couples to marry is also derived from the Fourteenth Amendment's guarantee of equal protection. The Due Process Clause and the Equal Protection Clause are connected in a profound way. Rights implicit in liberty and rights secured by equal protection may rest on different precepts and are not always co-extensive, yet each may be instructive as to the meaning and reach of the other. The Court has acknowledged the interlocking nature of these constitutional safeguards in the context of the legal treatment of gays and lesbians, and this dynamic also applies to same-sex marriage. The challenged laws burden the liberty of same-sex couples, and they abridge central precepts of equality. The marriage laws at issue are in essence unequal: Same-sex couples are denied benefits afforded opposite-sex couples and are barred from exercising a fundamental right. Especially against a long history of disapproval of their relationships, this denial works a grave and continuing harm, serving to disrespect and subordinate gays and lesbians. The right to marry is a fundamental right inherent in the liberty of the person, and under the Due Process and Equal Protection Clauses of the Fourteenth Amendment couples of the same-sex may not be deprived of that right and that liberty. Same-sex couples may exercise the fundamental right to marry, and the state laws challenged by the plaintiffs (P) are held invalid to the extent they exclude same-sex couples from civil marriage on the same terms and conditions as opposite-sex couples. There may be an initial inclination to await further legislation, litigation, and debate, but referenda, legislative debates, and grassroots campaigns; studies and other writings; and extensive litigation in state and federal courts have led to an enhanced understanding of the issue. While the Constitution contemplates that democracy is the appropriate process for change, individuals who are harmed need not await legislative action before asserting a fundamental right. Gays and lesbians have suffered pain and humiliation at the hands of state action, and the effects of these injuries no doubt have lingered. A ruling against same-sex couples would have the same effect and would be unjustified under the Fourteenth Amendment. The plaintiffs' (P) stories show the urgency of the issue they present to the Court, which has a duty to address these claims and answer these questions. The government defendants' (D) argument that allowing same-sex couples to wed will harm marriage as an institution rests on a counterintuitive view of opposite-sex couples' decisions about marriage and parenthood. Finally, the First Amendment ensures that religions, those who adhere to religious doctrines, and others have protection as they seek to teach the principles that are so fulfilling and so central to their lives and faiths. The Fourteenth Amendment requires states to recognize same-sex marriages validly performed out of state. Since same-sex couples may now exercise the fundamental right to marry in all states, there is no lawful basis for a state to refuse to recognize a lawful same-sex marriage performed in another state on the ground of its same-sex character.

DISSENT: (Roberts, C.J.) The plaintiffs' (P) arguments have appeal based on arguments rooted in social policy and considerations of fairness, but the Court is not a legislature, and whether same-sex marriage is a good idea should not be the Court's concern. The Court can only say what the law is, not what it should be. The majority's decision is not a pronouncement of a legal judgment, and

Continued on next page.

the right it announces has no basis in the Constitution or precedent. The core meaning of marriage has been that it is a union between a man and a woman, notwithstanding that this core has changed through history. The concept of marriage has been premised on the need for procreation as a means for the human race to survive, which is why, at its core it is about a union between a woman and a man, and this singular understanding of marriage has prevailed in the United States throughout its history. The majority's decision is bald judicial policymaking, which previously has been rejected in favor of judicial self-restraint, and that is why the majority's position is indefensible as a matter of constitutional law. Allowing unelected federal judges to select which unenumerated rights rank as "fundamental"—and to strike down state laws on the basis of that determination—raises significant concerns about the judicial role. Implied fundamental rights must be objectively and deeply rooted in the nation's tradition and history. The majority acknowledges none of this doctrinal background, and instead returns the Court to the long-discredited approach inherent in substantive due process. No precedents, including those that have guaranteed the privacy rights of same-sex couples, support the right to same-sex marriage. Unlike criminal laws banning contraceptives and sodomy, the marriage laws at issue here involve no government intrusion. They create no crime and impose no punishment. Same-sex couples remain free to live together, to engage in intimate conduct, and to raise their families as they see fit. Nothing interferes with these couples' right to be let alone. Given that the majority redefines the core meaning of marriage, its opinion invites the question of whether that core meaning can be expanded beyond just two individuals to many, since from the standpoint of history and tradition, a leap from opposite-sex marriage to same-sex marriage is much greater than one from a two-person union to plural unions, which have deep roots in some cultures around the world. Further, the opinion does not follow the usual framework for deciding equal protection cases, and, in any event, the marriage laws at issue here do not violate the Equal Protection Clause, because distinguishing between opposite-sex and same-sex couples is rationally related to the states' "legitimate state interest" in "preserving the traditional institution of marriage." The majority's manner of deciding this case will, in the long run, be detrimental to the Court as an institution, since the majority repeatedly and unabashedly exalts the role of the judiciary in delivering social change—a role it clearly does not have under the Constitution. Those who founded our country would not recognize the majority's conception of the judicial role. They after all risked their lives and fortunes for the precious right to govern themselves. They would never have imagined yielding that right on a question of social policy to unaccountable and unelected judges. By deciding the question of same-sex marriage under the Constitution, the Court removes it from the realm of democratic decision, which will have significant consequences in the loss of respect for the Court. Finally, the

majority needlessly sullies people of faith, who did nothing more than follow the understanding of marriage that has existed for our entire history, by characterizing them as bigoted and hurting gays and lesbians. In sum, the Constitution had nothing to do with the majority's decision.

DISSENT: (Scalia, J.) The majority's opinion is the furthest extension imaginable of the Court's power to create so-called liberties that do not exist in the Constitution. Thus, the majority usurps the power to govern, which should remain with the people and their elected officials. A system of government that makes the People subordinate to a committee of nine unelected lawyers does not deserve to be called a democracy. The majority makes clear that it believes in such judicial superiority, by finding that no matter what it was the People ratified, the Fourteenth Amendment protects those rights that the Judiciary, in its "reasoned judgment," thinks the Fourteenth Amendment ought to protect The Court's Justices do not represent a cross-section of America, and to let them decide the policy question of same-sex marriage violates a fundamental tenet of democracy: no social transformation without representation. The majority's opinion is both pretentious and egotistic, and lacking in logic and precision. It is judicial hubris, plain and simple. This decision should have been left to the People.

DISSENT: (Thomas, J.) The majority claims the plaintiffs (P) are deprived of "liberty," but the majority's concept of liberty is not one that can be found in the Due Process Clauses, under conceptions neither of substantive nor procedural due process. Based on the history of these Clauses, "liberty" was construed to refer only to freedom from physical restraint. Even assuming that "liberty" goes beyond such freedom, the American legal tradition has long understood "liberty" as individual freedom from governmental action, not as a right to a particular governmental entitlement. Not only does the majority's decision undermine democratic processes, it also threatens religious liberties since marriage is not simply a governmental institution but a religious institution as well.

DISSENT: (Alito, J.) The majority's decision usurps the constitutional right of the people to decide whether to keep or alter the traditional understanding of marriage and violates core federalism principles. The majority's view of marriage is not a traditional view, which rested for millennia on ideas tied to procreation. Admittedly, society's understanding of marriage is changing. However, there still are states that adhere to the traditional view of marriage and are afraid that departing from that view will erode the marriage institution. Although the views of citizens and states vary, what is clear is that it is far beyond the outer reaches of the Court's authority to say that a state may not adhere to the understanding of marriage that has

Continued on next page.

long prevailed, not just in this country and others with similar cultural roots, but also in a great variety of countries and cultures all around the globe. The majority, by imposing its view on the entire country, and taking the issue away from democratic processes, marginalizes those Americans who have traditional ideas. In attempting to make up for the harsh treatment of gays and lesbians in the past, the majority will inflict bitter and lasting wounds on the nation. The majority abuses its power, and its decision evidences a deep and perhaps irremediable corruption of our legal culture's conception of constitutional interpretation.

▶ ANALYSIS

The majority's decision will require states to issue marriage licenses to same-sex couples and to recognize same-sex marriages entered in other states largely based on a constitutional provision guaranteeing "due process" before a person is deprived of his "life, liberty, or property." The dissent characterizes this outcome as a result of substantive due process, which has been discredited as permitting judges to stray from the Constitution's text, guided only by their personal views. The dissent (Thomas, J.) also views the majority's use of equal protection (which the majority indicates acts synergistically with due process) as only a means to shore up its substantive due process analysis, which the dissent claims is an analysis both based on an imaginary constitutional protection and a revisionist view of history and tradition.

Quicknotes

DUE PROCESS CLAUSE Clauses, found in the Fifth and Fourteenth Amendments to the United States Constitution, providing that no person shall be deprived of "life, liberty, or property, without due process of law."

EQUAL PROTECTION CLAUSE A constitutional provision that each person be guaranteed the same protection of the laws enjoyed by other persons in like circumstances.

FOURTEENTH AMENDMENT Declares that no state shall make or enforce any law that shall abridge the privileges and immunities of citizens of the United States. No state shall deny to any person within its jurisdiction the equal protection of the laws.

JUDICIAL RESTRAINT Self-imposed discipline by judges making decision without indulging their own personal views or ideas that may not be consistent with existing law.

SUBSTANTIVE DUE PROCESS A constitutional safeguard limiting the power of the state, irrespective of how fair its procedures may be; substantive limits placed on the power of the state.

Washington v. Glucksberg

State (D) v. Doctor (P)

521 U.S. 707 (1997).

NATURE OF CASE: Appeal in case challenging the constitutionality of prohibition against assisted suicide.

FACT SUMMARY: Glucksberg (P), a Washington state physician, wished to assist his terminally ill patients to commit suicide.

RULE OF LAW
The "liberty" protections of the Due Process Clause of the Fourteenth Amendment do not include a right to commit suicide with another's assistance.

FACTS: Washington state law makes it a felony to knowingly cause or aid another person to attempt suicide. Glucksberg (P), a Washington state doctor, along with others, wanted to assist his terminally ill, mentally competent patients in ending their lives. In January of 1994, Glucksberg (P) filed a declaratory judgment action, asserting that Washington's (D) ban on assisted suicide violated the Fourteenth Amendment's protection of liberty interests. The district court ruled for Glucksberg (P) and the Ninth Circuit affirmed. Washington (D) appealed.

ISSUE: Do the "liberty" protections of the Due Process Clause include a right to commit suicide with another's assistance?

HOLDING AND DECISION: (Rehnquist, C.J.) No. The "liberty" protections of the Due Process Clause of the Fourteenth Amendment do not include a right to commit suicide with another's assistance. Therefore, Washington's (D) prohibition against assisting a suicide does not violate the Fourteenth Amendment. Here, unlike seeking an abortion or terminating lifesaving medical assistance, Washington's (D) state interests outweigh any personal issues of autonomy that Glucksberg (P) may assert. First, assisted suicide is not a deeply rooted tradition in American culture and the Supreme Court has required a careful description of liberty interests that are protected by the Fourteenth Amendment. No such historical guideposts exist for assisted suicide. Furthermore, an individual's interest in personal autonomy is outweighed by Washington's (D) interest in preventing coercion of patients and discrimination against the terminally ill. This Court has been very cautious in expanding rights under the Fourteenth Amendment, requiring asserted rights to meet a threshold so that those same rights do not ultimately get manipulated in the political process. The asserted right of assisted suicide does not meet any threshold. Reversed.

CONCURRENCE: (O'Connor, J.) While I agree that there is no general right to commit suicide, the narrower question of whether a mentally competent, terminally ill patient has the right to determine his own imminent death does not need to be answered today with the facial challenge to the Washington (D) law.

CONCURRENCE: (Stevens, J.) While there is no general right to commit suicide, the "unqualified interest in the preservation of human life" is not itself sufficient to outweigh the interest in liberty that may justify the only possible means of preserving a dying patient's dignity and alleviating her intolerable suffering. Some allowable circumstances may arise in the future.

CONCURRENCE: (Souter, J.) While assisted suicide may be an accepted right in the future, legislators are in a better position than the courts to determine if such a right is within the confines of the due process protections of the Constitution.

CONCURRENCE: (Ginsburg, J.) Substantially for the reasons stated by Justice O'Connor, I concur with the Court's judgment.

CONCURRENCE: (Breyer, J.) Our legal tradition may provide greater support for a plaintiff's right to "die with dignity," rather than a "right to commit suicide with another's assistance," but this Court does not need to decide now whether such a right is "fundamental."

ANALYSIS

This unanimous ruling by the Supreme Court decided the most closely watched case of its 1997 term. Note that the Court implied that states could choose to permit doctor-assisted suicide if they so desired. Oregon has in fact voted by referendum to do so. The Court will rule on a challenge to that law in 1998.

Quicknotes

FOURTEENTH AMENDMENT DUE PROCESS CLAUSE Provides that protections mandated by the U.S. Constitution and observed by the federal government are equally applicable, and therefore must be observed by the states.

Cleveland Board of Education v. Loudermill

Board of Education (D) v. Employee (P)

470 U.S. 532 (1985).

NATURE OF CASE: Appeal of order invalidating termination of public employee without hearing.

FACT SUMMARY: Loudermill (P), a public employee who could only be terminated for cause, was denied a pretermination hearing.

🏛 RULE OF LAW
A public employee who can be discharged only for cause is entitled to a pretermination hearing.

FACTS: It was discovered that Loudermill (P), an Ohio public servant, had falsified data on his employment application. He was discharged without a pretermination hearing. Under Ohio law, he could be discharged only for cause. Loudermill (P) challenged this as a deprivation of due process. Ohio law provided for termination without a hearing. The district court found that this did not violate due process, but the court of appeals reversed.

ISSUE: Is a public employee who can be discharged only for cause entitled to a pretermination hearing?

HOLDING AND DECISION: (White, J.) Yes. A public employee who can be discharged only for cause is entitled to a pretermination hearing. The Constitution does not create property rights; this is the province of the states. However, once a property right is created, the Constitution mandates that such property can be deprived only with due process. Due process requires that the concerned individual be given a predeprivation hearing. Here, Ohio by statute gave Loudermill (P) the right to continue employment, with good behavior, which is a property right. As Loudermill (P) was deprived of it without a hearing, due process was violated. Affirmed.

DISSENT: (Rehnquist, J.) When, as here, the statute conferring the property right provides its own procedures, those procedures are acceptable.

▶ ANALYSIS

The rule announced by the Court will only apply when an employee has a vested interest in continued employment. The Court has held that an employee who can be terminated without cause has no right to a hearing. *Roth v. Board of Regents of State Colleges*, 408 U.S. 564 (1972). It should be noted, however, that state laws have recently been expanding in terms of recognizing rights to employ-ment, so the scope of the present case would appear to be ever-expanding.

━━■

Quicknotes

DUE PROCESS CLAUSE Clauses found in the Fifth and Fourteenth Amendments to the United States Constitution providing that no person shall be deprived of "life, liberty, or property, without due process of law."

━━■

Mathews v. Eldridge

Government agency (D) v. Benefits recipient (P)

424 U.S. 319 (1976).

NATURE OF CASE: Appeal from order of evidentiary hearing.

FACT SUMMARY: [Eldridge's (P) benefits under the federal disability insurance benefits program were terminated after a state agency found that his disability had ceased to exist.]

🏛 RULE OF LAW
An evidentiary hearing is not required prior to the termination of disability benefits.

FACTS: [Eldridge (P), who had been receiving disability insurance benefits under the Social Security Act since 1968, received a questionnaire from the state agency charged with monitoring his medical condition in 1972. After considering Eldridge's (P) reply that he was still disabled as well as the reports of physicians and a psychiatric consultant, the agency informed Eldridge (P) by letter that it had made a tentative decision to terminate his disability payments and gave Eldridge (P) a reasonable time to reply. After Eldridge (P) replied, disputing the agency's findings, the state agency made a final determination against Eldridge (P), which was accepted by the Social Security Agency. Although Eldridge (P) had the right to seek reconsideration of the decision within six months, he instead filed suit challenging the constitutional validity of the administrative procedures used to assess the presence of a continued disability. The court of appeals held that Eldridge (P) had to be afforded an evidentiary hearing prior to termination of disability payments, and Mathews (D), on behalf of the Social Security Agency, appealed.]

ISSUE: Is an evidentiary hearing required prior to the termination of disability benefits?

HOLDING AND DECISION: (Powell, J.) No. An evidentiary hearing is not required prior to the termination of disability benefits. The determination of what due process requires in the way of specific procedures requires consideration of three distinct factors: (1) the private interest that will be affected by the official action; (2) the risk of an erroneous deprivation of such interest through the procedures used and the probable value, if any, of additional or substitute procedural safeguards; and (3) the government's interest, including the function involved and the fiscal and administrative burdens that the additional or substitute procedural requirement would entail. Here, while the deprivation from termination of disability benefits may be significant, the recipient may have access to other forms of private or government assistance. Second, because the decision whether to discontinue disability ben-

efits will usually turn upon routine and unbiased medical reports, there is little risk of an erroneous deprivation. Third, the government's and the public's interest in conserving scarce fiscal and administrative resources is a significant factor. Thus, the present administrative procedures fully comport with due process. Reversed.

DISSENT: (Brennan, J.) The very legislative determination to provide disability benefits, without any prerequisite determination of need in fact, presumes a need by the recipient that should not be denigrated.

▶ ANALYSIS

In *Sniadich v. Family Finance Corp.*, 395 U.S. 337 (1969), the Court invalidated a Wisconsin statutory garnishment procedure that gave no notice or opportunity to be heard before the in rem seizure of Sniadich's wages. The Court noted that because prejudgment garnishment may impose tremendous hardship on the wage earner and give the creditor enormous leverage, the general rule is that there must be notice and a prior hearing before garnishment.

Quicknotes

NOTICE Communication of information to a person by an authorized person or an otherwise proper source.

PROCEDURAL DUE PROCESS The constitutional mandate that if the state or federal government acts so as to deny a citizen of a life, liberty, or property interest the individual is first entitled to notice and the right to be heard.

Home Building & Loan Association v. Blaisdell

Lender (P) v. State (D)

290 U.S. 398 (1934).

NATURE OF CASE: Appeal from ruling upholding state mortgage moratorium law.

FACT SUMMARY: In the midst of the Depression, Minnesota (D) passed a mortgage moratorium law.

🏛 RULE OF LAW
Legislation postponing enforcement of mortgages, when tailored to an emergency situation, does not violate the Contracts Clause.

FACTS: In 1933, during the Depression, Minnesota (D) passed a mortgage moratorium law to provide emergency relief for homeowners threatened with foreclosure. The law allowed courts to postpone mortgage sales and periods of redemption through May 1, 1935, thus modifying lenders' (P) contractual rights of foreclosure. The Minnesota Supreme Court upheld the statute, and lenders (P) appealed.

ISSUE: Does legislation postponing enforcement of mortgages, when tailored to an emergency situation, violate the Contracts Clause?

HOLDING AND DECISION: (Hughes, C.J.) No. When tailored to an emergency situation, legislation postponing enforcement of mortgages does not violate the Contracts Clause. While the Contracts Clause prohibits impairment of contractual obligations, it does not follow that conditions may not arise in which a temporary restraint of enforcement may be constitutional. A court will not use the Contracts Clause to throttle the ability of states to protect their fundamental interests, and the reservation of a state's power to exercise its protection is read into all contracts. In this case, an emergency justified the state's (D) protection of the community's vital interest. The state's (D) legislation aimed to protect the entire society's basic interest, and the conditions are reasonable and temporary. Affirmed.

DISSENT: (Sutherland, J.) The Contracts Clause was adopted following the Revolution, when Americans found themselves impoverished and debtors began to rest their hopes on legislative interference. It cannot be urged that conditions that produced the rule may now be invoked to destroy it. If the provisions of the Constitution are not upheld when they pinch as well as when they comfort, they may as well be abandoned.

▶ ANALYSIS

A state law runs afoul of the Contracts Clause if it: (1) substantially impairs a contractual relationship; (2) serves no significant and legitimate public purpose; and (3) contains conditions that are not reasonable or appropriate to the public purpose.

Quicknotes

CONTRACT CLAUSE Article 1, section 10 of the U.S. Constitution prohibiting states from passing any "law impairing the Obligation of Contracts."

Pennsylvania Coal Co. v. Mahon

Coal mining company (D) v. Landowner (P)

260 U.S. 393 (1922).

NATURE OF CASE: Action by property owner to enjoin certain operations on adjacent property.

FACT SUMMARY: A Pennsylvania statute forbade the mining of coal in such fashion as to cause the subsidence of any structure used as a human habitation.

🏛 RULE OF LAW
While private property may be regulated to a certain degree, a taking under the Fifth Amendment will be found if the regulation results in a severe diminution of value. At a certain magnitude, there must be an exercise of eminent domain and compensation to sustain the regulatory act. While considerable deference is to be given the legislature's judgment, each case will turn upon its particular facts.

FACTS: In 1878, the Pennsylvania Coal Co. ("the Coal Co.") (D) conveyed some land but reserved in the deed the right to remove all coal under the land. The grantee agreed to assume any resulting damage. Mahon (P), who later acquired the land, was bound by the deed. Mahon (P), wanting to prevent further mining under the land, claimed that a 1922 state law (the Kohler Act, called "the Act") changed the coal company's (D) rights. The Act forbade the mining of coal in such manner as to cause the subsidence of any structure used as a human habitation with certain exceptions. Mahon's (P) injunction was denied, the trial court maintaining that the Act would be unconstitutional if applied to the present case. On appeal, the state Supreme Court reversed, holding that the statute was a legitimate exercise of the police power.

ISSUE: Must a state which, through legislation, destroys previously existing contractual and property rights between private parties to the extent of severe diminution of property value give compensation to the affected party?

HOLDING AND DECISION: (Holmes, J.) Yes. While private property may be regulated to a certain degree, a taking under the Fifth Amendment will be found if the regulation results in a severe diminution of value. At a certain magnitude, there must be an exercise of eminent domain and compensation to sustain the regulatory Act. While considerable deference is to be given the legislature's judgment, each case will turn upon its particular facts. Where damage is inflicted on a single private house, even if similar damage is inflicted on others in different places, there is no public interest. On the other hand, the damage to the Coal Co.'s (D) contractual and property rights is considerable. The Act cannot be sustained where, as an exercise of the police power, it affects reserved rights. To make coal mining commercially unprofitable is, in effect, to destroy it. The rights of the public in a street purchased by eminent domain are those it has paid for. A strong public desire to improve the public condition is not enough to justify achieving it by a shorter cut than the constitutional way of paying for the charge. This is a question of degree and cannot be disposed of by general propositions. So long as private individuals or communities take the risk of contracting for or purchasing only surface rights, they must bear the loss. Reversed.

DISSENT: (Brandeis, J.) Every restriction on the use of property is an abridgment by the state of rights in property without making compensation. Here, the restriction was only against a noxious use of property that remains in the Coal Co.'s (D) possession. The Coal Co. (D), once it discontinues its noxious use, is free to enjoy its property as before. A restriction does not cease to be public simply because some individuals may be benefited. The means chosen here may be the only way to prevent the subsistence of land. Because values are relative, the value of the coal kept in place by the restriction should be compared with the value of other parts of the land. The state should not have to follow a theory of reciprocal advantage to justify exercising its police power for the public good. The reciprocal advantage given by the Act to the Coal Co. (D) is that of doing business in a civilized community.

▶ ANALYSIS

Eventually, the same analysis of the "taking" issue was used in *United States v. Causby*, 328 U.S. 265 (1946). There, a group of chicken farmers who owned land adjacent to a military airport claimed that, as a result of the noise of planes flying over their property, their chickens were literally frightened to death and egg production fell off. Rejecting the government's argument that any damage was merely consequential of the public's right of freedom of transit, Justice Douglas, writing for the majority, stated: "It is the owner's loss, not the taker's gain, which is the measure of the value of the property taken. . . . The owner's right to possess and exploit the land—that is to say, his beneficial ownership of it—would be destroyed. . . . It would not be a case of incidental damages arising from a legalized nuisance." In dissent, Justice Black warned "the effect of the Court's decision is to limit, by the imposition of relatively absolute constitutional barriers, possible future adjustments through legislation and regulation which might become necessary with the growth of air

Continued on next page.

transportation, and [because] the Constitution does not contain such barriers."

Quicknotes

EMINENT DOMAIN The governmental power to take private property for public use so long as just compensation is paid therefor.

TAKING A governmental action that substantially deprives an owner of the use and enjoyment of his property, requiring compensation.

Miller v. Schoene

Private property owner (P) v. State entomologist (D)

276 U.S. 272 (1928).

NATURE OF CASE: Appeal from order to cut cedar trees.

FACT SUMMARY: A Virginia statute authorized a state official (D) to order, after study, the cutting down of cedar trees growing on private property so as to prevent the spread of rust disease to private apple orchards; no compensation was allowed the owner of the cedar trees.

RULE OF LAW
The state does not exceed its constitutional powers by deciding upon the destruction of one class of private property in order to save another, which, in the judgment of the legislature, is of greater value to the public. Where the choice is unavoidable, there is no denial of due process, and compensation need not be given the private owners affected.

FACTS: A Virginia statute authorized the state entomologist (D) (an official charged with studying and regulating insects) to determine if any cedar trees constituted a menace to the health of any apple orchard. Upon an affirmative finding, the state entomologist (D) could order private owners of property to cut down their cedar trees. No compensation is given by the state for the value of the cedars or any decrease in market value of the realty which results. The statute was designed to curb the spread of cedar rust, a disease fatal to apple orchards, but without effect on the value of the cedar. The disease is carried by spores up to two miles. Compared with the value of apple orchards, red cedar is not valued commercially, but for the most part, only as ornamental. On the other hand, apple growing is a principal crop of Virginia, involving multi-million-dollar investments, jobs, and attendant development. Miller (P) was ordered to cut down his red cedar trees and challenged the constitutionality of the statute as denying him due process of law as applied to the states through the Fourteenth Amendment. The trial court had affirmed the order after a hearing to consider whether his trees were, in fact, infected with rust disease.

ISSUE: May a state, acting through the police power, order the destruction of one class of private property so as to protect another class, which, in its estimation, is of greater value to the public interest?

HOLDING AND DECISION: (Stone, J.) Yes. Virginia had to choose between two classes of private property, in close proximity to one another, which were incompatible. If the state had chosen not to pass a statute, this would have been a poor choice, since the apple orchards would almost certainly have been destroyed. There

may be a preponderant public interest favoring one property class over another: more is involved than a conflict of private interests and a shifting of loss between them. The police power may place the public interest over the property interest of an individual even to the extent of destroying private property. The Virginia statute is constitutional. Reversed.

ANALYSIS

Although the Fifth Amendment provides that no private property shall "be taken for private use, without just compensation," the Supreme Court has consistently held that a state, acting through its police powers, may restrict the use of private property; such impositions, even if producing a substantial loss in market value of the property, is not tantamount to a "taking," and so the state is not required to compensate the owner for incidental losses that are the consequence of legitimate regulations infused with the public interest.

Quicknotes

FIFTH AMENDMENT Provides that no person shall be compelled to serve as a witness against oneself or be subject to trial for the same offense twice, or be deprived of life, liberty, or property without due process of law.

POLICE POWER The power of a government to impose restrictions on the rights of private persons, so long as those restrictions are reasonably related to the promotion and protection of public health, safety, morals, and the general welfare.

TAKING A governmental action that substantially deprives an owner of the use and enjoyment of his property, requiring compensation.

Penn Central Transportation Co. v. New York City

Transportation company (P) v. Municipality (D)

438 U.S. 104 (1978).

NATURE OF CASE: Appeal of action challenging application of municipal landmark preservation law.

FACT SUMMARY: Penn Central Transportation Co. (P) was denied a permit to erect a skyscraper over Grand Central Station, a designated landmark.

RULE OF LAW

A city may, as part of a comprehensive landmark preservation scheme, place restrictions on development affecting the landmark without paying "just compensation."

FACTS: New York City (D) enacted a comprehensive landmark preservation ordinance requiring Landmark Preservation Commission ("the Commission") approval prior to development affecting a designated landmark. In exchange for losing development rights, the owners of designated property were permitted to transfer development rights to other property. Grand Central Station, belonging to Penn Central Transportation Co. (Penn Central) (P), was designated a landmark. The Commission denied an application for the erection of a skyscraper over the station. Penn Central (P) filed suit, claiming that the ordinance constituted a "taking" in the Fifth Amendment sense. Penn Central (P) did not argue that Grand Central Station was profitable. The New York Court of Appeals held for New York City (D), and Penn Central (P) appealed.

ISSUE: May a city, as part of a comprehensive landmark preservation scheme, place restrictions on development affecting the landmark without paying "just compensation?"

HOLDING AND DECISION: (Brennan, J.) Yes. A city may, as part of a comprehensive landmark preservation scheme, place restrictions on development affecting the landmark without paying "just compensation." No precise rule exists for determining when regulation of private property becomes a taking in the constitutional sense. Some factors include whether a physical invasion occurred, whether the interference is arbitrary or part of a common plan, and whether any reasonable return is left on the property. An analysis of these factors leads to the conclusion that no taking occurred. There was no invasion. The regulation was part of a comprehensive plan. Analysis also reveals that a reasonable return on the property still remains. This is especially true in light of the fact Penn Central (P) is the beneficiary of transferred development rights. It is settled that a government may deny an owner the most profitable use of his property without a taking occurring, and this rule applies here. Affirmed.

DISSENT: (Rehnquist, J.) The type of legislation involved here was not zoning in the true sense, so rules formulated regarding zoning should not apply. The law imposes an affirmative duty on the part of Penn Central (P) to maintain the property, and this is more than the usual type of zoning regulation. The burden of landmark preservation should not so disproportionately fall on the owner.

ANALYSIS

The Court has been highly deferential to state authority in this area of the law. While examples of holdings in favor of owners do exist (e.g., *Pennsylvania Coal Co. v. Mahon*, 260 U.S. 393 (1922)), it is difficult for an owner to prevail. Generally speaking, in the absence of an invasion or outright destruction, the regulation will not be held to constitute a taking.

Quicknotes

TAKING A governmental action that substantially deprives an owner of the use and enjoyment of his property, requiring compensation.

Lucas v. South Carolina Coastal Council

Developer (P) v. State agency (D)

505 U.S. 1003 (1992).

NATURE OF CASE: Appeal of reversal of compensation award for government "taking."

FACT SUMMARY: The South Carolina Coastal Council (D) prevented Lucas (P) from building homes on his beachfront property.

RULE OF LAW

Where regulation prohibits all economically beneficial use of land, and the proscribed use could not have been prohibited under state nuisance law, the regulation is a "taking" that requires "just compensation" to be paid to the landowner.

FACTS: In 1986, Lucas (P) purchased two vacant beachfront lots in a residential area. In 1988, South Carolina passed a law creating a coastal zone in which no occupiable improvements could be built. The law's stated purpose was to protect property from storms, tides, and beach erosion, and as an environmental protection. The law prevented Lucas (P) from constructing two homes he had planned. In suing the South Carolina Coastal Council (D), Lucas (P) did not challenge the state's right to pass the law or its justifications for doing so. He simply claimed the law rendered his property valueless, which amounted to a "taking" under the Fifth Amendment, and, thus, entitled him to just compensation. The trial court agreed, the South Carolina Supreme Court reversed, and Lucas (P) appealed.

ISSUE: Where regulation prohibits all economically beneficial use of land, and the proscribed use could not have been prohibited under state nuisance law, is the regulation a "taking" that requires "just compensation" to be paid to the landowner?

HOLDING AND DECISION: (Scalia, J.) Yes. Where regulation prohibits all economically beneficial use of land, and the proscribed use could not have been prohibited under state nuisance law, the regulation is a "taking" that requires "just compensation" be paid to the landowner. Mandated preservation of private land looks like a conversion of private property to public, a classic "taking." Government cannot be permitted to regulate in this manner without compensation simply by reciting some police power or "prevention of harmful use" rationale. Such regulations must account for owners' traditional understandings as to the state's power over their property rights. The source of these understandings is state public and private nuisance law. Thus, the owner of a lake bed always is aware he may be stopped by law from flooding adjacent property to create a landfill. If the state restricts this use, even to deprive him of all economic benefit, he is not entitled to compensation. Here, however, South Car-

olina common-law principles probably would not prevent Lucas (P) from building homes on his land. If the state court determines they would not, Lucas (P) is entitled to just compensation. Reversed and remanded.

CONCURRENCE: (Kennedy, J.) Where all economic value is deprived, the issue of compensation turns on the owner's reasonable, investment-backed expectations. However, reasonable expectations must be based on our whole legal tradition, not just nuisance law. Coastal property may present unique concerns not addressed by nuisance law.

DISSENT: (Blackmun, J.) The Court should not create a category that precludes a case-specific inquiry when all economic value is lost. It is well recognized that government may regulate property without compensation no matter how adverse the financial effect on the owner. The Court's injection of nuisance considerations into takings doctrine is misguided and goes beyond what is necessary to secure Lucas's (P) benefit.

DISSENT: (Stevens, J.) Under the Court's new rule, a landowner who loses 95 percent of his property value gets nothing, while one who loses 100 percent recovers the land's full value. The Court's holding today denies the legislature its traditional power to revise property laws. Even assuming Lucas's (P) land was rendered valueless, the risks inherent in Lucas's (P) type of investment, the generality of the statute, and the compelling purpose motivating the legislature demonstrate that no taking was affected.

ANALYSIS

Traditionally, "takings" were limited to direct appropriation of property by the government. Since this view was rejected in *Pennsylvania Coal Co. v. Mahon*, 260 U.S. 393 (1922), the Court has engaged in a case-by-case, ad hoc determination of when regulation becomes "taking." The *Lucas* majority identified two categories of regulations that constitute takings regardless of the public interest in the regulation. One category is defined in the holding. The other is where the government physically invades the owner's property (e.g., where a city law requires landlords to place cable television facilities in their buildings).

Quicknotes

TAKING A governmental action that substantially deprives an owner of the use and enjoyment of his property, requiring compensation.

Palazzolo v. Rhode Island

Property owner (P) v. State (D)

533 U.S. 606 (2001).

NATURE OF CASE: Appeal from a decision denying compensation in adverse condemnation suit.

FACT SUMMARY: Anthony Palazzolo made several proposals for developing his property to the Rhode Island Coastal Resources Management Council, which rejected his proposals. Palazzolo (P) brought an inverse condemnation suit against Rhode Island (D).

RULE OF LAW
A landowner not deprived of all economic use of property by a state's designation as coastal wetlands, has not had the property taken in violation of the Takings Clause of the Fifth Amendment.

FACTS: Anthony Palazzolo (P) owned a waterfront parcel of land in Rhode Island (D), most of which was designated as protected coastal wetlands. Palazzolo (P) made several proposals to the Rhode Island Coastal Resources Management Council ("the Council") to develop his property. His proposals were rejected, with the exception that he could build a substantial residence on an 18-acre parcel. The Council stated that his application was "vague and inadequate for a project of this size and nature" and that it would adversely impact the waters and wetlands on and around the prospective development area. Palazzolo (P) brought an inverse condemnation suit against Rhode Island (D), arguing that denial of his application without just compensation constituted a violation of the Takings Clause of the Fifth Amendment. The trial court found against Palazzolo (P), and the Rhode Island Supreme Court affirmed. Palazzolo (P) appealed to the United States Supreme Court.

ISSUE: Has a landowner who has not been deprived of all economic use of his or her property by the state's designation as coastal wetlands had the property taken in violation of the Takings Clause of the Fifth Amendment?

HOLDING AND DECISION: (Kennedy, J.) No. A landowner not deprived of all economic use of his or her property by the state's designation as coastal wetlands has not had the property taken in violation of the Takings Clause of the Fifth Amendment. Just as a prospective enactment, such as a new zoning ordinance, can limit the value of land without effecting a taking because it may be reasonable to all concerned, other enactments are unreasonable and do not become less so because of the passage of time. While the right to improve property, however, is indeed subject to the reasonable exercise of state authority, including the enforcement of valid zoning and land-use restrictions, the Takings Clause in certain circumstances

allows the landowner to assert that a particular exercise of the state's regulatory power is so unreasonable or onerous as to compel compensation. Here, Rhode Island (D), by designation of the property as coastal wetlands, prevented Palazzolo (P) from using any fill, effectively precluding commercial development of his property in his desired manner. With no fill, there can be no structures and no development on the wetlands. A regulation that denies all economically beneficial or productive use of land will require compensation under the Takings Clause. Even where regulation places limitations on land that fall short of eliminating all economically beneficial use, a taking may nonetheless have occurred, depending on a complex of factors, including the regulation's economic effect on the landowner, the extent to which the regulation interferes with reasonable investment-backed expectations, and the character of the government action. Here, however, the regulation permitted Palazzolo (P) to build a substantial residence on an 18-acre parcel, which does not leave the property "economically idle." This constitutes far more than simply leaving Palazzolo (P) with "a few crumbs of value" or a token interest. While the Rhode Island Supreme Court did not err in finding that Palazzolo (P) failed to establish a deprivation of all economic value since it is undisputed the parcel retains significant worth for construction of a residence, the latter court did err in finding the claims were unripe because Palazzolo (P) failed to apply for further building permits subsequent to the coastal wetlands designation. Affirmed in part, reversed in part, and remanded.

CONCURRENCE: (O'Connor, J.) Courts properly consider the effect of existing zoning and land-use regulations under the rubric of investment-backed expectations in determining whether a compensable taking has occurred. The salience of these facts cannot be reduced to any set formula. The temptation to adopt what amounts to per se rules in either direction must be resisted.

CONCURRENCE: (Scalia, J.) The fact that a restriction existed at the time the purchaser of property took title should have no bearing upon the determination of whether the restriction is so substantial as to constitute a taking.

CONCURRENCE AND DISSENT: (Stevens, J.) While future generations have a right to challenge unreasonable limitations on the use and value of land, it does not follow that, as the Court assumes, a succeeding property owner may obtain compensation for a taking of property from his or her predecessor in interest. A taking is a

Continued on next page.

discrete event, a governmental acquisition of private property for which the state is required to provide just compensation. Like other transfers of property, it occurs at a particular time, the time being the moment when the relevant property interest is alienated from its owner.

▶ *ANALYSIS*

In *Palazzolo*, the Supreme Court makes clear the determination that whether an existing, general law can limit all economic use of property must turn on objective factors, such as the nature of the land use proscribed.

▰▰▰

Quicknotes

FIFTH AMENDMENT Provides that no person shall be compelled to serve as a witness against oneself or be subject to trial for the same offense twice, or be deprived of life, liberty, or property without due process of law.

TAKINGS CLAUSE Provision of the Fifth Amendment to the United States Constitution, prohibiting the government from taking private property for public use without providing just compensation therefore.

▰▰▰

Freedom of Expression

Quick Reference Rules of Law

Masses Publishing Co. v. Patten

Publishing company (P) v. Postmaster General (D)

244 F. 535 (S.D.N.Y. 1917).

NATURE OF CASE: Action for preliminary injunction.

FACT SUMMARY: Patten (D) refused Masses Publishing Co.'s (P) magazine access to the mails for violating the 1917 Espionage Act.

🏛 RULE OF LAW

An opinion critical of a draft statute, no matter how seditious in nature, cannot be deemed to be advocacy of the violation of that statute unless there is a direct urging of such violation.

FACTS: Masses Publishing Co. (Masses) (P) published a monthly magazine called "The Masses," which contained cartoons and text of a politically revolutionary nature. During the First World War, Masses (P) ran political material in the magazine violently attacking the draft and the war and expressing sympathy for conscientious objectors. In July of 1917, under directions from the Postmaster General, Patten (D), Postmaster of New York, told Masses (P) that their August issue would be denied use of the mails. Patten (D) stated that the magazine violated the Espionage Act of 1917 by: (1) making false statements with the intent to interfere with the operation of the military forces of the United State; (2) arousing discontent among potential draftees and thereby promoting insubordination among troops already in the war; and (3) counseling resistance and disobedience to the law. Masses (P) brought this suit for a preliminary injunction against Patten's (D) refusal to accept the magazine in the mails.

ISSUE: Where a person's publications or utterances stop short of directly advocating resistance to a law, is that person nonetheless to be held responsible for attempting to cause its violation?

HOLDING AND DECISION: (Hand, J.) No. An opinion critical of a draft statute, no matter how seditious in nature, cannot be deemed to be advocacy of the violation of that statute unless there is a direct urging of such violation. Unless there is some direct advocacy by a person for others to resist a particular law, then that person may not be held responsible for attempting to cause a violation of the law. Here, the publications of Masses (P) may have created national dissension and thereby assisted, indirectly, the cause of the enemy. But the statute in question provided that such publications be willfully false and made with the intent to interfere with military operations. The publications were mere opinions and not publications of facts. Thus, they fell within the scope of the right to criticize, normally the privilege of individuals in countries depen-dent on free expression of opinions as an ultimate source of authority. The statute was intended to prevent the spreading of false rumors embarrassing to the military, not the dissemination of inflammatory public opinion. It is also contended by Patten (D) that to allow Masses (P) to arouse discontent among the public as to the conduct of the war and draft caused insubordination among wartime troops. But to interpret the word "causes" too broadly would be to suppress all hostile criticism of the war except those offi-cially sanctioned opinions. There are recognized limits to criticisms of existing laws or policies of war. One may not counsel or advise others to violate the law as it stands. The present statute is limited to punishing direct advocacy of resistance to recruiting and enlistment. Neither the car-toons nor the text of Masses' (P) publications fell with this test. Injunction granted.

▶ ANALYSIS

The present test, later supplanted with the "clear and present danger" test as to what type of conduct constitutes advocacy of resistance to law, focuses on the speaker and the value of the speech. This decision weighs the value of content of freely spoken opinions against its impact on the orderly conduct of governmental policy. The burden is on the government as accuser to show that such speech or publication is so detrimental to the orderly process of government that freedom of speech should bow to gov-ernmental will. The *Masses* case takes a liberal view of First Amendment rights and allows the free expression of opin-ion that falls short of direct advocacy of resistance to governmental authority. Judge Hand's decision in this case was overturned by the court of appeals on the ground a person would be held accountable for the natural con-sequences of his words. If his words strongly imply a particular law should be violated, that person will not be immune from prosecution merely because he omitted a direct appeal for violations. Judge Hand later wrote to a friend that his opinion in this case had apparently received little or no professional approval.

■▬■

Quicknotes

FIRST AMENDMENT Prohibits Congress from enacting any law respecting an establishment of religion, prohibiting the free exercise of religion, abridging freedom of speech or the press, the right of peaceful assembly and the right to petition for a redress of grievances.

■▬■

Schenck v. United States

Publisher (D) v. Federal government (P)

249 U.S. 47 (1919).

NATURE OF CASE: Appeal from conviction for conspiracy to violate the Espionage Act, conspiracy to use the mails for transmissions of nonmailable material, and unlawful use of the mails.

FACT SUMMARY: During a time of war, Schenck (D) mailed circulars to draftees that were calculated to cause insubordination in the armed services and to obstruct the U.S. recruiting and enlistment program in violation of military laws.

🏛 RULE OF LAW
The test to determine the constitutionality of a statute restricting free speech is whether, under the circumstances, the speech is of such a nature as to create a clear and present danger that it will bring about the substantive evils that Congress has a right to prevent.

FACTS: During a time of war, Schenck (D) mailed circulars to draftees. The circulars stated that the Conscription Act was unconstitutional and likened conscription to conviction. The circulars intimated that conscription was a monstrous wrong against humanity in the interest of Wall Street's chosen few and described nonconscription arguments as coming from cunning politicians and a mercenary capitalist press. They urged: "Do not submit to intimidation," but advised only peaceful actions such as a petition to repeal the Conscription Act. Schenck (D) did not deny that the jury could find the circulars could have no purpose except to influence draftees to obstruct the carrying out of the draft.

ISSUE: Does the right to freedom of speech depend upon the circumstances in which the speech is spoken?

HOLDING AND DECISION: (Holmes, J.) Yes. The test to determine the constitutionality of a statute restricting free speech is whether, under the circumstances, the speech is of such a nature as to create a clear and present danger that it will bring about the substantive evils Congress has a right to prevent. The character of every act depends on the circumstance in which it is done. The most stringent protection of free speech would not protect a person's falsely shouting "fire" in a theatre and causing a panic. "The question in every case is whether the words are used in such circumstances and are of such a nature as to create a clear and present danger that they will bring about the substantive evils Congress has a right to prevent. It is a question of proximity and degrees." During a war, things that could be said during peaceful times may be such a hindrance to the war effort they will not be permitted. Affirmed.

▶ ANALYSIS

The Court's first significant encounter with the problem of articulating the scope of constitutionally protected speech came in a series of cases involving agitation against the draft and war during World War I (*Schenck, Frohwerk* (249 U.S. 204 (1919)), and *Debs* (249 U.S. 211 (1919)). *Schenck* announces the "clear and present danger" test, the test for determining the validity of legislation regulating speech. In *Schenck*, Justice Holmes rejected perfect immunity for speech. But he also rejected a far more restrictive, far more widely supported, alternative test: that "any tendency in speech to produce bad acts, no matter how remote, would suffice to validate a repressive statute."

■==■

Quicknotes

FIRST AMENDMENT Prohibits Congress from enacting any law respecting an establishment of religion, prohibiting the free exercise of religion, abridging freedom of speech or the press, the right of peaceful assembly and the right to petition for a redress of grievances.

■==■

Abrams v. United States

Publisher (D) v. Federal government (P)

250 U.S. 616 (1919).

NATURE OF CASE: Appeal of conviction for publishing materials with intent to hinder American war efforts.

FACT SUMMARY: In response to American military intervention in post-czarist Russia, Abrams (D) circulated a leaflet calling for a strike.

 RULE OF LAW
[Rule of law not stated in casebook excerpt.]

FACTS: Following the Marxist takeover of Russia, the United States sent a military expedition to that country. Abrams (D) circulated a leaflet decrying the U.S. efforts to undercut the Russian revolution and calling for a general strike by U.S. workers. Abrams (D) was convicted of "publishing materials with the intent to hinder American war efforts." Abrams (D) appealed.

ISSUE: [Issue not stated in casebook excerpt.]

HOLDING AND DECISION: (Clarke, J.) [The Court summarily rejected Abrams's (D) First Amendment claims.]

DISSENT: (Holmes, J.) The First Amendment is meant to encourage the free exchange of ideas in the marketplace, and this applies to all ideas, no matter how unpopular. Only when expression presents an immediate danger may it be curtailed, and this was not the case here.

▶ **ANALYSIS**

Justice Holmes's dissent was, at the time, probably the most libertarian treatise on the First Amendment that a Court member had made. The concept of "clear and present danger" being the only basis for curtailment of expression first saw its pronouncement here. This concept would later be expanded upon by the Court itself.

▬▬■

Quicknotes

FIRST AMENDMENT Prohibits Congress from enacting any law respecting an establishment of religion, prohibiting the free exercise of religion, abridging freedom of speech or the press, the right of peaceful assembly and the right to petition for a redress of grievances.

▬▬■

Gitlow v. New York

Publisher (D) v. State (P)

268 U.S. 652 (1925).

NATURE OF CASE: Appeal from a conviction for criminal anarchy.

FACT SUMMARY: Gitlow (D) printed and circulated literature advocating a Communist revolt against the U.S. government.

🏛 RULE OF LAW
Under its police powers, a state may validly forbid any speech or publication that has tendency to produce action dangerous to public security, even where such speech or publication presents no "clear and present danger" to the security of the public.

FACTS: Gitlow (D) was a member of the Left Wing Section of the Socialist Party in New York, and he was responsible for printing the official organ of the Left Wing called the Revolutionary Age. In this paper, Gitlow (D) printed articles advocating the accomplishment of the Communist revolution through militant revolutionary socialism. Gitlow (D) further advocated a class struggle, mobilization of the proletariat through mass industrial revolts and political strikes to conquer and destroy the U.S. government and replace it with a dictatorship of the proletariat. Although there was no evidence that these writings resulted in any such action, Gitlow (D) was arrested, tried, and convicted for advocating the overthrow of the government by force under a New York (P) criminal anarchy statute. At trial, Gitlow's (D) counsel urged that since there was no resulting action flowing from the publication of the Gitlow (D) "Manifesto," the statute penalized the mere utterance of doctrine having no propensity toward incitement of concrete action.

ISSUE: Is a state statute punishing the mere advocacy of overthrowing the government by force an unconstitutional denial of the freedom of speech and press as protected under the First Amendment and applied to the states by the Fourteenth Amendment?

HOLDING AND DECISION: (Sanford, J.) No. Under its police powers, a state may validly forbid both speech and publication if they have tendency to result in action that is dangerous to public security, even though such utterances present no "clear and present danger" to the security of the public. The New York (P) criminal anarchy statute did not punish the utterance of abstract doctrine, having no quality of incitement to action. It prohibits advocacy to overthrow organized government by unlawful means. These words imply advocacy of action. Clearly, Gitlow's (D) "Manifesto," which spoke in terms of "mass action" of the proletariat for the "Communist re-construction of society" is language of direct incitement. The means suggested imply force and violence and are inherently unlawful in a constitutional form of government based on law and order. Although freedom of speech and press are protected by the First and Fourteenth Amendments, it is fundamental that this freedom is not absolute. The police power extends to a state the right to punish those who abuse this freedom by advocating action inimical to the public welfare, tending to corrupt public morals, to incite crime, or to threaten the public security. The state need not wait for such dangers to arise. It may punish utterances likely to bring about such substantive evils. The "clear and present danger" test announced in the *Schenck* case, 249 U.S. 47 (1919), does not apply here since the legislature has previously determined the danger of the substantive evils that may arise from specified utterances. So long as the statute is constitutional and the use of the language sought to be penalized comes within the prohibition, the statute will be upheld. And it is not necessary the defendant advocate some definite or immediate act of force or violence. It is sufficient if they were expressed in general terms. Affirmed.

DISSENT: (Holmes, J.) The "clear and present danger" test applies, and there was no clear and present danger here. The followers of Gitlow (D) were too few to present one. Every idea is an incitement. The only meaning of free speech is to allow everyone to have their say.

▶ ANALYSIS

The *Gitlow* case is an example of what has been termed the "bad tendency" test. This test punishes utterances whose meaning lies somewhere between "clear and present danger" and mere advocacy of abstract ideas. The key question here is whether the language "tends" to produce action resulting in a danger to public security. The holding of the Court in this case, while recognizing Gitlow's (D) constitutional rights of free speech and press, bypassed these rights by saying that the New York (P) statute did not unduly restrict such freedom. However, in light of the modern test of "clear and present danger," it seems that the "bad tendency" test is all but dead. The "clear and present danger" test requires language that results in imminent lawless action. Tendency is not enough. It is important to note that the "bad tendency" test has not been used by the Court since *Gitlow*.

Continued on next page.

Quicknotes

POLICE POWERS The power of a state or local government to regulate private conduct for the health, safety and welfare of the general public.

Whitney v. California

Communist Party member (D) v. State (P)

274 U.S. 357 (1927).

NATURE OF CASE: Appeal from conviction for violation of criminal syndicalism act.

FACT SUMMARY: Whitney (D), organizer and member of the Communist Labor Party of California, was convicted of aiding in that organization's violation of the Criminal Syndicalism Act.

🏛 RULE OF LAW
A state may, in the exercise of its police power, punish abuses of freedom of speech where such utterances are inimical to the public welfare as tending to incite crime, disturb the peace, or endanger organized government through threats of violent overthrow.

FACTS: In 1919, Whitney (D) attended a convention of the Socialist Party. When the convention split into factions, Whitney (D) went with the radicals and helped form the Communist Labor Party (CLP). Later that year, Whitney (D) attended another convention to organize a new California unit of CLP. There Whitney (D) supported a resolution that endorsed political action and urged workers to vote for CLP member-candidates at all elections. This resolution was defeated and a more extreme program of action was adopted, over Whitney's (D) protests. At trial, upon indictment for violation of the California Criminal Syndicalism Act ("the Act"), which held it unlawful to organize a group that advocated unlawful acts of violence as a means of effecting change in industrial ownership and in political change, Whitney (D) contended that she never intended the CLP to become a terrorist organization. Whitney (D) further contended that since she had no intent to aid the CLP in a policy of violent political reform, her mere presence at the convention was not a crime. Whitney (D) contended that the Act thus deprived her of her liberty without due process, and freedom of speech, assembly and association.

ISSUE: Is a state statute that punishes a person for becoming a knowing member of an organization that advocates the use of unlawful means to affect its aims, a violation of due process and a restraint of freedom of speech, assembly and association secured by the Constitution?

HOLDING AND DECISION: (Sanford, J.) No. A state may, in the exercise of its police power, punish abuses of freedom of speech where such utterances are inimical to the public welfare as tending to incite crime, disturb the peace, or endanger organized government through threats of violent overthrow. At her trial, Whitney (D) testified it was not her intention that the Communist Labor Party of California should be an instrument of terrorism or violence. Nevertheless, by its enactment of the Criminal Syndicalism Act, California (P) has declared that for an individual to knowingly be or become a member of an organization that advocates criminal syndicalism, involves such danger to the public peace and security of the state that these acts should be penalized in the exercise of California's (P) police power. That determination must be given great weight. Here, the essence of the offense denounced by the legislation is of the nature of a criminal conspiracy. It is clear such united and joint action involves even greater danger to the public peace and security than the mere isolated utterances and acts of individual persons. Accordingly, the Court cannot hold that, as here applied, the Criminal Syndicalism Act constitutes an unreasonable or arbitrary exercise of California's (P) police power. Affirmed.

CONCURRENCE: (Brandeis, J.) Whitney (D) is here punished for a step in the preparation of incitement that only threatens the public remotely. The Criminal Syndicalism Act of California aims at punishing those who propose to preach not put into action, criminal syndicalism. The right of freedom of speech, assembly and association, protected by the Due Process Clause of the Fourteenth Amendment and binding on the states, are restricted if they threaten political, moral or economic injury to the state. However, such restriction does not exist unless speech would produce a clear and imminent danger of some substantive evil to the state. The Court has not yet fixed standards in determining when a danger shall be clear. But no danger flowing from speech can be deemed clear and present unless the threatened evil is so imminent that it may strike before an opportunity for discussion on it. There must be, however, a probability of serious injury to the state. As to review by this court of an allegation of unconstitutionality of a criminal syndicalism act, whenever fundamental rights of free speech and assembly are alleged to have been invaded, the defendant must be allowed to present the issue of whether a clear and present danger was imminent by his actions. Here, mere advocacy of revolution by mass action at some future date was within the Fourteenth Amendment protection. But our power of review was lacking since there was evidence of a criminal conspiracy and such precludes review by this court of errors at a criminal trial absent a showing that constitutional rights were deprived.

Continued on next page.

▶ *ANALYSIS*

The *Whitney* case is important for having added to the *Schenck* test of "clear and present danger" the further requirement that the danger must be "imminent." *Schenck v. United States*, 249 U.S. 47 (1919). The opinion by Justice Brandeis in the *Whitney* case should be viewed as a dissenting opinion. His addition of "imminent," flew directly in the face of the majority opinion which punished "mere advocacy" of threatened action against the state. The "mere advocacy" test has not survived. Modernly, through the Smith Act that continues to punish criminal syndicalism, "mere advocacy" is not punishable. The urging of action for forcible overthrow is necessary before punishment will be imposed. Thus, the "urging of action" is the modern test of "clear and present imminent danger" espoused by Justice Brandeis in *Whitney*.

■■■■

Quicknotes

DUE PROCESS CLAUSE Clauses found in the Fifth and Fourteenth Amendments to the United States Constitution providing that no person shall be deprived of "life, liberty, or property, without due process of law."

FOURTEENTH AMENDMENT Declares that no state shall make or enforce any law that shall abridge the privileges and immunities of citizens of the United States. No state shall deny to any person within its jurisdiction the equal protection of the laws.

Dennis v. United States

Communist Party members (D) v. Federal government (P)

341 U.S. 494 (1951).

NATURE OF CASE: Appeal from conviction of violating the Smith Act.

FACT SUMMARY: Ringleaders (D) of the American Communist Party were convicted, under the Smith Act, of knowingly advocating the overthrow of government by violent means, and conspiracy.

RULE OF LAW
In reviewing legislation that restricts freedom of speech, the court, in determining whether a "clear and present danger" exists, must ask whether the gravity of the evil, discounted by its improbability, justifies such invasion of free speech as is necessary to avoid the evil.

FACTS: The Smith Act, passed by Congress in 1940, made it a crime for anyone to knowingly advocate the overthrow of government by force or violence, or by the assassination of any officer. The Act also prohibited an attempt or conspiracy to accomplish the same. Dennis (D) and other ringleaders (D) of the American Communist Party had been conducting seminars, making speeches, and writing articles advocating the overthrow of the U.S. government (P). They were charged with conspiracy in violation of the Smith Act. At their trial, the judge instructed the jury that its only duty was to determine whether a violation of the Act had occurred, and if so, as a matter of law, he had determined there is sufficient danger of a substantive evil that Congress had a right to prevent that justified the Act's application under the First Amendment. Dennis (D) and the other leaders (D) were convicted, and they appealed.

ISSUE: Is the Smith Act, as applied against the leaders of the American Communist Party, constitutional?

HOLDING AND DECISION: (Vinson, C.J.) Yes. In reviewing legislation that restricts freedom of speech, the court, in determining whether a "clear and present danger" exists, must ask whether the gravity of the evil, discounted by its improbability, justifies such invasion of free speech as is necessary to avoid the evil. [The Court initially held Congress has the power to pass the Smith Act since government has a right to protect itself against armed rebellion.] Congress, by passing the Act, intended not to prohibit the free discussion of political theories, but only advocacy of a dangerous nature. The words of the standard test, "clear and present danger," cannot mean that before the government may act, it must wait until the rebellion is about to be executed, the plans have been laid, and the signal is awaited. The fact those plotting the rebellion are

small and weak, while the government is strong, is irrelevant; success or probability of success is not the criterion. In determining whether a "clear and present danger exists," the court must determine the gravity of the evil as discounted by the improbability of its occurrence. In the present case, the trial court concluded that the Communist Party, composed of rigidly disciplined members subject to call at the will of the leaders, posed a sufficient danger to justify an intrusion on First Amendment rights. Furthermore, the doctrine that there must be a clear and present danger of a substantive evil that Congress has a right to prevent is a judicial rule to be applied as a matter of law by the courts. The convictions are affirmed.

CONCURRENCE: (Frankfurter, J.) The independence of the judiciary would be jeopardized were courts to become embroiled in the passions of the day and assume primary responsibility in choosing between competing political, economic, and social pressures. How best to reconcile competing interests is the business of legislatures and should not be second-guessed by the judiciary if there is any reasonable basis to sustain it.

CONCURRENCE: (Jackson, J.) The "clear and present danger" test should be applied only in those cases where the issue is criminality of a hot-headed speech on a street corner or circulation of a few pamphlets, etc. It should not be applied in cases like the instant one where the Court must appraise imponderables, including international and national phenomena that baffle the best-informed foreign offices and our most experienced politicians.

DISSENT: (Black, J.) The First Amendment as construed in the light of "reasonableness" is not likely to protect any but those safe or orthodox views that rarely need its protection.

DISSENT: (Douglas, J.) Defendants here were indicted for organizing people to teach, and themselves teach, certain books. These books, by Marx and Lenin, may lawfully remain on library shelves. Thus, the Smith Act punishes not what is said, but on the intent with which it is said. Furthermore, pure speech, without seditious conduct, is prohibited. The "clear and present danger" test requires that before speech can be curtailed, conditions must be so critical there will be no time to avoid the evil that is threatened. That is not the situation here; while the force of Communism may be prevalent in the world, its strength in this country is minimal.

Continued on next page.

▶ ANALYSIS

After *Dennis*, the Court retreated from its apparent carte blanche approval of congressional attempts to fight domestic Communism. In *Yates v. United States*, 354 U.S. 298 (1957), the Court held that in order for a defendant to be convicted under the Smith Act, the trial judge must instruct the jury to acquit, unless it found there had been some advocacy of action and not merely an argument for the desirability of the action.

━━━

Quicknotes

SMITH ACT Federal law prohibiting the violent overthrow of government.

━━━

Brandenburg v. Ohio

Ku Klux Klan member (D) v. State (P)

395 U.S. 444 (1969).

NATURE OF CASE: Appeal from conviction for violation of the Ohio Criminal Syndicalism statute.

FACT SUMMARY: Brandenburg (D) was convicted under a state statute that proscribes advocacy of the duty, necessity, or propriety of crime, sabotage, violence, or unlawful methods of terrorism as a means of accomplishing reform.

🏛 RULE OF LAW
The constitutional guarantees of freedom of speech and freedom of press do not permit a state to forbid or proscribe advocacy of the use of force or of law violation, except where such advocacy is directed to inciting or producing imminent lawless action and is likely to produce or incite such action.

FACTS: Brandenburg (D), a Klu Klux Klan leader, was convicted under Ohio's Criminal Syndicalism statute. The statute prohibits advocacy of the duty, necessity, or propriety of crime, sabotage, violence, or unlawful methods of terrorism as a means of accomplishing reform, and the assembling with any group formed to teach or advocate the doctrine of criminal syndicalism. The case against Brandenburg (D) rested on some films. One film showed 12 hooded figures, some carrying firearms, gathered around a wooden cross they burned. Scattered words could be heard that were derogatory to Jews and blacks. Brandenburg (D) made a speech and stated, "We are not a revengent group, but if our President, our Congress, and our Supreme Court, continues to suppress the white, Caucasian race, it's possible there might have to be some revengence taken."

ISSUE: Does a statute that proscribes advocacy of the use of force or of law violation violate the rights guaranteed by the First and Fourteenth amendments?

HOLDING AND DECISION: (Per curiam) Yes. The constitutional guarantees of freedom of speech and freedom of press do not permit a state to forbid or proscribe advocacy of the use of force or of law violation, except where such advocacy is directed to inciting or producing imminent lawless action and is likely to incite or produce such action. The mere abstract teaching of the moral propriety or even moral necessity for a resort to force and violence is not the same as preparing a group for violent action steering it to such action. A statute that fails to draw this distinction impermissibly intrudes upon the freedoms guaranteed by the First and Fourteenth Amendments. It sweeps within its condemnation speech the Constitution has immunized from governmental control. The Ohio statute purports to punish mere advocacy and to forbid assembly with others merely to advocate the described type of action. Hence, it cannot be sustained. Brandenburg's (D) conviction is reversed.

CONCURRENCE: (Black, J.) The doctrine of "clear and present danger" should have no place in the interpretation of the First Amendment.

CONCURRENCE: (Douglas, J.) It is doubtful that the "clear and present danger" is congenial with the First Amendment. "The line between what is permissible and not subject to control and what may be made impermissible and subject to regulation is the line between ideas and overt acts." Apart from where "speech is brigaded with action," speech should be immune from prosecution.

▎ ANALYSIS

This case demonstrates that the imminence of danger is an essential requirement to the validity of any statute curbing freedom of speech. This requirement was reiterated in *Bond v. Floyd*, 385 U.S. 116 (1966), in which the Court reversed a state legislature's resolution excluding Bond from membership. The exclusion was based on the ground Bond could not take the oath to support the state and U.S. Constitutions given his endorsement of a statement issued by the Student Nonviolent Coordinating Committee (SNCC) and his remarks criticizing the draft and the Vietnam War. The Court found no incitement to violation of law in Bond's remarks.

Quicknotes

FIRST AMENDMENT Prohibits Congress from enacting any law respecting an establishment of religion, prohibiting the free exercise of religion, abridging freedom of speech or the press, the right of peaceful assembly and the right to petition for a redress of grievances.

FOURTEENTH AMENDMENT Declares that no state shall make or enforce any law that shall abridge the privileges and immunities of citizens of the United States. No state shall deny to any person within its jurisdiction the equal protection of the laws.

Cantwell v. Connecticut

Jehovah's Witness (D) v. State (P)

310 U.S. 296 (1940).

NATURE OF CASE: Appeal of conviction for breach of the peace.

FACT SUMMARY: Cantwell (D), on a public street, played a recording of virulent anti-Catholic nature, for which he was convicted of breach of the peace.

🏛 RULE OF LAW
Speech not amounting to a clear and present danger to public health or security may not be abridged under the guise of preserving public peace.

FACTS: Cantwell (D), a Jehovah's Witness, positioned himself on a sidewalk and then played to passersby a recording denouncing all other religions in general and Catholicism in particular. Cantwell (D) did not attempt to intimidate anyone into listening against their will. The recording, while insulting, did not call for violence. Cantwell (D) was convicted of breaching the peace, and he appealed.

ISSUE: May speech not amounting to a clear and present danger to public health or security, be abridged under the guise of preserving public peace?

HOLDING AND DECISION: (Roberts, J.) No. Speech not amounting to a clear and present danger to public health or security may not be abridged under the guise of preserving public peace. The Constitution holds that the free communication of ideas is an important value, and something more than a desire to conserve desirable conditions is required to suppress it. An immediate threat to the public is required. Here, the recording in question may have been offensive to some, but it was not a call to violence or other threat to the public. Reversed.

▶ ANALYSIS

A portion of the Court's opinion is interesting to note. Justice Roberts pointed out that Cantwell (D) was not convicted because of the noise his phonograph made, but rather the ideas therein. The inference could be that regulation of the noise would have been permissible. This can be viewed as an intimation of the doctrine that content-neutral abridgments of speech will be given greater latitude than content-regulatory ones.

━━━

Quicknotes

FIRST AMENDMENT Prohibits Congress from enacting any law respecting an establishment of religion, prohibiting the free exercise of religion, abridging freedom of speech or the press, the right of peaceful assembly and the right to petition for a redress of grievances.

Feiner v. New York

Public speaker (D) v. State (P)

340 U.S. 315 (1951).

NATURE OF CASE: Appeal from conviction for disorderly conduct.

FACT SUMMARY: Feiner (D) gave an open-air speech before a racially mixed audience. The crowd that gathered forced pedestrians into the street. Feiner (D) urged black people to rise up in arms against whites and fight for equal rights. He refused to stop when asked to do so by a police officer and was arrested.

> ## 🏛 RULE OF LAW
> When clear and present danger of riot, disorder, interference with traffic on the streets, or other immediate threat to public safety, peace, or order appears, the state has the power to punish or prevent such disorder.

FACTS: Feiner (D) addressed an open-air meeting. A racially mixed crowd of about eighty people gathered. The crowd forced pedestrians walking by into the street. In response to a complaint about the meeting, two police officers arrived. They heard Feiner (D) urge black people to take up arms and fight against whites for equal rights. The remarks stirred up the crowd a little, and one person commented on the police's inability to control the crowd. Another threatened violence if the police did not act. The officers finally "stepped in to prevent it all resulting in a fight." They asked Feiner (D) twice to stop speaking. He ignored them, and they arrested him.

ISSUE: When clear and present danger of riot, disorder, interference with traffic on the streets, or other immediate threat to public safety, peace, or order appears, does the state have the power to punish or prevent such disorder?

HOLDING AND DECISION: (Vinson, C.J.) Yes. When clear and present danger of riot, disorder, interference with traffic on the streets, or other immediate threat to public safety, peace, or order appears, the state has the power to prevent or punish such disorder. Here, the crowd's behavior and Feiner's (D) refusal to obey the police requests presented a sufficient danger to warrant his arrest and to persuade the court that Feiner's (D) conviction for violation of public peace, order and authority does not exceed the bounds of proper state police action. Feiner (D) was neither arrested nor convicted for the making or the content of his speech. Rather, it was the reaction it engendered. The community's interest in maintaining peace and order on its streets must be protected. Hence, Feiner's (D) conviction is affirmed.

DISSENT: (Black, J.) Disagreement, mutterings, and objections from a crowd do not indicate imminent threat of a riot; nor does one threat to assault the speaker. Even assuming a critical situation existed, it was the duty of the police to protect Feiner's (D) right to speak, which they made no effort to do. Finally, a person making a lawful address is not required to be silent merely because an officer so directs. Here, Feiner (D) received no explanation as to why he was being directed to stop speaking. This decision means the police have the discretion to silence minority views in any city as soon as the customary hostility to such views develops.

▶ ANALYSIS

As *Feiner* demonstrates, free speech is not an absolute right. The conflicting interest of community order must also be considered. *Feiner* points out the question of whether the boundaries of protected speech depend on the content of the speech and the speaker's words or on the environment, the crowd reaction or potential crowd reaction. This question arose again in *Gregory v. Chicago*, 394 U.S. 111 (1969), which reversed convictions of disorderly conduct. There, participants in a "peaceful and orderly procession" to press their claims for desegregation were arrested when, after the number of bystanders increased, and some became unruly, they were asked to disperse and did not. The majority asserted this was a simple case as the marchers' peaceful conduct was a protected activity within the First Amendment. The concurring opinion saw *Gregory* as involving some complexities, since, as the judge noted, both the demonstrators and the officers had tried to restrain the hecklers but were unable to do so. He concluded that "this record is a crying example of a need for some narrowly drawn law," rather than the sweeping disorderly conduct law.

■=■

Quicknotes

FIRST AMENDMENT Prohibits Congress from enacting any law respecting an establishment of religion, prohibiting the free exercise of religion, abridging freedom of speech or the press, the right of peaceful assembly and the right to petition for a redress of grievances.

■=■

Chaplinsky v. New Hampshire

Jehovah's Witness (D) v. State (P)

315 U.S. 568 (1942).

NATURE OF CASE: Appeal of a conviction for violation of statute forbidding utterance of words derisive or annoying to another.

FACT SUMMARY: Chaplinsky (D), a Jehovah's Witness, first denounced all other religions as "rackets" and then called a Marshall a "fascist" and "racketeer."

RULE OF LAW
A government may proscribe language tending to incite violence.

FACTS: Chaplinsky (D), a Jehovah's Witness, had been calling other religions "rackets." An unfriendly crowd began to assemble. A Marshall warned Chaplinsky (D) that the crowd was getting ugly, whereupon Chaplinsky (D) called the Marshall a "racketeer" and a "fascist." Chaplinsky (D) was convicted under an ordinance prohibiting the utterance of words tending to harass, annoy, or deride another. Chaplinsky (D) appealed.

ISSUE: May a government proscribe language tending to incite violence?

HOLDING AND DECISION: (Murphy, J.) Yes. A government may proscribe language tending to incite violence. It is established that words constituting a clear and present danger to the public health may be banned. So-called "fighting words" do constitute such a danger. The ordinance in question basically is a prohibition of fighting words, and therefore the ordinance is valid. Affirmed.

ANALYSIS

This case presents one of the first enunciations of the concept of "protected" and "unprotected" speech, among them libel, obscenity, and "fighting words." The scope of the former two categories has been the subject of much subsequent analysis.

▬▬

Quicknotes

FIGHTING WORDS Unprotected speech under the First Amendment, which is likely to instigate a violent reaction.

▬▬

New York Times Co. v. United States;
United States v. Washington Post Co.

Federal government (P) v. Press (D)

403 U.S. 713 (1971).

NATURE OF CASE: Review of denial of injunctions against newspapers.

FACT SUMMARY: The United States (P) sought to enjoin the further publication of a top secret Defense Department study of the Vietnam War, known as the *Pentagon Papers*.

RULE OF LAW
There is a special presumption that the First Amendment does not permit the use of prior restraints.

FACTS: When the *Washington Post* (D) and the *New York Times* (D) began publishing the *Pentagon Papers*, the Government (P) sought to enjoin further publication, claiming that further publication of the top secret study would endanger national security and prolong the Vietnam War. The district court and the Court of Appeals for the District of Columbia Circuit held the Government (P) had not met the heavy burden of showing justification for the imposition of a prior restraint. The New York district court had also ruled the Government (P) had not met its burden, but the Second Circuit Court of Appeals reversed. Restraining orders were issued while the two cases were appealed. The Supreme Court granted certiorari.

ISSUE: Is there a special presumption that the First Amendment does not permit the use of prior restraints?

HOLDING AND DECISION: (Per curiam) Yes. There is a special presumption that the First Amendment does not permit the use of prior restraints. The Government (P) has not met its heavy burden of showing justification for the imposition of a prior restraint on speech. The Second Circuit's decision is reversed and the other judgments are affirmed.

CONCURRENCE: (Black, J.) The First Amendment abolished the government's power to censor the press. The judiciary cannot make laws enjoining publication of current news and abridging freedom of the press in the name of "national security."

CONCURRENCE: (Douglas, J.) That these disclosures may have a serious impact is no basis for sanctioning a previous restraint on the press. Open debate and discussion of public issues are vital to the national health.

CONCURRENCE: (Brennan, J.) It was error to grant any injunctive relief whatever, interim or otherwise.

The First Amendment does not tolerate any prior judicial restraints of the press predicated upon surmise or conjecture that untoward consequences may result. Unless and until the Government (P) has clearly made its case, the First Amendment commands that no injunction may issue.

CONCURRENCE: (Stewart, J.) The executive branch may promulgate and enforce executive regulations to protect the confidentiality necessary to carry out its responsibilities in international relations and national defense. In the absence of specific regulations or laws, it cannot be said that disclosure of the documents at issue will surely result in direct, immediate, and irreparable damage to the nation. That being so there is only one judicial resolution under the First Amendment.

CONCURRENCE: (White, J.) The Government's (P) failure to justify prior restraints does not measure its constitutional entitlement to a conviction for criminal publication. That the Government (P) mistakenly chose to proceed by injunction does not mean it could not have successfully proceeded in another way.

CONCURRENCE: (Marshall, J.) Congress has specifically rejected passing legislation that would have clearly given the President the power he seeks here to prevent publication of sensitive material damaging to "national security." It is not for this Court to overrule Congress.

DISSENT: (Burger, C.J.) These are not easy cases because no one knows all the facts. We are in this posture because these cases have been conducted in unseemly haste. When judges are pressured as in these cases the result is a parody of the judicial function.

DISSENT: (Harlan, J.) The Court has been almost irresponsibly feverish in dealing with these cases. The doctrine of separation of powers permits the judiciary to review the initial executive determination that disclosure of these documents would irreparably impair the national security, but it does not permit the judiciary to redetermine for itself the probable impact of disclosure on the national security.

DISSENT: (Blackmun, J.) I would remand to allow the orderly presentation of evidence from both sides. The publication of some of these documents could clearly result in great harm to the nation because it could lead to the death of soldiers, the destruction of alliances, the increased difficulty of negotiations with our enemies, the prolongation of

Continued on next page.

the war, and the further delay in the freeing of U.S. prisoners.

▶ *ANALYSIS*

These cases illustrate the fact that injunctions are considered to be prior restraints. A prior restraint may be invalid even if the speech at issue would result in a criminal prosecution. The doctrine of prior restraint reflects the historical right of the press to be free from licensing or censorship.

Quicknotes

FIRST AMENDMENT Prohibits Congress from enacting any law respecting an establishment of religion, prohibiting the free exercise of religion, abridging freedom of speech or the press, the right of peaceful assembly and the right to petition for a redress of grievances.

PRIOR RESTRAINT A restriction imposed on speech imposed prior to its communication.

Gooding v. Wilson

State (P) v. Antiwar demonstrator (D)

405 U.S. 518 (1972).

NATURE OF CASE: Appeal of grant of federal habeas corpus.

FACT SUMMARY: Wilson (D), arrested during an antiwar demonstration, was convicted under a statute proscribing words tending to cause a breach of the peace.

🏛 RULE OF LAW
Statutes abridging freedom of speech must be narrowly drawn to abridge only unprotected expression.

FACTS: Wilson (D) was arrested during an antiwar demonstration. Wilson (D) used threatening and highly derisive language to the officers. He was convicted under a statute proscribing words tending to cause a breach of the peace. Wilson (D) sought and obtained habeas corpus, which was appealed.

ISSUE: Must statutes abridging freedom of speech be narrowly drawn to abridge only unprotected expression?

HOLDING AND DECISION: (Brennan, J.) Yes. Statutes abridging freedom of speech must be narrowly drawn to abridge only unprotected expression. A state may regulate, for instance, "fighting words," which are unprotected. However, this statute, while admittedly pertaining to such language, impermissibly covers other types of language, as the expression of ideas can breach the peace. While it may be true the speech here would be properly abridged under a more narrowly drawn statute, the statute itself must fall here. Affirmed.

DISSENT: (Burger, C.J.) No danger for sweeping application of the statute in question exists, so it should be upheld.

▶ ANALYSIS

The present case presents an example of the "overbreadth" doctrine. As the name implies, a court in a First Amendment case will look to the language of a statute. If the statute can be applied to cover protected speech, it will be struck down, even if the speech in question could have been properly circumscribed.

Quicknotes

FIRST AMENDMENT Prohibits Congress from enacting any law respecting an establishment of religion, prohibiting the free exercise of religion, abridging freedom of speech or the press, the right of peaceful assembly and the right to petition for a redress of grievances.

Lovell v. Griffin

Literature distributor (D) v. Municipality (P)

303 U.S. 444 (1938).

NATURE OF CASE: Appeal from conviction of violation of city ordinance prohibiting the distribution of circulars, handbooks, advertising, or literature of any kind without first obtaining written permission from the City Manager.

FACT SUMMARY: Lovell (D) distributed religious tracts and magazines in the City of Griffin (P), without first obtaining a permit from the City Manager.

🏛 RULE OF LAW
An ordinance that prohibits the distribution of literature of any kind at any time, at any place, and in any manner without a prior permit is unconstitutional in that it subjects the right of freedom of the press to license and censorship.

FACTS: A City of Griffin (P) ordinance provided that no circulars, handbooks, advertising, or literature of any kind will be distributed within the city limits without first obtaining written permission from the City Manager. Lovell (D) distributed a pamphlet and a magazine in the nature of religious tracts, without obtaining written permission from the City Manager. She (D) contended first that the ordinance abridged freedom of the press and the free exercise of her religion.

ISSUE: Does an ordinance that prohibits the distribution of literature of any kind without first obtaining a written permit violate the constitutional right of freedom of the press?

HOLDING AND DECISION: (Hughes, C.J.) Yes. An ordinance that prohibits the distribution of literature of any kind at any time, at any place, and in any manner without a prior permit is unconstitutional in that it subjects the right of freedom of the press to license and censorship. The City of Griffin (P) ordinance was in no way limited to literature that is obscene or offensive to public morals or that advocates unlawful conduct. It embraced literature in the widest sense without any restriction in its application with respect to time or place. It prohibited the distribution of literature of any kind, at any time, at any place, and in any manner without a permit from the City Manager. The ordinance was invalid on its face in that it subjected the freedom of the press to license and censorship. Reversed.

▶ ANALYSIS

What a state may not do by direct regulation, it may not do indirectly through licensing, permit, or registration statutes. As *Lovell* demonstrates, just as a state may not constitu-tionally ban all speech in public places, it may not require, as a condition precedent to the exercise of free speech in public, that a citizen first obtain a permit, the granting or denial of which is discretionary with local authorities. The Court also invalidated an ordinance that banned the unli-censed communication of any views from door to door. It made canvassing in public subject to a police officer's determination of what could be distributed and who could distribute it. Likewise, it has been held a requirement that one must register before making a speech in public to enlist support for a lawful movement is quite incompatible with the First Amendment.

Quicknotes

FIRST AMENDMENT Prohibits Congress from enacting any law respecting an establishment of religion, prohibiting the free exercise of religion, abridging freedom of speech or the press, the right of peaceful assembly and the right to petition for a redress of grievances.

Near v. Minnesota

News publisher (D) v. State (P)

283 U.S. 697 (1931).

NATURE OF CASE: Action to abate publication of a newspaper as a public nuisance.

FACT SUMMARY: Minnesota (P) sought an injunction issued against the Saturday Press (D), which was publishing articles charging public officials with dereliction and complicity in dealing with gangsters.

RULE OF LAW
A state statute that authorizes previous restraints on publication violates the liberty of the press guaranteed by the Fourteenth Amendment if such publication relates to the malfeasance of public officials.

FACTS: A Minnesota (P) statute authorized abatement as a public nuisance of a "malicious, scandalous and de-famatory" newspaper. The law permitted the defense of good motives and justifiable ends. The Saturday Press (D) had published a series of articles charging that gangsters were in control of gambling, bootlegging, and racketeering in Minneapolis, and that public officials were either derelict in their duties or had illicit relations with the gangsters. Minnesota (P) sought to abate further publication of the Saturday Press (D), which was "malicious, scandalous, or defamatory." The trial court issued a permanent injunction, and the Saturday Press (D) appealed.

ISSUE: Is a state statute that authorizes abatement of a newspaper publication dealing with the corruption of public officials unconstitutional?

HOLDING AND DECISION: (Hughes, C.J.) Yes. A state statute that authorizes previous restraints on publication violates the liberty of the press guaranteed by the Fourteenth Amendment if such publication relates to the malfeasance of public officials. It is the chief purpose of the constitutional guaranty of freedom of press to prevent previous restraint on publication. Placing previous restraints on the press endangers the very nature of a free state. Only in exceptional circumstances may previous restraints be imposed. These would include where a government seeks to prevent actual obstruction to its recruiting service or the publication of the sailing dates of transports or the number and location of troops. Similarly, obscene publications and incitements to acts of violence or the overthrow by force of orderly government may be enjoined. However, previous restraint on a publication that seeks to expose the malfeasance of public officials is prohibited by the Fourteenth Amendment. Public officials have recourse against false accusations under the libel law. Finally, requiring newspapers to present proof of their

good intentions is merely an additional step to a complete system of censorship. So far as the Minnesota (P) statute authorized the abatement proceedings against the Saturday Press (D), it was unconstitutional. Reversed.

DISSENT: (Butler, J.) The Minnesota (P) statute does not operate as a "previous restraint on publication" within the proper meaning of that phrase. It does not authorize administrative control in advance such as was formerly exercised by the licensors and censors but prescribes a remedy to be enforced by a suit in equity. Existing libel laws are ineffective to suppress the evils occasioned by false and malicious publications.

ANALYSIS

"The issue is not whether the government may impose a particular restriction of substance in an area of public expression, such as forbidding obscenity in newspapers, but whether it may do so by a particular method, such as advance screening of newspaper copy. In other words, restrictions that could be validly imposed when enforced by subsequent punishment are, nevertheless, forbidden if attempted by prior restraint." Emerson, "The Doctrine of Prior Restraint," 20 *L. & Contemp. Prob.* 648 (1956). Traditionally, the judicial concern in prior restraint cases is on the broad discretion over free expression vested in administrative officers.

Quicknotes

FOURTEENTH AMENDMENT Declares that no state shall make or enforce any law that shall abridge the privileges and immunities of citizens of the United States. No state shall deny to any person within its jurisdiction the equal protection of the laws.

New York Times v. Sullivan

News publisher (D) v. Public official (P)

376 U.S. 254 (1964).

NATURE OF CASE: Appeal of defamation judgment.

FACT SUMMARY: The *New York Times* (D) published an editorial advertisement in which false statements were made that concerned Sullivan (P).

🏛 RULE OF LAW
The First Amendment requires that a public official may not recover damages for defamatory falsehoods relating to his official conduct unless he proves the statement involved was made with "actual malice—that is, with knowledge it was false or with reckless disregard of whether it was false or not."

FACTS: Sullivan (P) was a commissioner in the city of Montgomery, Alabama, charged with supervision of the Police Department. During a series of civil rights demonstrations in that city in 1960, the *New York Times* (D) published an editorial advertisement entitled "Heed Their Rising Voices," in which several charges of terrorism were leveled at the Police Department. The falsity of some of these statements is uncontroverted. The advertisement charged that nine students at a local college had been expelled for leading a march on the state capitol when, in fact, the reason had been an illegal lunch counter sit-in. The advertisement charged the police had padlocked the dining hall of the college to starve the demonstrators into submission when, in fact, no padlocking had occurred. Other false statements also were made. Sullivan (P) brought a defamation action against the *New York Times* (D) for these statements and recovered $500,000. Under Alabama law, a publication is libel per se (no special damages need be proved—general damages are presumed), whenever a defamatory falsehood is shown to have injured its subject in his public office or impute misconduct to him in his office. The *New York Times* (D) appealed the Alabama judgment, challenging this rule.

ISSUE: Are defamatory falsehoods regarding public officials protected by constitutional guarantees of freedom of speech and press?

HOLDING AND DECISION: (Brennan, J.) Yes. The First Amendment requires that a public official may not recover damages for defamatory falsehoods relating to his official conduct unless he proves the statement involved was made with "actual malice—that is, with knowledge it was false or with reckless disregard of whether it was false or not." First Amendment protections do not turn upon the truth, popularity, or social utility of ideas and beliefs that are involved. Rather, they are based upon the theory

erroneous statements are inevitable in free debate and must be protected if such freedom is to survive. Only where malice is involved do such protections cease. Here, the Alabama rule falls short of this standard and the evidence at trial was insufficient to determine its existence. The decision must, therefore, be reversed and remanded.

CONCURRENCE: (Black, J.) The federal Constitution has dealt with this deadly danger to the press in the only way possible without leaving the free press open to destruction—by granting to the press an absolute immunity for criticism of the way public officials do their public duty. "Malice," even as defined by the Court, is an elusive, abstract concept, hard to prove and hard to disprove. The requirement that malice be proved provides at best an evanescent protection for the right critically to discuss public affairs and certainly does not measure up to the sturdy safeguard embodied in the First Amendment.

▶ ANALYSIS

New York Times v. Sullivan is the landmark case in constitutional defamation law. Subsequent cases have expanded this concept even further. In *Rosenblatt v. Baer*, 383 U.S. 75 (1966), the Court defined "public official" as anyone having substantial responsibility for conduct of government affairs. In *Curtis Publishing Co. v. Butts* (decided together with) *Associated Press v. Walker*, 388 U.S. 130 (1967), *New York Times v. Sullivan* was extended to "public figures" as well as officials. In *Gertz v. Robert Welch, Inc.*, 418 U.S. 323 (1974), however, the Court retreated a bit by stating, "As long as they do not impose liability without fault, the states may define for themselves the appropriate standard of liability for (a) publisher . . . of defamatory falsehood injurious to a private individual." The Court also has taken steps to toughen the *New York Times v. Sullivan's* recklessness standard. In *St. Amont v. Thompson*, 390 U.S. 727 (1968), the Court ruled recklessness was not to be measured by the reasonable person standard, but rather by the subjective standard of whether or not the defendant in the case subjectively entertained serious doubts about the truth of his statements.

■■■◼■■

Quicknotes

DEFAMATION PER SE An intentional false publication of words which, standing alone without proof, communicated

Continued on next page.

publicly in either oral or written form, subject a person to scorn, hatred or ridicule.

FIRST AMENDMENT Prohibits Congress from enacting any law respecting an establishment of religion, prohibiting the free exercise of religion, abridging freedom of speech or the press, the right of peaceful assembly and the right to petition for a redress of grievances.

MALICE The intention to commit an unlawful act with the intent to inflict injury without justification or excuse.

Cox Broadcasting Corp. v. Cohn

Broadcasting company (D) v. Father of rape victim (P)

420 U.S. 469 (1975).

NATURE OF CASE: Appeal from conviction for invasion of privacy.

FACT SUMMARY: Cohn (P) sued Cox Broadcasting Corp. (D) for invading his privacy by identifying his daughter as a rape victim.

RULE OF LAW

The First and Fourteenth Amendments prevent state sanctions for publication of truthful information contained in official court records that are open to public inspection.

FACTS: Cohn's (P) daughter was a murder and rape victim. The Georgia code prohibited the publication of the name or identity of a rape victim. At the trial a reporter for Cox Broadcasting Corp. (D) obtained Cohn's (P) daughter's name by examining public records. The girl's name was broadcast during a news report concerning the crime and the trial. Cohn (P) sued Cox Broadcasting Corp. (D) for violating the Georgia code that protects the privacy of rape victims. The trial court granted a judgment for Cohn (P). The Georgia Supreme Court affirmed for Cohn (P). Cox Broadcasting Corp. (D) appealed.

ISSUE: May a state impose sanctions upon the publication of truthful information contained in official court records open to public inspection?

HOLDING AND DECISION: (White, J.) No. The First and Fourteenth Amendments prevent state sanctions for publication of truthful information contained in official court records open to public inspection. The right to privacy is not invaded by any publication made in a court of justice, and reports of any such proceedings that are open to public inspection may be published without invading a person's right to privacy. If there are privacy interests to be protected in judicial proceedings, the states must respond by means that avoid public documentation or other exposure of private information. Here, the defendant simply published truthful information contained in official court records that were open to public inspection; it did not invade the plaintiff's privacy. Judgment is entered for Cox Broadcasting Corp. (D). Reversed.

ANALYSIS

By declaring that persons have no reasonable expectation of privacy in information contained in public records, the Court in *Cox* materially constricted the constitutional right to privacy. Note this rule runs contrary to the well-established defamation rule that the scope of publication of any statement may increase liability. Note also that this rule

runs the risk of motivating and justifying (especially on the facts of *Cox*) government secrecy "gag orders," etc., under the subterfuge of protecting citizens from press embarrassment. *Cox* appears, at least theoretically, to threaten the privacy cause of action based on unauthorized disclosure of privileged information—since disclosure here, though not subject to privilege, was illegal.

■=■

Quicknotes

FIRST AMENDMENT Prohibits Congress from enacting any law respecting an establishment of religion, prohibiting the free exercise of religion, abridging freedom of speech or the press, the right of peaceful assembly and the right to petition for a redress of grievances.

FOURTEENTH AMENDMENT Declares that no state shall make or enforce any law that shall abridge the privileges and immunities of citizens of the United States. No state shall deny to any person within its jurisdiction the equal protection of the laws.

GAG ORDER Court order, mandating that the parties or reporters not discuss or publicize the case, so the defendant may receive a fair trial.

■=■

Virginia State Board of Pharmacy v. Virginia Citizens Consumer Council

State agency (D) v. Public interest group (P)

425 U.S. 748 (1976).

NATURE OF CASE: Action for declaratory relief.

FACT SUMMARY: A Virginia statute made it illegal for pharmacists to advertise the prices of prescription drugs.

🏛 RULE OF LAW
The consumer's interest in the free flow of commercial information makes such information the type of expression the First Amendment is designed to protect—even if it does no more than propose a commercial transaction.

FACTS: By Virginia law, the advertising of prescription drug prices by pharmacists was deemed "unprofessional conduct" subjecting offending pharmacists to various penalties. The Consumer Council (P), a private public interest organization, filed this action in federal district court, to have the Virginia law declared an unconstitutional violation of the First Amendment rights of both pharmacists and consumers. The Consumer Council (P) offered evidence that the advertising ban had resulted in wide price variations from outlet to outlet. From a declaration of unconstitutionality, this appeal followed.

ISSUE: Does the First Amendment protect such purely commercial speech activity as price advertising?

HOLDING AND DECISION: (Blackmun, J.) Yes. The consumer's interest in the free flow of commercial information makes such information the type of expression the First Amendment is designed to protect, even if it does no more than propose a commercial transaction. If there is a kind of speech that lacks all First Amendment protection, it must be distinguished by its content. Yet the speech whose content deprives it of protection cannot simply be speech on a commercial subject. No one would contend a pharmacist may be prevented from being heard on the subject of whether, in general, pharmaceutical prices should be regulated, or their advertisement forbidden. Nor can it be dispositive that a commercial advertisement is noneditorial, and merely reports a fact. Purely factual matter of public interest may claim protection. Even though an advertiser's interest is a purely economic one, such fact does not disqualify the advertiser from First Amendment protection. A particular consumer's interest in the free flow of commercial information may be as keen, if not keener by far, than his interest in the day's most urgent political debate. As applied to the instant case, when drug prices vary as strikingly as they do, information as to who is charging what becomes more than a convenience. It could mean the alleviation of pain or the enjoyment of basic necessities. Affirmed.

DISSENT: (Rehnquist, J.) The Court's extraordinary decision today not only usurps the power of the state legislature to make policy decisions about professionals, it also opens the door to possible irresponsible advertising and interference in the doctor-patient relationship.

▶ ANALYSIS

This case finally did away with the often-criticized rule that the First Amendment does not protect pure commercial speech. In *Bigelow v. Virginia*, 421 U.S. 809 (1975), the Court had invalidated a Virginia statute that made the advertising of abortions illegal. The Court there indicated abortion was of "public interest" and therefore information about it was constitutionally protected. *Consumer Council* expands that to cover all commercial advertising. Note this case has stimulated speculation that advertising bans on attorneys are also unconstitutional. Indeed, several state bar associations have recently begun drafting new regulations in this regard.

Quicknotes

FIRST AMENDMENT Prohibits Congress from enacting any law respecting an establishment of religion, prohibiting the free exercise of religion, abridging freedom of speech or the press, the right of peaceful assembly and the right to petition for a redress of grievances.

Miller v. California

Advertisement distributor (D) v. State (P)

413 U.S. 15 (1973).

NATURE OF CASE: Criminal prosecution for knowingly distributing obscene matter.

FACT SUMMARY: Miller (D) sent out advertising brochures for adult books to unwilling recipients.

RULE OF LAW
Material is obscene and not protected by the First Amendment if: (1) the average person, applying contemporary community standards, would find the work, taken as a whole, appeals to the prurient interest; (2) the work depicts in a patently offensive way sexual conduct specifically defined by the applicable state law; and (3) the work, taken as a whole, lacks serious literary, artistic, political, or scientific value.

FACTS: Miller (D) conducted a mass mailing campaign to advertise the sale of adult books. The advertising brochures were themselves found obscene. These brochures were sent to unwilling recipients who had not requested the material. Miller (D) was convicted of violating a statute that forbade knowingly distributing obscene matter.

ISSUE: Is material that is obscene protected by the First Amendment?

HOLDING AND DECISION: (Burger, C.J.) No. Material is obscene and not protected by the First Amendment if: (1) the average person, applying contemporary community standards, would find the work, taken as a whole, appeals to the prurient interest; (2) the work depicts in a patently offensive way sexual conduct specifically defined by the applicable state law; and (3) the work, taken as a whole, lacks serious literary, artistic, political, or scientific value. If material meets this definition of obscenity, then the state can prohibit its distribution if the mode of distribution entails the risk of offending unwilling recipients or exposing the material to juveniles. The burden of proof of the *Memoirs* test, (*Memoirs v. Massachusetts*, 383 U.S. 413 (1966)), that the material is utterly without redeeming value, is virtually impossible for the prosecution to meet and must be abandoned. There is no fixed national standard of "prurient interest" or "patently offensive" and these first two parts of the test are questions of fact to be resolved by the jury by applying contemporary community standards. Vacated and remanded.

DISSENT: (Douglas, J.) Courts were never given the constitutional power to make definitions of obscenity. The idea the First Amendment permits punishment for ideas that are "offensive" is astounding. No greater leveler of speech or literature has ever been designed.

DISSENT: (Brennan, J.) The statute in question is unconstitutionally overbroad and therefore invalid on its face.

ANALYSIS

Under the *Miller* test of obscenity, if the three requirements are met, the material in question is considered obscene and outside the protection of the First Amendment. *Miller* is a turnaround from *Memoirs* for many reasons: the *Memoirs* standard was too difficult to prove; the lower courts had no clear-cut guidelines because *Memoirs* was a plurality opinion; the Court decided to use local community standards to allow greater jury power; and the Court was beginning to feel institutional pressures, since every obscenity question was a constitutional question. Therefore, *Miller* was an attempt by the Court to decentralize decision-making.

Quicknotes

FIRST AMENDMENT Prohibits Congress from enacting any law respecting an establishment of religion, prohibiting the free exercise of religion, abridging freedom of speech or the press, the right of peaceful assembly and the right to petition for a redress of grievances.

Paris Adult Theatre I v. Slaton

Movie theatres (D) v. State (P)

413 U.S. 49 (1973).

NATURE OF CASE: Civil proceeding to enjoin continued showing of two adult films.

FACT SUMMARY: Two adult films were shown at theaters that advertised the nature of the films and required proof all patrons were over 21.

🏛 RULE OF LAW
A state can forbid the dissemination of obscene material to consenting adults in order to preserve the quality of the community and to prevent the possibility of resulting antisocial behavior.

FACTS: Two movie theatres in Atlanta showed "adult" films exclusively. The state of Georgia sought to enjoin the showing of sexually explicit movies in these theatres under an obscenity statute. It was determined the exterior advertising was not obscene or offensive, but that there were signs at the entrance stating that patrons must be 21 years of age and able to prove it. There was a further warning that those who would be offended by nudity should not enter. However, the films in question included, in addition to nudity, various simulated sex acts.

ISSUE: Can a state prohibit the dissemination of obscene material if the material is distributed only to consenting adults?

HOLDING AND DECISION: (Burger, C.J.) Yes. A state can forbid the dissemination of obscene material to consenting adults in order to preserve the quality of the community and to prevent the possibility of resulting antisocial behavior. A state has a valid interest in preventing exposure of obscene material to consenting adults. Even if exposure to juveniles and unwilling observers is prevented, the state has a further interest in preserving the quality of life, the community environment, and possible threats to public safety, which will allow the regulation of obscenity. Even if there is no conclusive scientific proof that exposure to obscenity adversely affects either an individual or society, it is for the legislature, not the courts, to resolve these empirical uncertainties. A legislature can determine a connection between obscenity and antisocial behavior exists, even in the absence of conclusive proof. Here, even though only consenting adults are involved, the state can make a judgment that public exhibition of obscenity has tendency to injure the community and can, therefore, enjoin the distribution of obscenity. Vacated and remanded.

DISSENT: (Brennan, J.) Prior obscenity standards have proved unworkable because they fail to give adequate notice of the definition of obscenity, producing a chilling effect on constitutionally protected speech. Because of the vague nature of these standards, every case is marginal, producing a vast number of constitutional questions, which creates institutional stress in the judicial system. States do have a valid interest in protecting children and unconsenting adults from exposure to allegedly obscene material, but other possible state interests, as discussed in the majority opinion, are vague, speculative, and cannot be proven. Therefore, in the absence of threat of exposure to juveniles or unconsenting adults, material cannot be suppressed, but the state can regulate the manner of distribution.

▶ ANALYSIS

The Court, in three companion cases to the principal case, also upheld obscenity convictions on seizures involving the importation of films from a foreign country, the interstate transportation of obscene materials for private use, and the sale of an obscene book that contained no pictures. In 1974, however, the Court overturned an obscenity conviction for the showing of *Carnal Knowledge*, a film with an MPAA rating of "R." While asserting the finding of obscenity was essentially a question of fact for the jury, the Court warned the jury did not have unbridled discretion in this area. In another case, the Court also stated the community standard to be applied was local, not national. Justice Brennan dissented, arguing that requiring a national distributor to comply with numerous local standards was totally unreasonable.

■=■

Quicknotes

FIRST AMENDMENT Prohibits Congress from enacting any law respecting an establishment of religion, prohibiting the free exercise of religion, abridging freedom of speech or the press, the right of peaceful assembly and the right to petition for a redress of grievances.

OBSCENITY Indecency, lewdness or offensive behavior in appearance or expression.

■=■

Cohen v. California

Wearer of jacket with text (D) v. State (P)

403 U.S. 15 (1971).

NATURE OF CASE: Criminal prosecution for violation of disturbing the peace statute.

FACT SUMMARY: Cohen (D) wore a jacket with the words "Fuck the Draft" on it in a courthouse corridor and was arrested and convicted under a disturbing the peace statute.

RULE OF LAW

A state cannot bar the use of offensive words either because such words are inherently likely to cause a violent reaction or because the state wishes to eliminate such words to protect the public morality.

FACTS: Cohen (D) was arrested in a courthouse because he was wearing a jacket bearing the words "Fuck the Draft." Cohen (D) did not engage in any act of violence or any other unlawful act. There was also no evidence that anyone who saw the jacket became violently aroused or even protested the jacket. Cohen (D) testified that he wore the jacket to inform people of his feelings against the Vietnam War and the draft. He was convicted under a statute prohibiting "maliciously and willfully disturbing the peace or quiet ... by offensive conduct." The state court held "offensive conduct" meant conduct that had a tendency to provoke others to disturb the peace.

ISSUE: Can a state constitutionally prevent the use of certain words on the ground that the use of such words is offensive conduct?

HOLDING AND DECISION: (Harlan, J.) No. A state cannot constitutionally prohibit the use of offensive words. Here, Cohen (D) could not be punished for criticizing the draft, so the statute could be upheld, if at all, only as a regulation of the manner, not the substantive content, of his speech. Cohen's (D) speech does not come within any of the exceptions to the general rule that the form and content of speech cannot be regulated: (1) this is not a prohibition designed to protect courthouse decorum because the statute is not so limited; (2) this is not an obscenity case because Cohen's (D) words were not erotic; (3) this is not a case of fighting words that are punishable as inherently likely to provoke a violent reaction because here the words were not directed as a personal insult to any person; and (4) this is not a captive audience problem since a viewer could merely avert his eyes, there is no evidence of objection by those who saw the jacket, and the statute is not so limited. The state tries to justify the conviction because the words are inherently likely to cause a violent reaction, but this argument cannot be upheld because these

are not fighting words and there is no evidence words that are merely offensive would cause such a response. Next the state justifies the conviction on the ground the state is guardian of the public morality. This argument is unacceptable because "offensive" is an unlimited concept and forbidding the use of such words would also cause the risk of suppressing the accompanying ideas. Therefore, there are no valid state interests that support the regulation of offensive words in public. Reversed.

DISSENT: (Blackmun, J.) Cohen's (D) conviction can be upheld both because his speech was fighting words and also because his act was conduct and not speech. Additionally, the state court subsequently restricted the statute in question to the fighting words context, so the case should be remanded and reconsidered under this construction.

ANALYSIS

This case reasserts the *Chaplinsky v. New Hampshire*, 315 U.S. 568 (1942), holding that fighting words are not protected by the First Amendment. Fighting words, then, are only those words that are likely to cause an immediate breach of the peace by another and are not just offensive words. More importantly, this case holds that a state has no valid interest in preventing the use of offensive words when there is no competing privacy interest. Here, the public in general has no right to protection from hearing either offensive words or offensive ideas.

■━■

Quicknotes

FIGHTING WORDS Unprotected speech that inflicts injury by its very utterance and provokes violence from the audience.

■━■

Beauharnais v. Illinois

Publisher (D) v. State (P)

343 U.S. 250 (1952).

NATURE OF CASE: Appeal from a criminal conviction.

FACT SUMMARY: Beauharnais (D) was convicted under an Illinois (P) statute making it a crime to publish any material criticizing members of a group in a way that subjects them to ridicule or invites civil unrest.

RULE OF LAW

A statute that makes it a crime to libel the members of any class or group is not repugnant to the Constitution.

FACTS: An Illinois (P) law made it a crime to publish or exhibit any lithograph, movie, play or sketch that attributed depravity, criminality, or other conduct lacking in virtue to a racial or religious group in such a way as to expose the members of that group to derision or cause a breach of the peace. Beauharnais (D), president of the White Circle League, arranged for the distribution of lithographs that urged whites to prevent further encroachment by blacks and that described the alleged criminality, violence, and drug use rampant among blacks. Beauharnais (D) was charged with violating the state statute but argued that the enactment deprived him of freedom of speech and press and was unconstitutionally vague. Beauharnais (D) was found guilty and his conviction was affirmed by the Illinois Supreme Court, which identified the challenged statute as "a form of criminal libel law." The U.S. Supreme Court then agreed to review the conviction.

ISSUE: Is a statute that makes it a crime to libel the members of any class or group repugnant to the Constitution?

HOLDING AND DECISION: (Frankfurter, J.) No. A statute that makes it a crime to libel the members of any class or group is not repugnant to the Constitution. Originally, libel was a common-law crime to which even truth was not a defense. In Illinois (P), as in most states, truth is now a defense to a criminal libel charge only if publication was made "with good motives and for justifiable ends." Since Beauharnais's (D) offers of proof made no effort to establish motive or justification, the trial court properly concluded the lithographs were libelous as a matter of law and permitted the jury to decide only the issue of publication. Profane or cruelly pejorative expressions may be punished by a state without interfering with anyone's constitutionally guaranteed privileges. Historically, violence and bloodshed have accompanied racial disputes in Illinois (P). Whether or not the contested statute is the best way of dealing with the problem, it is a reasonable exercise of the legislature's power to preserve the peace and protect the public. The statute is drawn with sufficient narrowness and clarity and punishes only utterances that are indisputably libelous. Therefore, the law is constitutional and Beauharnais's (D) conviction must be affirmed.

DISSENT: (Black, J.) This "group libel law" exemplifies an invidious form of censorship. Traditional criminal libel laws apply only to attacks upon individuals, not groups. In racial controversies, angry accusations are so prevalent virtually anyone could end up violating a statute such as enacted by Illinois (P). This law precludes free public discussion, and thus stifles cherished First Amendment rights. It is argued judicial discretion could prevent Illinois (P) from abusing the statute, but the rights secured to all citizens by the Constitution should not be dispensed at the whim of an arbitrary and sometimes capricious tribunal.

DISSENT: (Douglas, J.) If the First Amendment is to be overridden, the peril of the speech must be so clear and present that failure to curb it will result in disaster.

ANALYSIS

Common-law criminal libel statutes were apparently designed to discourage feuding individuals from launching personal attacks upon one another in public. Such laws were not applied to punish allegedly libelous assaults upon groups. Nevertheless, some contemporary commentators argue group libel laws would be an effective and desirable method of preventing scurrilous public campaigns of hatred against particular races or religious groups. Although such laws would tend to stifle protected First Amendment rights, it may be possible to imagine situations similarly to that cited by the *Beauharnais* majority in which such restraint would be justified by a need to protect against threats to the public peace and tranquility.

Quicknotes

FIRST AMENDMENT Prohibits Congress from enacting any law respecting an establishment of religion, prohibiting the free exercise of religion, abridging freedom of speech or the press, the right of peaceful assembly and the right to petition for a redress of grievances.

LIBEL A false or malicious publication subjecting a person to scorn, hatred or ridicule, or injuring him or her in relation to his or her occupation or business.

R.A.V. v. City of St. Paul

Vandal (D) v. Municipality (P)

505 U.S. 377 (1992).

NATURE OF CASE: Appeal of reversal of dismissal of disorderly conduct charge.

FACT SUMMARY: R.A.V. (D) burned a cross and was charged with violating St. Paul's (P) hate crime law.

RULE OF LAW
The government may not proscribe some fighting words and permit others, where the distinction is based on content or viewpoint.

FACTS: R.A.V. (D) allegedly burned a cross in the yard of a black family and was charged under the "fighting words" ordinance. R.A.V. (D) facially challenged the ordinance on grounds it was overbroad and impermissibly content-based. The state trial court dismissed the charges. The Minnesota Supreme Court reversed, finding the ordinance not overbroad because prior Minnesota cases had limited the phrase "anger, alarm or resentment in others" to "fighting words" (under the doctrine of *Chaplinsky v. New Hampshire*, 315 U.S. 568 (1942)), i.e., "conduct that itself inflicts injury or tends to incite immediate violence." R.A.V. (D) appealed.

ISSUE: May the government proscribe some fighting words and permit others, where the distinction is based on content or viewpoint?

HOLDING AND DECISION: (Scalia, J.) No. The government may not proscribe some fighting words and permit others where the distinction is based on content or viewpoint. The government may proscribe fighting words, but proscribable categories of speech are not beyond the First Amendment. Speech may be proscribable for one reason, but not for another. For example, a city may ban obscenity, but not just obscenity that criticizes city government. Here, St. Paul (P) may prohibit the conduct that is fighting words, but may not, as it has, ban fighting words only if they go to the topics of "race, color, creed, religion or gender." This ordinance goes beyond content to viewpoint discrimination, prohibiting, for example, fighting words aimed at religion, while permitting fighting words aimed at religious opponents. Content discrimination may permissibly single out speech presenting a heightened version of the harm that is the basis for the category of proscribable speech (e.g., an obscenity law prohibiting only the most lascivious displays of sexual activity). Or it may single out speech with secondary effects (e.g., a law only prohibiting live obscene performances by minors, the secondary effect being harm to minors). These bases for distinction ensure the restriction is not based on opposi-

tion to the speaker's message. Here, however, St. Paul (P) certainly attempted to suppress particular ideas. Reversed.

CONCURRENCE: (White, J.) The majority strikes down the ordinance for the wrong reason. This Court has long held fighting words and other categories of unprotected speech outside the First Amendment. Fighting words are worthless to society. It is inconsistent to hold fighting words may be completely proscribed, but the government may not treat some fighting words differently than others. The irrationally discriminatory laws the majority is concerned about would be prohibited by the Equal Protection Clause. The majority's exceptions are designed to cover obvious flaws. The St. Paul (P) ordinance singles out certain fighting words that present a special threat of violence. The ordinance should be struck down as overbroad. This approach, unlike the majority's, avoids chilling protected speech. *Chaplinsky* identifies words "which by their very utterance inflict injury." The only injury identified in the ordinance is "anger, alarm or resentment." The mere fact that expression causes hurt feelings, offense, or resentment does not render it unprotected.

CONCURRENCE: (Blackmun, J.) First Amendment values are compromised by prohibiting attempts to drive minorities from their homes by cross burning, but there is great harm in preventing St. Paul (D) from specifically punishing race-based fighting words that prejudice the community. Nevertheless, the ordinance is overbroad and invalid.

CONCURRENCE: (Stevens, J.) St. Paul's (P) ordinance does not regulate speech based on content or viewpoint. The ordinance regulates a subcategory of speech that causes harm based on race, color, creed, religion or gender. The Court narrowly construes St. Paul's (P) ordinance as not banning all hate speech. R.A.V. (D) is therefore free to burn a cross to announce a rally or express race supremacy views, so long as the burning is not so directed at an individual as to inflict injury. Such proscription scarcely offends the First Amendment.

▶ ANALYSIS

The majority also held the ordinance did not survive strict scrutiny review. St. Paul (P) had a compelling interest in protecting the rights of certain group members to live where they wish in peace, but the ordinance was held not necessary to achieve this interest. The majority ruled

Continued on next page.

a content-neutral ordinance could have achieved the same results. Justice White disagreed, stating that the Court, as recently as *Burson v. Freeman*, 504 U.S. 191 (1992), has always rejected the view a narrowly drawn, content-based ordinance is unconstitutional if the object of legislation could be achieved by banning a wider category of speech.

■■■

Quicknotes

CONTENT-BASED Refers to statutes that regulate speech based on its content.

CONTENT-NEUTRAL Refers to statutes that regulate speech regardless of their content.

FIGHTING WORDS Unprotected speech under the First Amendment, which is likely to instigate a violent reaction.

OVERBREADTH Refers to a statute that proscribes lawful as well as unlawful conduct.

■■■

Virginia v. Black

State (P) v. Person convicted under cross-burning statute (D)

538 U.S. 343 (2003).

NATURE OF CASE: Appeal from a criminal conviction.

FACT SUMMARY: When Black (D) was prosecuted and convicted under Virginia's (P) cross-burning statute, he argued its unconstitutionality because of a provision treating any cross burning as prima facie evidence of intent to intimidate.

RULE OF LAW
A provision in a state's cross-burning statute treating any cross burning as prima facie evidence of intent to intimidate is unconstitutional.

FACTS: Black (D) was prosecuted and convicted by a jury under Virginia's (P) cross-burning statute, which bans cross burning with intent to intimidate a person or group of persons. The statute contains a provision that any burning of a cross constitutes prima facie evidence of intent to intimidate a person or group of persons. The Supreme Court of Virginia upheld the conviction, and Black (D) appealed to the U.S. Supreme Court on the grounds the prima facie evidence provision was unconstitutional.

ISSUE: Is a provision in a state's cross-burning statute treating any cross burning as prima facie evidence of intent to intimidate unconstitutional?

HOLDING AND DECISION: (O'Connor, J.) Yes. A provision in a state's cross burning statute treating any cross burning as prima facie evidence of intent to intimidate is unconstitutional. To this day, regardless of whether the message is a political one or whether the message is also meant to intimidate, the burning of a cross is a symbol of hate. While cross burning sometimes carries no intimidating message, at other times the intimidating message is the only message conveyed. The Court has long held the government may regulate certain categories of expression consistent with the Constitution and indeed intimidation in the constitutionally proscribable sense of the word is a type of true threat. The First Amendment, accordingly, permits Virginia (P) to outlaw cross burnings done with the intent to intimidate because burning a cross is a particularly virulent form of intimidation. Furthermore, instead of prohibiting all intimidating messages, Virginia (P) may choose to regulate this subset of intimidating messages, in light of cross burnings long and pernicious history, as a signal of impending violence. However, this particular cross-burning statute is unconstitutionally overbroad due to its provision stating that any burning of a cross is prima facie evidence of intent to intimidate a person or group of persons. The prima facie provision strips away the very reason why a state may ban cross burning with the intent to intimidate because this provision permits a jury to convict in every cross-burning case in which defendants exercise their constitutional right not to put on a defense. It is apparent the provision as so interpreted "would create an unacceptable risk of the suppression of ideas." Anger or hatred is not sufficient to ban all cross burnings in the absence of actual intimidation or threat. The First Amendment does not permit shortcuts.

CONCURRENCE: (Stevens, J.) Cross burning with "an intent to intimidate" unquestionably qualifies as the kind of threat that is unprotected by the First Amendment.

DISSENT: (Thomas, J.) The majority errs in imputing an expressive component to the activity in question. In our culture, cross burning has almost invariably meant lawlessness and understandably instills in its victims well-grounded fear of physical violence. Those who hate cannot terrorize and intimidate to make their point.

CONCURRENCE AND DISSENT: (Souter, J.) While agreeing the statute makes a content-based distinction within the category of punishable intimidating or threatening expression, I disagree that any exception should save the statute from unconstitutionality. No content-based statute should survive without a high probability that no official suppression of ideas is being encouraged.

► ANALYSIS

As articulated by the plurality in the *Black* decision, the prima facie evidence provision in the Virginia cross-burning statute ignored all the contextual factors that would be necessary in order for a court or jury to decide whether a particular cross burning was in fact intended to intimidate. On the other hand, some legal commentators express the viewpoint such as conveyed in Justice Thomas's dissent, that a cross burning always and necessarily represents intimidation.

Quicknotes

FIFTH AMENDMENT Provides that no person shall be compelled to serve as a witness against oneself, or be subject to trial for the same offense twice, or be deprived of life, liberty, or property without due process of law.

OVERBREADTH That quality or characteristic of a statute, regulation, or order that reaches beyond the problem it was meant to solve causing it to sweep within it activity it cannot legitimately reach.

Adderley v. Florida

Students (D) v. State (P)

385 U.S. 39 (1966).

NATURE OF CASE: Grant of certiorari after conviction on a charge of trespass with a malicious and mischievous intent upon the premises of another.

FACT SUMMARY: Adderley (D) and other students marched to the jail to protest segregation policies. They were told to leave. When they refused, they were arrested.

RULE OF LAW
Demonstrators do not have a constitutional right to expound their views whenever, wherever, and however they choose.

FACTS: Adderley (D) and 200 other students went to a jail to protest the arrest of other demonstrators the day before and segregation policies. They stood or sat singing, clapping, and dancing on a jail driveway that was normally used to transport prisoners and was not used by the public. They were blocking the driveway and, when the sheriff arrived, he told them they were trespassing on jail property and would be arrested if they did not leave within ten minutes. Ten minutes later, he warned them again, and arrested the 107 persons who remained.

ISSUE: Do demonstrators have a constitutional right to expound their views whenever, wherever, and however they choose?

HOLDING AND DECISION: (Black, J.) No. Demonstrators do not have a constitutional right to expound their views whenever, wherever, and however they choose. In this case Adderley (D) and the other demonstrators were convicted under a narrowly drawn statute aimed at one limited kind of conduct, trespass upon the property of another with a malicious intent. The statute does not suffer from overbreadth or vagueness. Secondly, the protesters went to the jail. Jails generally are not open to the public. Finally, they entered the jail through a driveway used only for jail purposes and not generally used by the public. Hence, the jury was authorized to find the State (P) had proven every element of the crime of trespass. This conviction did not deprive Adderley (D) of any constitutional rights. The state may control the use of its own property for its own lawful nondiscriminatory purpose. There is no evidence Adderley (D) was arrested because the sheriff objected to what was being sung or said. Rather, he objected to their presence on that part of the jail grounds. The assumption, demonstrators have a constitutional right to expound their views whenever, wherever, and however they please, was vigorously rejected in *Cox*

(*Cox v. Louisiana*, 379 U.S. 559 (1965)), and is rejected again here. Adderley's (D) conviction is affirmed.

DISSENT: (Douglas, J.) A trespass law is being used to penalize people for exercising their constitutional right. There was no violence here, nor any threats of violence. The jailhouse routine was uninterrupted. This case gives the sheriff the power to decide in his discretion when public places can be used for demonstrations. It does damage to the First Amendment to allow a trespass statute to bar a person from going onto public property.

ANALYSIS

State statutes cannot be invoked arbitrarily to defeat First Amendment freedoms. State trespass convictions have been reversed where the only acts involved were the peaceable assembly at and refusal to leave a public facility or public place. The "sit-in demonstration" cases state peaceful presence in a place held open to the public cannot be made a crime. In *Wright v. Georgia*, 373 U.S. 284 (1962), the Court found the distinguishing factor in *Adderley* to be that a jail is not a place held open to the public. In *Food Employees v. Logan Valley Plaza*, 391 U.S. 308 (1968), private property that had been held open to public use was treated like a public place meaning neither state nor private trespass rules could be applied to limit the reasonable exercise of First Amendment rights. There, the Court reversed trespass convictions that arose out of union members' peaceful picketing of a grocery store in a privately-owned shopping center.

Quicknotes

FIRST AMENDMENT Prohibits Congress from enacting any law respecting an establishment of religion, prohibiting the free exercise of religion, abridging freedom of speech or the press, the right of peaceful assembly and the right to petition for a redress of grievances.

Police Department of Chicago v. Mosley

Municipality (D) v. Picketer (P)

408 U.S. 92 (1972).

NATURE OF CASE: Action to enjoin enforcement of a statute.

FACT SUMMARY: An ordinance prohibited all picketing around schools during school hours except for labor disputes.

> ## RULE OF LAW
> A state may not permit or prohibit peaceful picketing based on the content of the sign.

FACTS: Mosley (P) peacefully picketed a high school, claiming it discriminated against blacks. Chicago (D) then enacted an ordinance that prohibited the picketing of schools from one-half hour before school to one-half hour after it had ended. Only those involved in labor disputes were exempted from the ordinance. Mosley (P) brought suit to enjoin enforcement of the statute as applied to him. Mosley (P) alleged once an exception has been made to a reasonable regulation concerning the time and place of picketing, other picketing may not be prohibited merely because of the content of the sign.

ISSUE: May a state permit or prohibit picketing based on the content of the sign?

HOLDING AND DECISION: (Marshall, J.) No. A state may not permit or prohibit peaceful picketing based on the content of the sign. A state may reasonably regulate the time, place, and manner of picketing if necessary to protect a valid interest. Content may not be regulated. A state may not prohibit or permit picketing based on the content of the sign, i.e., the nature of the ideas expressed. The ordinance herein finds those having labor grievances do not constitute an interference with school operations because of the nature of their message. All other pickets are deemed to interfere with such operations because of the nature of their messages. This is violative of the Equal Protection Clause and First Amendment rights. Once exceptions are made, all must be allowed to express their rights. The statute is unconstitutional. Affirmed.

ANALYSIS

In *Madison School District v. Wisconsin Employment Relations Comm.*, 429 U.S. 167 (1976), the Court held a state may not enjoin a dissident member of a teacher's union from speaking at a public meeting of the Board of Education while permitting the unit representative to do so. If there are conflicting demands for use of the same place, a state may make a choice among potential users. *Cox v. Louisiana*, 379 U.S. 559 (1965).

Quicknotes

EQUAL PROTECTION CLAUSE A constitutional provision that each person be guaranteed the same protection of the laws enjoyed by other persons in like circumstances.

FIRST AMENDMENT Prohibits Congress from enacting any law respecting an establishment of religion, prohibiting the free exercise of religion, abridging freedom of speech or the press, the right of peaceful assembly and the right to petition for a redress of grievances.

Lehman v. City of Shaker Heights

Political candidate (P) v. Municipality (D)

418 U.S. 298 (1974).

NATURE OF CASE: On writ of certiorari after denial of declaration and injunctive relief.

FACT SUMMARY: Lehman (P), a political candidate, challenged a City of Shaker Heights (D) policy that does not allow political advertising on its transit vehicles.

RULE OF LAW

A city that operates a public rapid transit system and sells advertising space on its vehicles is not required by the First and Fourteenth Amendments to accept paid political advertising on behalf of a candidate for public office.

FACTS: Lehman (P), a candidate for state office, sought to promote his candidacy by purchasing advertising space on the City of Shaker Heights' (D) buses. He was refused space because the City (D) had a policy that did not permit political advertising on its transit vehicles.

ISSUE: Is a city that operates a public rapid transit system and sells advertising space on its vehicles required by the First and Fourteenth Amendments to accept paid political advertising on behalf of a candidate for public office?

HOLDING AND DECISION: (Blackmun, J.) No. A city that operates a public rapid transit system and sells advertising space on its vehicles is not required by the First and Fourteenth Amendments to accept paid political advertising on behalf of a candidate for public office. No First Amendment forum is present in a case such as this where a city operates a public transit system and sells advertising space on its vehicles. It is true that because state action exists, the policies and practices governing access to the transit systems advertising space must not be arbitrary, capricious or invidious. Here, the City of Shaker Heights (D) decided only to accept nonpolitical advertising. This decision minimizes chances of abuse, the appearance of favoritism, and the risk of imposing upon a captive audience. A city may reasonably limit access to advertising space, and such a limitation, in this case, did not violate the First Amendment. Affirmed.

CONCURRENCE: (Douglas, J.) The ownership and operation of a bus by a city does not without more make it a forum for communication. The right of commuters to be free from forced intrusions on their privacy precludes the city from transforming its vehicles of public transportation into forums for the dissemination of ideas upon this captive audience.

DISSENT: (Brennan, J.) The City (D) created a forum for the dissemination of information and expression of ideas when it accepted and displayed commercial and public service advertisements on its rapid transit vehicles. Once a public forum is established, both free speech and equal protection principles prohibit discrimination based solely on subject matter or content. That the discrimination is among entire classes of ideas, rather than among points of view within a particular class, does not render it any less odious.

ANALYSIS

Justice Blackmun's reluctance to recognize a public forum claim in *Lehman* should be compared with his majority opinion less than a year later in *Southeastern Promotions, Ltd. v. Conrad*, 420 U.S. 546 (1975). There, the Court found that First Amendment rights had been violated by a municipal board managing City Theater's refusal of permission to present the musical "Hair." The refusal was based on the ground the production would not be in the community's best interest. Blackmun did not reach the issue of "Hair's" alleged obscenity, but found the refusal constituted a prior restraint imposed without affording the rigorous procedural safeguards required. He noted municipal theaters were public forums designed for expressive activities, and neither the *Lehman* captive audience nor any other circumstances, qualifying as exceptions to the prior restraint doctrine, were present.

Quicknotes

PUBLIC FORUM Refers to lands upon which speech may be made.

United States v. O'Brien

Federal government (P) v. Draft protestor (D)

391 U.S. 367 (1968).

NATURE OF CASE: Appeals from a conviction for burning a draft card.

FACT SUMMARY: O'Brien (D) burned his draft card during a public demonstration and was subsequently convicted of violating the Universal Military Training and Service Act.

RULE OF LAW
When speech and nonspeech elements are combined in the same course of conduct, a sufficiently important governmental interest in regulating the nonspeech element can justify incidental limitations on First Amendment freedoms.

FACTS: O'Brien (D) burned his Selective Service registration certificate on the steps of a courthouse and was subsequently convicted of violating the Universal Military Training and Service Act of 1948, as amended in 1965. In pertinent part the Act makes it a federal offense to knowingly destroy or mutilate such certificates. O'Brien (D) maintained he burned his draft card publicly to express his opposition to the Vietnam conflict and to influence others to adopt his antiwar beliefs and the Act was an unconstitutional abridgement of his free speech rights. The district court rejected this argument, but on appeal the court of appeals held the 1965 amendment abridged freedom of speech. Nonetheless the court affirmed O'Brien's (D) conviction under that part of the Act that in its view effectively made violation of the nonpossession regulation a crime. Both O'Brien (D) and the Government (P) appealed.

ISSUE: When speech and nonspeech elements are combined in the same course of conduct, can a sufficiently important governmental interest in regulating the nonspeech element justify incidental limitations on First Amendment freedoms?

HOLDING AND DECISION: (Warren, C.J.) Yes. When speech and nonspeech elements are combined in the same course of conduct, a sufficiently important governmental interest in regulating the nonspeech element can justify incidental limitations on First Amendment freedoms. This Court cannot accept the view an apparently limitless variety of conduct can be labeled speech whenever the person engaging in the conduct intends thereby to express an idea. However, even on the assumption the alleged communicative element in O'Brien's (D) conduct is sufficient to bring into play the First Amendment, it does not necessarily follow that the destruction of a registration certificate is constitutionally protected activity. A govern-

ment regulation is sufficiently justified if it is within the constitutional power of the government; if it furthers an important governmental interest; if it is unrelated to the suppression of free expression; and if the incidental restriction is no greater than is essential to the furtherance of that interest. Congress has the power to raise and support armies. Pursuant to this power, Congress may establish a system of registration for individuals. The issuance of certificates indicating the registration of individuals is a legitimate and substantial administrative aid in the functioning of this system. Reversed.

CONCURRENCE: (Harlan, J.) It is my understanding that the Court does not foreclose consideration of First Amendment claims in those rare instances when the "incidental" restriction imposed on expression by a regulation furthering an "important or substantial" governmental interest has the practical effect of entirely preventing a "speaker" from reaching a significant audience with whom he could not otherwise lawfully communicate. Because O'Brien (D) could have communicated his message in many ways other than burning his draft card, this is not such a case.

DISSENT: (Douglas, J.) The underlying issue in this case is whether conscription is permissible absent a state of war. This case should be reargued to address this point. Further, "symbolic speech" deserves more protection than the Court has given it.

ANALYSIS

Justice Harlan wrote a brief concurring opinion, expressing concern the Court's rationale might, in a different case, have the effect of entirely preventing a speaker from reaching a significant audience with whom he could not otherwise lawfully communicate. Justice Douglas dissented on the ground the underlying and basic problem was whether conscription is permissible in the absence of a declaration of war.

Quicknotes

FIRST AMENDMENT Prohibits Congress from enacting any law respecting an establishment of religion, prohibiting the free exercise of religion, abridging freedom of speech or the press, the right of peaceful assembly and the right to petition for a redress of grievances.

Buckley v. Valeo

Senator (P) v. Federal government (D)

424 U.S. 1 (1976).

NATURE OF CASE: Action for declaration of unconstitutionality.

FACT SUMMARY: Senator Buckley (P) and others challenged the Federal Election Campaign Act's contribution and expenditure limitation, reporting and disclosure requirements and public financing of presidential elections.

🏛 RULE OF LAW
The strong governmental interest in preventing election corruption does not justify imposition of substantial restrictions on the effective ability of any individual to express his political beliefs and engage in political association.

FACTS: In order to curtail political corruption, Congress in the Federal Election Campaign Act of 1971, as amended in 1974, developed an intricate statutory scheme for the regulation of federal political campaigns. Inter alia, Congress imposed a $1,000 limitation on individual contributions "to a single candidate" in § 608(b)(1); a $5,000 limitation on "contributions" to a single candidate by political committees in § 608(b)(2); a $25,000 limitation on total "contributions" by any individual in one year to political candidates in § 608(b)(3); a $1,000 ceiling in "expenditures" relative to a known candidate in § 608(e)(1); and similar ceilings on "expenditures" by the candidate and his family and on overall campaign "expenditures" in § 608(a) and (c). In addition, Congress required disclosure by candidates of all "contributions" greater than $10, and by individuals of all "contributions and expenditures" aggregating over $1,000—§ 434(e). In a separate action, Congress provided for federal financing of presidential elections. Senator Buckley (D) and others, pursuant to a special section in the Act of 1971, brought this action to have all the above-mentioned sections declared an unconstitutional violation of their First Amendment rights of freedom of expression and association. This appeal followed.

ISSUE: Does the strong governmental interest in preventing election corruption justify imposition of substantial restrictions on the effective ability of any individual to express his political beliefs and engage in political association?

HOLDING AND DECISION: (Per curiam) No. The strong governmental interest in preventing election corruption does not justify imposition of substantial restrictions on the effective ability of any individual to express his political beliefs and engage in political association.

Although "the [F]irst [A]mendment protects political association as well as political expression . . . a limitation upon the amount any one person or group may contribute to (and associate with) a candidate or a political committee entails only a marginal restriction on the contributor's ability to engage in free communication (and association)"; but "a restriction on the amount of money a person or group can spend on political communication (as a whole) during a campaign (excessively) reduces the quantity of expression by restricting the number of issues discussed, the depth of their exploration, and the size of the audience reached." As such, the so-called "contribution" (i.e., to candidates) limitations here (§ 608(b)1–3) may be upheld as valid means for limiting political corruption by large financial contributors. The so-called "expenditure" (on political expression) limitations (§ 608(a),(c),(e)), however, places too broad a restriction on the individual's ability to speak out and must therefore be voided. As for the reporting and disclosure requirements, broad as they are, they are clearly upheld by the "compelling government interest" in deterring corruption by getting important information to the voters and providing records for enforcement of the law. Finally, the challenge to the public financing of presidential elections is simply unfounded since it entails no abridgment of speech whatsoever. Affirmed in part, reversed in part.

CONCURRENCE AND DISSENT: (Burger, C.J.) The disclosure requirements for small contributions are unnecessarily broad intrusions into First Amendment rights since only large contributions are likely to cause the corruption the Act is supposed to remedy. The contribution limitations upheld by the Court place just as great a burden on political expression as expenditure limitations. Finally, there is no constitutional justification for the "incestuous" relationship between government and politics that the public financing law, upheld by the Court, creates.

CONCURRENCE AND DISSENT: (White, J.) Since the expenditure limitations, struck down by the Court, are neutral as to the content of speech, are not motivated by the fear of political expression, and reflect the well-founded conclusion of Congress that regulation of campaign finances are essential to protect the integrity of the system, the First Amendment is not violated by them.

CONCURRENCE AND DISSENT: (Marshall, J.) A limitation on the amount of personal assets a candidate may use in an election is an important method

Continued on next page.

of insuring public office does not become a domain of the wealthy only.

CONCURRENCE AND DISSENT: (Blackmun, J.) The Court does not properly distinguish between contribution limitations and expenditure limitations.

ANALYSIS

In *Buckley* the Court has identified one of the few "compelling governmental interests" that may be employed to justify congressional regulation of an area subject to strict judicial scrutiny. That interest is the interest in maintaining the integrity of the political process. Note, however, even though the interest is held compelling, the Court does not automatically affirm its imposition. Note the Court's decision left the Federal Election Campaign Act rift with loopholes. Perhaps the most exploited was that which permitted individuals to "expend" (i.e., separately from any candidate or his organization) large sums to endorse a vote for a particular candidate.

Quicknotes

FIRST AMENDMENT Prohibits Congress from enacting any law respecting an establishment of religion, prohibiting the free exercise of religion, abridging freedom of speech or the press, the right of peaceful assembly and the right to petition for a redress of grievances.

Citizens United v. Federal Election Commission

Nonprofit corporation (P) v. Government agency (D)

558 U.S. 310 (2010).

NATURE OF CASE: Appeal in action challenging the constitutionality of federal laws prohibiting "electioneering communications" by corporations and unions.

FACT SUMMARY: Citizens United (P), a nonprofit organization that wanted to distribute a film that expressed opinions about whether Hillary Rodham Clinton would make a good president, sought to enjoin the Federal Election Commission (D) from enforcing federal law that prohibited the distribution on the grounds it constituted prohibited "electioneering communication." [The procedural posture of the case is not presented in the casebook extract.]

🏛 **RULE OF LAW**
The government may not suppress political speech on the basis of the speaker's corporate identity, and the government may not restrict corporate independent expenditures.

FACTS: Citizens United (P), a nonprofit corporation, released a film entitled *Hillary: The Movie*. The movie expressed opinions about whether Hillary Rodham Clinton would make a good president. Then-senator Clinton was a candidate in the 2008 Democratic Party's Presidential primary election. Federal law 2 U.S.C. § 441b prohibits corporations and unions from using general treasury funds to make direct contributions to candidates or independent expenditures that expressly advocate the election or defeat of a candidate through any form of media in connection with certain federal elections. Section 441b makes it a felony for all corporations either to expressly advocate the election or defeat of candidates or to broadcast electioneering communications within 30 days of a primary election and 60 days of a general election. Section 203 of the Bipartisan Campaign Reform Act of 2002 (BCRA) prohibits any "electioneering communication." The Federal Election Commission (D) held the movie was an electioneering communication within the meaning of BCRA § 203. *McConnell v. Federal Election Commn.*, 540 U.S. 93 (2003), upheld limits on electioneering communications, relying on the Court's holding in *Austin v. Michigan Chamber of Commerce*, 494 U.S. 652 (1990), which held that political speech may be banned based on the speaker's corporate identity. The Supreme Court granted certiorari. [The procedural posture of the case is not presented in the casebook extract.]

ISSUE: May the government suppress political speech on the basis of the speaker's corporate identity, and may

the government restrict corporate independent expenditures?

HOLDING AND DECISION: (Kennedy, J.) No. The government may not suppress political speech on the basis of the speaker's corporate identity, and the government may not restrict corporate independent expenditures. *Austin* and portions of *McConnell* are overruled. Section 441b's prohibition on corporate independent expenditures is an outright ban on speech, backed by criminal sanctions. If § 441b applied to individuals, it would clearly violate the First Amendment. Laws burdening political speech are subject to strict scrutiny, which requires the Government (D) to prove the restriction "furthers a compelling interest and is narrowly tailored to achieve that interest." The First Amendment stands against attempts to disfavor certain subjects or viewpoints or to distinguish among different speakers, which may be a means to control content. The Government (D) may also commit a constitutional wrong when by law it identifies certain preferred speakers. There is no basis for the proposition that, in the political speech context, the Government may impose restrictions on certain disfavored speakers. The Court has recognized that the First Amendment applies to corporations. Pre-*Austin* cases reasoned that political speech did not lose its protections simply because the speech was made by a corporate entity, rather than a natural person. *Austin* bypassed these cases by recognizing a new governmental interest in preventing "the corrosive and distorting effects of immense aggregations of wealth that are accumulated with the help of the corporate form and that have little or no correlation to the public's support for the corporation's political ideas." Neither *Austin's* antidistortion rationale nor the Government's (D) other justifications support § 441b's restrictions. The First Amendment prohibits Congress from fining or jailing citizens, or associations of citizens, for engaging in political speech, but *Austin's* antidistortion rationale would permit the Government (D) to ban political speech because the speaker is an association with a corporate form. This protection is inconsistent with *Austin's* rationale, which is meant to prevent corporations from obtaining "an unfair advantage in the political marketplace" by using "resources amassed in the economic marketplace." Distinguishing wealthy individuals from corporations based on the latter's special advantages of, e.g., limited liability, does not suffice to allow laws prohibiting speech. The censorship at issue is vast in its reach. When Government (D) seeks to use its full power, including the criminal law, to command where a person may get his or her

Continued on next page.

information or what distrusted source he or she may not hear, it uses censorship to control thought, which is unlawful under the First Amendment, which confirms the freedom to think for ourselves. The Government's (D) other arguments are also unsound. The Government (D) reasons that corporate political speech can be banned to prevent corruption or its appearance. The Court in prior precedent found this rationale "sufficiently important" to allow contribution limits but refused to extend that reasoning to expenditure limits. Independent expenditures, including those made by corporations, do not give rise to corruption or the appearance of corruption. That speakers may have influence over or access to elected officials, does not mean those officials are corrupt. Additionally, the appearance of influence or access will not cause the electorate to lose faith in this democracy. This is because the fact a corporation, or any other speaker, is willing to spend money to try to persuade voters presupposes the people have the ultimate influence over elected officials. Even if there is a problem of undue influence, Congress may not remedy that problem by using unconstitutional means. Thus, an outright ban on corporate political speech is not a permissible remedy. Additionally, the Government's (D) asserted interest in protecting dissenting shareholders from being compelled to fund corporate political speech would allow the Government (D) to ban the political speech even of media corporations, which is also not constitutionally permissible. [The procedural outcome of the case is not presented in the casebook extract.]

CONCURRENCE: (Roberts, C.J.) This case raises the issue of whether stare decisis requires adherence to *Austin*; it does not. Although stare decisis is the preferred course, from which departure requires a special justification, stare decisis is neither an "inexorable command" nor "a mechanical formula of adherence to the latest decision. Here there are several justifications for departing from *Austin*. First, it was an aberration from the robust protections previously granted to political speech. Its reasoning was inconsistent with prior precedent's repudiation of any government interest in "equalizing the relative ability of individuals and groups to influence the outcome of elections." It was also inconsistent with the clear rejection of the idea that speech that otherwise would be within the protection of the First Amendment loses that protection simply because its source is a corporation. Second, *Austin* has been a source of disagreement on the Court ever since it was decided, thus undermining its ability to contribute to the stable and orderly development of the law.

CONCURRENCE: (Scalia, J.) Justice Stevens's dissent tries to show the majority decision is not supported by the original understanding of the First Amendment, but he doesn't show how the freedom of speech that was the right of Englishmen did not include the freedom to speak in association with other individuals, including association in the corporate form. Moreover, Justice Stevens's analysis is made in isolation from the text of the Amendment, and he offers no textual evidence corporations' speech could be

censored, even back when the Constitution was enacted. Further, Justice Stevens concludes the Founders did not like corporations, and further concludes that is the reason they had no rights of free speech, but that is relevant only insofar as it can be thought to be reflected in the understood meaning of the text they enacted, not as a freestanding substitute for that text. And, even if the Founders dislike of founding-era corporations is relevant, the Founders may not have disliked modern corporations, which do not have the type of state-granted monopoly privileges individually chartered corporations enjoyed during the founding era and which was the trait the Founders dislike about corporations at the time. Ultimately, and most importantly, the constitutional text makes no distinction between types of speakers, from single individuals to partnerships of individuals, to unincorporated associations of individuals, to incorporated associations of individuals.

CONCURRENCE AND DISSENT: (Stevens, J.) The majority's basic premise—that the First Amendment bars regulatory distinctions based on a speaker's identity, including its "identity" as a corporation—is not a correct statement of the law. Corporations are not members of our society, and they cannot vote or run for office. The financial resources, legal structure, and instrumental orientation of corporations raise legitimate concerns about their role in the electoral process, and lawmakers have a compelling constitutional basis, if not also a democratic duty, to take measures designed to guard against the potentially deleterious effects of corporate spending in local and national races. The majority's approach to corporate electioneering marks a dramatic break from over a hundred years of precedent and legislative limitations on corporate electoral spending. The principle of stare decisis requires a significant justification from precedent, but no such justification exists for departing from *Austin*. Ultimately, the majority's rejection of *Austin* and *McConnell* comes down to nothing more than its disagreement with their results. The only relevant thing that has changed since *Austin* and *McConnell* were decided is the composition of this Court. Accordingly, this decision strikes at the heart of stare decisis. The majority's disembowelment of stare decisis is wrong, as are the premises underpinning its rulings on the merits. First, the majority claims the First Amendment precludes regulatory distinctions based on speaker identity, including the speaker's identity as a corporation. However, precedent recognizes the Government's (D) interests may be more or less compelling with respect to different classes of speakers, and the authority of legislatures to enact viewpoint-neutral regulations based on content and identity is well settled. The distinctive potential of corporations to corrupt the electoral process has long been recognized, and the majority fails to explain why corporate identity demands the same treatment as individual identity. Second, the majority claims *Austin* and *McConnell* are radical outliers. In fact, it is the majority's

Continued on next page.

opinion that is the outlier which represents a radical departure from settled First Amendment law. Looking at the Framers' understanding of the First Amendment, there is absolutely no evidence anyone believed it would preclude regulatory distinctions based on the corporate form. In any event, the Framers—to the extent their position on the matter is knowable—would have disagreed with the majority's position. The Framers took it as a given corporations could be comprehensively regulated in the service of the public welfare, and when they constitutionalized the right to free speech in the First Amendment, it was the free speech of individuals they had in mind. Justice Scalia adduces no evidence that undermines the basic point that members of the founding generation held a cautious view of corporate power and a narrow view of corporate rights, and they thought of speech in terms of individuals. Since 1907, when Congress passed the Tillman Act banning all corporate contributions to candidates, both legislative and judicial pronouncements have recognized the express distinction between corporate and individual political spending on elections. This century of more recent history puts to rest any notion the majority's ruling is faithful to our First Amendment tradition. In addition, to repudiate *Austin*, the majority relies on precedent [*Bellotti v. Baird*, 443 U.S. 622 (1979)] that clearly declined to adopt the majority's position, and that ruled, in an explicit limitation on the scope of its holding, that "our consideration of a corporation's right to speak on issues of general public interest implies no comparable right in the quite different context of participation in a political campaign for election to public office." That precedent based this distinction on the rationale that the state has a greater interest in regulating independent corporate expenditures on candidate elections than on referenda, because in a functioning democracy the public must have faith its representatives owe their positions to the people, not to the corporations with the deepest pockets. Thus, *Austin* and *McConnell* sit perfectly well with established First Amendment precedent. Finally, as to the interests involved, the majority rides roughshod over Congress's legitimate interest in preventing the money that is spent on elections from exerting an undue influence on an officeholder's judgment and from creating the appearance of such influence. The majority offers very little serious analysis to support its rejection of the anticorruption rationale. The majority suggests that BCRA § 203 may be little more than an incumbency protection plan intended to protect the interests of the legislators who passed it. However, there is no a solid basis for believing that this legislative action was motivated by the desire to protect incumbents or that it will degrade the competitiveness of the electoral process. Further, the majority fails to appreciate that *Austin's* antidistortion rationale is itself an anticorruption rationale tied to the special concerns raised by corporations. Understood properly, antidistortion is simply a variant on the classic governmental interest in protecting against improper influences on officeholders that debilitate the democratic process. The unique position of corporations, as opposed to individuals, including significant financial resources and limited liability, may make a corporation a formidable political presence, even though the power of the corporation may be no reflection of the power of its ideas. These basic differences between individuals and corporations help explain why corporate electioneering is not only more likely to impair compelling governmental interests, but also why restrictions on that electioneering are less likely to encroach upon First Amendment freedoms. Taking away a corporation's speech will not affect individuals' self-expression, which is what the First Amendment seeks fundamentally to protect. Recognizing the weakness of a speaker-based critique of *Austin*, the majority places primary emphasis not on the corporation's right to electioneer, but rather on the listener's interest in hearing what every possible speaker may have to say. There are many flaws in this argument, as it has been recognized that corporate spending on elections may drown out noncorporate voices, and that corporate "domination" of electioneering can generate the impression corporations dominate our democracy, leading citizens to lose faith in their capacity to influence public policy. The majority brushes these real-world concerns and complexities aside, or simply chooses to ignore them. Finally, Congress has an interest in protecting dissenting shareholders and union members from coerced speech that does not reflect their views. *Austin's* acceptance of restrictions on general treasury spending "simply allows people who have invested in the business corporation for purely economic reasons"—the vast majority of investors, one assumes—"to avoid being taken advantage of, without sacrificing their economic objectives." This concern has a long history in campaign finance reform, and it has been endorsed in a long line of cases.

▶ *ANALYSIS*

The Supreme Court's decision in *Citizens United* called into question laws in many states, though before the case was decided, 26 allowed unlimited corporate spending in elections. After the decision in *Citizens United*, many states introduced bills that, among other things, would repeal the independent expenditure ban, require stockholder approval prior to an independent expenditure, or establish corporate disclosure requirements for independent expenditures.

■■■

Quicknotes

CORPORATE SPEECH Speech, the source of which is a corporation and not an individual.

POLITICAL SPEECH Speech pertaining to the political process that is afforded the greatest amount of protection under the First Amendment.

■■■

Branzburg v. Hayes

News reporters (D) v. State and federal government (P)

408 U.S. 665 (1972).

NATURE OF CASE: Appeal from contempt citations for failure to testify before state and federal grand juries.

FACT SUMMARY: Newsmen refused to testify before state and federal grand juries, claiming that their news sources were confidential.

RULE OF LAW

The First Amendment's freedom of press does not exempt a news reporter from disclosing to a grand jury information he has received in confidence.

FACTS: Branzburg (D), who had written articles for a newspaper about drug activities he had observed, refused to testify before a state grand jury regarding his information. [No further facts are stated in casebook excerpt.]

ISSUE: Does the First Amendment protect a news reporter from disclosing to a grand jury, information that he has received in confidence?

HOLDING AND DECISION: (White, J.) No. The First Amendment's freedom of press does not exempt a news reporter from disclosing to a grand jury information he has received in confidence. The First Amendment does not invalidate every incidental burdening of the press that may result from the enforcement of civil or criminal statutes of general applicability. News reporters cannot invoke a testimonial privilege not enjoined by other citizens. The Constitution should not shield criminals who wish to remain anonymous from prosecution through disclosure. Forcing news reporters to testify will not impede the flow of news. The news reporter may never be called to testify. Many political groups will still turn to the reporter because they are dependent on the media for exposure. Grand jury proceedings are conducted in secret and the police are experienced in protecting informants. More important, the public's interest in news flow does not override the public's interest in deterring crime. Here, the grand juries were not probing at will without relation to existing need; the information sought was necessary to the respective investigations. A grand jury is not restricted to seeking information from non-newsmen; it may choose the best method for its task. The contempt citations are affirmed.

CONCURRENCE: (Powell, J.) It must be emphasized the Court's holding is a limited one and a newsman who is called upon to give information bearing only a remote and tenuous relationship to the subject of the investigation, or who has some other reason to believe his testimony implicates confidential source relationships without a legitimate need of law enforcement, will have

access to the court on a motion to quash the subpoena and an appropriate protective order may be entered. In short, the courts will be available to newsmen under circumstances where legitimate First Amendment interests require protection.

DISSENT: (Douglas, J.) To mandate disclosure of a reporter's confidential sources will seriously impede the dissemination of ideas a free press offers.

DISSENT: (Stewart, J.) A corollary of the right to publish is the right to gather news. The right to gather news implies, in turn, a right to a confidential relationship between a reporter and his or her source. Since informants are necessary to the news-gathering business as we know it today, the promise of confidentiality may be a necessary-prerequisite to a productive relationship between newspersons and their informants. First Amendment rights require special safeguards.

ANALYSIS

Guidelines promulgated by the Attorney General for federal officials to follow when subpoenaing members of the press to testify before grand juries or at criminal trials included the following test for information: whether there is "sufficient reason to believe the information sought is essential to a successful investigation" and cannot be obtained from non-press sources. However, in "emergencies and other unusual situations," "subpoenas which do not conform to the guidelines may be issued."

■═■

Quicknotes

FIRST AMENDMENT Prohibits Congress from enacting any law respecting an establishment of religion, prohibiting the free exercise of religion, abridging freedom of speech or the press, the right of peaceful assembly and the right to petition for a redress of grievances.

■═■

The Constitution and Religion

Quick Reference Rules of Law

Lee v. Weisman

School officials (D) v. Father of student (P)

505 U.S. 577 (1992).

NATURE OF CASE: Appeal of permanent injunction.

FACT SUMMARY: Daniel Weisman (P), father of student Deborah (P), sought a permanent injunction barring the Providence public school officials (D) from inviting clergy to deliver invocations and benedictions at graduation ceremonies.

RULE OF LAW
Religious invocations and benedictions may not be given at a public primary or secondary school graduation ceremony.

FACTS: As allowed by the Providence School Committee (D), Principal Lee (D) invited Rabbi Gutterman to give the invocation and benediction at Lee's (D) middle school's graduation. Attendance at graduation exercises at Providence public schools is voluntary. Following school procedure, Lee (D) gave Rabbi Gutterman written guidelines for nonsectarian prayers. David Weisman (P), on behalf of himself and his daughter Deborah (P), sought a temporary restraining order (TRO) against school officials (P) to prevent Rabbi Gutterman from delivering prayers at Deborah's (P) graduation. The TRO was denied, and Deborah (P) went through the ceremonies. The students stood for a few minutes while Rabbi Gutterman delivered prayers. The Weismans' (P) suit continued since Deborah (P) was a student at a Providence public high school and would likely face the same situation at high school graduation. Applying the test of *Lemon v. Kurtzman*, 403 U.S. 602 (1971), the district court held the prayers violated the Establishment Clause because they had a primary effect of advancing religion. The district court permanently enjoined the school officials (D) from inviting clergy to give invocations and benedictions at future graduations. The court of appeals affirmed.

ISSUE: May religious invocations and benedictions be given at a public primary or secondary school graduation ceremony?

HOLDING AND DECISION: (Kennedy, J.) No. Religious invocations and benedictions may not be given at a public primary or secondary school graduation ceremony. Here, state officials (D) directed the performance of a formal, explicit religious exercise at public school graduation. Principal Lee (D) decided the prayers should be given, selected the cleric, and gave written guidelines for the prayer. Even for students who object to religious exercise, attendance and participation was in every practical sense obligatory. High school graduation is one of life's most significant occasions. To say that attendance is "voluntary" is formalistic in the extreme. Such prayers in public schools carry a particular risk of coercion. There is public and peer pressure on attending students to stand as a group or maintain respectful silence. A dissenter is injured by his reasonable perception others view his standing as approval and he is being forced by the state to pray. The First Amendment protects the objector from having to take unilateral, private action to avoid compromising religious principles at a state function. The fact the prayer was "nonsectarian" does not make government involvement acceptable. Affirmed.

CONCURRENCE: (Blackmun, J.) The Establishment Clause not only prohibits government coercion, but also any government engagement in religious practices. The simple issue is whether the state placed a stamp of approval on a religious activity. Here, it did.

DISSENT: (Scalia, J.) The Establishment Clause must be construed in light of government policies of accommodation and support for religion that are an accepted part of our political and cultural heritage. Nonsectarian prayers at graduations and other public celebrations are a long-standing American tradition. From the Framers to our current President, Congress, and Supreme Court, government leaders have opened public functions with prayer. The Establishment Clause only bars state religious activity backed by threat of penalty for nonparticipation. The coercion involved in school prayer cases is that students are compelled to attend school. No coercion exists here.

ANALYSIS

The dissent claimed that the Court's failure to apply the three-part *Lemon* test means the test is no longer good law. However, Justice Kennedy's opinion for the Court expressly declined to reconsider *Lemon*. Justices Kennedy and Souter both cited *Lemon* with approval, though they did not apply the test. Justice Blackmun's concurrence, joined by Justices Stevens and O'Connor, expressed the view that *Lemon* still applies in all Establishment Clause cases.

■ ═ ■

Quicknotes

ESTABLISHMENT CLAUSE The constitutional provision prohibiting the government from favoring any one religion

Continued on next page.

over others or engaging in religious activities or advocacy.

FIRST AMENDMENT Prohibits Congress from enacting any law respecting an establishment of religion, prohibiting the free exercise of religion, abridging freedom of speech or the press, the right of peaceful assembly and the right to petition for a redress of grievances.

Lynch v. Donnelly

Municipality (D) v. Residents (P)

465 U.S. 668 (1984).

NATURE OF CASE: Appeal from judgment finding a violation of the Establishment Clause.

FACT SUMMARY: The district court held that Pawtucket (D) violated the Establishment Clause by including a nativity scene in its Christmas display.

RULE OF LAW
The Establishment Clause does not prohibit the inclusion of a nativity scene in a municipal Christmas display.

FACTS: Donnelly (P) and other residents (P) of Pawtucket, Rhode Island ("the City") (P) sued to enjoin the City (D) from including a nativity scene in its annual Christmas display, as it had done for over 40 years. They contended the inclusion violated the Establishment Clause by bestowing a benefit on the Christian religion. The district court granted a permanent injunction forbidding the City (P) from including the scene in the display. The court of appeals affirmed, and the Supreme Court granted certiorari.

ISSUE: Does the Establishment Clause prohibit the inclusion of a nativity scene in a municipal Christmas display?

HOLDING AND DECISION: (Burger, C.J.) No. The Establishment Clause does not prohibit the inclusion of a nativity scene in a municipal Christmas display. The scene confers no more benefit on religion than other innocuous symbols recognizing the existence of religion in our society. The City's (D) purpose in including the display was to celebrate and depict the origin of the Christmas holiday. This clearly was a legitimate secular purpose. As a result, the inclusion of the scene was not unconstitutional. Reversed.

CONCURRENCE: (O'Connor, J.) Pawtucket (D) did not endorse Christianity by including the scene in its display. Therefore, it did not violate the Establishment Clause.

DISSENT: (Brennan, J.) The nativity scene recreates an event that lies at the heart of the Christian faith. Therefore, its inclusion clearly constituted an impermissible government involvement in religion.

DISSENT: (Blackmun, J.) Use of the religious symbol in a municipally sponsored display compels Christians to acknowledge its symbolic meaning and to alienate non-Christians. This is misuse of a sacred symbol.

► ANALYSIS

The Court articulated a three-part test to use in determining whether particular governmental action violates the Establishment Clause in *Lemon v. Kurtzman*, 403 U.S. 602 (1970). The test requires the Court to determine: (1) whether the action has a secular purpose; (2) whether it advances or inhibits religion; and (3) whether it creates an excessive government entanglement in religion. In the present case, the Court stated such a test is not to be blindly followed, and ad hoc line-drawing must be performed.

Quicknotes

ESTABLISHMENT CLAUSE The constitutional provision prohibiting the government from favoring any one religion over others or engaging in religious activities or advocacy.

Mueller v. Allen

Resident (P) v. State (D)

463 U.S. 388 (1983).

NATURE OF CASE: Action challenging the constitutionality of a state tax deduction law.

FACT SUMMARY: Mueller (P) instituted suit challenging the constitutionality of a Minnesota law allowing taxpayers, in computing their state income tax, to deduct certain expenses incurred in providing for their children's education, whether or not the children attended public schools or private parochial schools.

🏛 RULE OF LAW
A state's decision to defray the cost of educational expenses incurred by parents evidences a purpose that is both secular and understandable, and does not violate the Establishment Clause.

FACTS: Minnesota passed a law allowing taxpayers, in figuring their state income tax, to deduct actual expenses incurred for the "tuition, textbooks and transportation" of dependents attending elementary or secondary schools," whether or not the schools were nonsectarian or sectarian. A maximum $500 deduction for each dependent in grades Kindergarten through six and $700 for each dependent in grades seven through twelve was permitted. Mueller (P) brought suit challenging the validity of the law under the Establishment Clause. The court of appeals held the statute did not violate the Establishment Clause.

ISSUE: Does a state's decision to defray the cost of educational expenses incurred by parents violate the Establishment Clause?

HOLDING AND DECISION: (Rehnquist, J.) No. A state's decision to defray the cost of educational expenses incurred by parents evidences a purpose that is both secular and understandable and does not violate the Establishment Clause. A three-part test was laid down in *Lemon v. Kurtzman*, 403 U.S. 602 (1971), and is the means by which can be ascertained whether a particular program that in some manner aids parochial schools (either directly or indirectly) violates the Establishment Clause. The first part inquires whether the program has a secular purpose. In this case, the answer is yes. The tax deduction attempts to give to parents an incentive to educate their children and this serves the secular purpose of ensuring a well-educated citizenry. The second part of the test asks the related question of whether the program has "the primary effect of advancing the sectarian aims of the nonpublic schools." Here, the answer is no. The deduction is available to all parents, including those sending their children to public schools and it channels whatever funds available to such schools only as a result of numerous, private choices of individual parents of school-age children. The third part of the test to which this program must be put inquires whether or not the program "excessively entangles" the state in religion. It does not. The only decision that might remotely involve state officials in state surveillance of religious type issues would be the decisions state officials have to make in determining whether particular textbooks qualify for the deduction. In making this decision, they must disallow deductions taken from "instructional materials used in the teaching of religious tenets, doctrines or worship, the purpose of which is to inculcate such tenets, doctrines or worship." Making this type of decision does not differ substantially from making the types of decisions approved in early opinions of this Court. Thus, the program at issue here must be considered constitutional, as it has passed the three parts of the appropriate test. Affirmed.

DISSENT: (Marshall, J.) That the statute here makes some small benefit available to all parents does not alter the fact the most substantial benefit provided is available only to those parents who send their children to schools that charge tuition. The statute is, therefore, little more than a subsidy of tuition masquerading as a subsidy of general educational expenses. The other expenses are de minimis in comparison to tuition expenses.

▶ ANALYSIS

In the previously decided *Committee for Public Education v. Nyquist* case, 413 U.S. 756 (1973), on which the constitutional challenge to this tax deduction program relied heavily, New York had passed a statute that gave the parents of children attending private schools thinly disguised "tax benefits" that actually amounted to tuition grants. This was found to violate the Establishment Clause. By simply providing in its tax deduction statute that all parents could take such tuition deductions, Minnesota kept its tax deduction scheme from being declared unconstitutional. Yet, it is really a change in form more than in substance, for most public school parents do not have to pay tuition. So, giving them the opportunity to deduct tuition expenses is of little practical consequence and does little to change the effect of the program in providing indirect aid to mostly parochial schools.

■=■

Continued on next page.

Quicknotes

DE MINIMIS Insignificant; trivial; not of sufficient significance to require legal action.

ESTABLISHMENT CLAUSE The constitutional provision prohibiting the government from favoring any one religion over others or engaging in religious activities or advocacy.

Employment Division, Department of Human Resources v. Smith

State agency (D) v. Unemployment benefits applicant (P)

494 U.S. 872 (1990).

NATURE OF CASE: Review of decision reversing denial of unemployment compensation.

FACT SUMMARY: Smith (P) was denied unemployment compensation because he had been terminated for misconduct, this being the religious ingestion of peyote, a controlled substance under state law.

🏛 RULE OF LAW
A state may proscribe the use of psychoactive substances even in a religious context.

FACTS: Smith (P), an American Indian, was a member of a religious sect that included in its worship services the ingestion of peyote, a controlled substance under state law. Smith (P) was fired from his job for using the drug. He (P) was denied unemployment benefits as his termination was for misconduct. Smith (P) filed an action challenging this denial, contending that Oregon's proscription of peyote in all contexts violated the Free Exercise Clause of the First Amendment. The Oregon Supreme Court so held and ordered Smith (P) be given unemployment compensation. The U.S. Supreme Court granted certiorari.

ISSUE: May a state proscribe the use of psychoactive substances even in a religious context?

HOLDING AND DECISION: (Scalia, J.) Yes. A state may proscribe the use of psychoactive substances even in a religious context. A state may not enact a law that has the effect of specifically burdening a religion; to do so would violate the Free Exercise Clause of the First Amendment. However, there is nothing in the clause to exempt religiously based conduct from the reach of a general law of regulation. If an act is illegal, the fact it is religiously based will not make it otherwise. Where a religious act implicates some other constitutional right, the rule is in some cases to the contrary. Here, however, the ingestion of peyote is certainly not a right and the fact it is religiously based does not make it so. Reversed.

CONCURRENCE: (O'Connor, J.) Any burden on religiously based conduct must be shown by the government to serve a compelling interest. The deferential standard adopted by the Court is a major departure from free exercise jurisprudence.

DISSENT: (Blackmun, J.) A proscription such as at issue here must be supported by a compelling state interest, something not present here.

▶ ANALYSIS

A few examples exist in the area of free exercise jurisprudence wherein religiously based conduct was held to be exempt from state interference. However, as the opinion states, this was when other rights were also implicated. An example of this is *Pierce v. Society of Sisters*, 268 U.S. 510 (1925), where it was held a state could not proscribe religious education. The right of parents to direct their children was implicated there.

Quicknotes

FIRST AMENDMENT Prohibits Congress from enacting any law respecting an establishment of religion, prohibiting the free exercise of religion, abridging freedom of speech or the press, the right of peaceful assembly and the right to petition for a redress of grievances.

FREE EXERCISE CLAUSE The guarantee of the First Amendment to the United States Constitution prohibiting Congress from enacting laws regarding the establishment of religion or prohibiting the free exercise thereof.

Corporation of Presiding Bishop of the Church of Jesus Christ of Latter-Day Saints v. Amos

Religious organization (D) v. Employee (P)

483 U.S. 327 (1987).

NATURE OF CASE: Appeal from award of damages for wrongful termination.

FACT SUMMARY: In Amos's (P) suit for damages against the Church of Latter-Day Saints (D), the district court ruled that § 702 of the 1964 Civil Rights Act, which exempts religious organizations from Title VII's prohibition against discrimination in employment on the basis of religion, violates the Establishment Clause of the First Amendment when applied to the secular nonprofit activities of religious organizations.

RULE OF LAW
Where the legislature fashions a law to accommodate religious adherents' concerns, the law must have a primary effect that does not advance their religion so as to comply with the Establishment Clause of the First Amendment.

FACTS: Amos (P) was a janitor at the Desert Gymnasium, a nonprofit facility open to the public and run by the Mormon Church. Amos (P) was fired because he failed to qualify for a certificate stating he was a member of the Church eligible to attend its temples because he observed the Church's standards involving church attendance, tithing, and abstinence from coffee, tea, alcohol, and tobacco. As a result, Amos (P) brought this action for damages against the Church of Latter-Day Saints (D), contending that § 702, as amended, of the 1964 Civil Rights Act, which exempts religious organizations from Title VII's prohibition against discrimination in employment on the basis of religion, violates the Establishment Clause of the First Amendment when applied to the secular nonprofit activities of religious organizations. The district court, in agreement with this contention, awarded Amos (P) damages. The Church of Latter-Day Saints (D) appealed.

ISSUE: Where the legislature fashions a law to accommodate religious adherents' concerns, must the law have a primary effect that does not advance their religion so as to comply with the Establishment Clause of the First Amendment?

HOLDING AND DECISION: (White, J.) Yes. Where the legislature fashions a law to accommodate religious adherents' concerns, the law must have a primary effect that does not advance their religion so as to comply with the Establishment Clause of the First Amendment. This rule was derived from the second prong of the *Lemon v. Kurtzman*, 403 U.S. 602 (1971), three-part analysis regarding the constitutionality of religious legislation.

This relevant part of *Lemon's* analysis, in effect, prohibits the legislature from advancing or inhibiting religion through its own activities and influence. That is, the legislature is prohibited from having as its purpose the advancement or suppression of religion when it creates religious legislation. Moreover, even when legislative purpose isn't clear, if this form of legislation has the primary effect of advancing or inhibiting, then it will be implied this was the desired effect the legislature intended, thereby making the legislation unconstitutional. Ideally, religious legislation should allow religious organizations to advance religion, in contrast to the legislature directly advancing religion. In the instant case, the purpose of the amendment to § 702 is clear. Prior to this amendment, religious organizations were merely allowed to discriminate in employment on the basis of religion with respect to religious activities. However, these activities were difficult to distinguish from secular activities, thereby affecting the way an organization may carry out its religious mission for fear of potential liability. Consequently, the legislature allowed religious organizations to discriminate in employment on the basis of religion with respect to religious or secular activities, for the purpose of limiting governmental interference with the decision-making process in religions. Clearly, then, the legislature intended to remove restraints upon religious organizations' abilities to carry out their religious missions, which is a permissible religious legislative purpose. Aside from this, the 1972 amendment to § 702 was merely intended to extend to secular activities that advance a religious organization's mission. In this respect, the nonprofit activity involved here clearly advances a religious mission since it was formed to benefit an organization member's health and spirituality. Hence, applying § 702 as amended to the nonprofit activities of the religious employer involved here is rationally related to the legitimate purpose of alleviating significant governmental interference with the ability of religious organizations to define and carry out their religious missions. Reversed.

CONCURRENCE: (Brennan, J.) The cases involved here challenge the application of § 702's categorical exemption to the activities of a nonprofit organization. The particular character of nonprofit activity, which is most likely religious, makes inappropriate a case-by-case determination whether its nature is religious or secular.

CONCURRENCE: (O'Connor, J.) The cases here involve a government decision to lift from a nonprofit

Continued on next page.

activity of a religious organization the burden of demonstrating the particular nonprofit activity is religious, as well as the burden of refraining from discriminating on the basis of religion. Because there is a probability the nonprofit activity of a religious organization will itself be involved in the organization's religious mission, the objective observer should perceive the government action as an accommodation of the exercise of religion rather than a government endorsement of religion.

▶ *ANALYSIS*

In connection with the above decision, see McConnel, "Accommodation of Religion," 1985 *Sup. Ct. Rev.* 1, 1-3, where McConnel states the "much discussed 'tension' between the two Religion Clauses largely arises from the Court's substitution of a misleading formula (the three-part *Lemon* [test]) and subsidiary, instrumental values (especially the separation of church and state) in the place of the central value of religious liberty. [Between] the accommodations compelled by the Free Exercise Clause and the benefits to religion prohibited by the Establishment Clause there exists a class of permissible government actions toward religion, which have as their purpose and effects the facilitation of religious liberty. Neither strict neutrality nor separationism can account for the idea of accommodation or define its limits. Only an interpretation of the Religion Clauses based on religious liberty [satisfactorily] distinguishes permissible accommodations from impermissible establishments."

Quicknotes

ESTABLISHMENT CLAUSE The constitutional provision prohibiting the government from favoring any one religion over others or engaging in religious activities or advocacy.

FREE EXERCISE CLAUSE The guarantee of the First Amendment to the United States Constitution prohibiting Congress from enacting laws regarding the establishment of religion or prohibiting the free exercise thereof.

State Action

Quick Reference Rules of Law

Flagg Brothers v. Brooks

Storage company (D) v. Property owner (P)

436 U.S. 149 (1978).

NATURE OF CASE: Class action seeking damages and an injunction against unconstitutional state action.

FACT SUMMARY: Brooks (P) sought to enjoin the sale of the furnishings that had been picked up and stored with Flagg Brothers (D) pursuant to an eviction from her apartment.

🏛 RULE OF LAW
Action of a private party is considered state action where the state has delegated to that party a function traditionally exclusively reserved to the state.

FACTS: During her eviction, Brooks (P) instructed workmen from Flagg Brothers (Flagg) (D) to proceed to move and store her goods as arranged by the City Marshall even though she felt the cost too high. Eventually, a dispute over payment of the bill resulted in a threat by Flagg (D) to sell Brooks's (P) goods if the bill was not paid. Brooks (P) brought a class action suit for damages, an injunction against such sale, and a declaration the sale would violate the Due Process and Equal Protection Clauses. The court of appeals reversed a dismissal of the complaint for failure to state a claim for relief. It found there had been state action in that New York had delegated a portion of its sovereign monopoly power over conflict resolution to warehousemen and had, by statutorily acquiescing to their selling stored goods, permitted them to execute a lien and thus perform a function that was traditionally associated with sovereignty (in this case, a sheriff's function).

ISSUE: Are acts of a private party considered state action where they result from the state's delegating to that party a function traditionally exclusively reserved to the state?

HOLDING AND DECISION: (Rehnquist, J.) Yes. Action of a private party is considered state action where the state has delegated to that party a function traditionally exclusively reserved to the state. Settlement of disputes between creditors and debtors is not traditionally an exclusive public function, so the line of sovereign function cases does not support a finding of state action here. Furthermore, the statute at issue simply reflects the state's acquiescence in a private action, which does not convert such action into that of the state. Reversed.

DISSENT: (Stevens, J.) The test of what is a state function for purposes of the Due Process Clause is not whether there has been a delegation of an exclusive sovereign function but whether, as here, there has been a delegation of a function traditionally and historically associated with sovereignty.

▶ ANALYSIS

Prior cases indicate there are few functions that are considered exclusively reserved to the states, although there are many that have been traditionally performed by governments. One area the courts have continually recognized as involving a function exclusively reserved to the states is the conducting of public elections.

■━■

Quicknotes

DUE PROCESS CLAUSE Clauses found in the Fifth and Fourteenth Amendments to the United States Constitution providing that no person shall be deprived of "life, liberty, or property, without due process of law."

EQUAL PROTECTION CLAUSE A constitutional provision that each person be guaranteed the same protection of the laws enjoyed by other persons in like circumstances.

■━■

Shelley v. Kraemer

Buyer of real property (D) v. Covenantee (P)

334 U.S. 1 (1948).

NATURE OF CASE: Action to enforce a restrictive covenant in the sale of real property.

FACT SUMMARY: Kraemer (P) sought to void a sale of real property to Shelley (D) from a Mr. Fitzgerald relying on a racially restrictive covenant.

RULE OF LAW
Judicial enforcement of a private racially restrictive covenant is considered state action for Fourteenth Amendment purposes.

FACTS: On February 16, 1911, 30 out of a total of 39 owners of property fronting both sides of Labadie Avenue between Taylor Avenue and Cora Avenue in St. Louis signed an agreement, which was subsequently recorded. The agreement provided in part that the property could not be used or occupied by "people of the Negro or Mongolian race" for a period of 50 years. This covenant was to be valid whether it was included in future conveyances or not and was to attach to the land as a condition precedent to the sale of the property. On August 11, 1945, petitioners Shelley (D), who are black, purchased a parcel of land subject to the restrictive covenant from a Mr. Fitzgerald. The Shelleys (D) did not have any actual knowledge of the restrictive agreement at the time of the purchase. On October 9, 1945, Kraemer (P), an owner of other property subject to the terms of the restrictive covenant, brought suit in the Circuit Court of St. Louis to enjoin the Shelleys (D) from taking possession of the property and to divest title from the Shelleys (D) and revest title in Fitzgerald or in such person as the court should direct. The trial court held for the Shelleys (D), but on appeal the Supreme Court of Missouri reversed their decision. The Shelleys (D) contended that the restrictive covenant violated the Equal Protection Clause of the Fourteenth Amendment. Kraemer (P) contended that no state action was involved in the private restrictive covenant and even if there were state action, the courts would enforce a restrictive covenant barring whites from purchasing certain land and so there was equal protection of the law. Kraemer (P) further contended that if he was not allowed to enforce the covenant that he would be denied equal protection of the law.

ISSUE: Does the Equal Protection Clause of the Fourteenth Amendment prevent judicial enforcement by state courts of restrictive covenants based on race or color?

HOLDING AND DECISION: (Vinson, C.J.) Yes. Judicial enforcement of a private racially restrictive covenant is considered state action for Fourteenth Amendment

purposes. Because the restrictive covenants did not involve any action by the state legislature or City Council, the restrictive covenant itself did not violate any rights protected by the Fourteenth Amendment, since it was strictly a private covenant. But the judicial enforcement of the covenant did qualify as state action. From the time of the adoption of the Fourteenth Amendment until the present, the court has consistently ruled that the action of the states to which the amendment has reference includes action of state courts and state judicial officers. In this case because there was a willing buyer and seller, the Shelleys (D) would have been able to enforce the restrictive covenants only with the active intervention of the state courts. The court rejected Kraemer's (P) argument that since the state courts would enforce restrictive covenants excluding white persons from ownership of property there was no denial of equal protection. The court stated equal protection of the law is not achieved through indiscriminate imposition of inequalities. As to Kraemer's (P) contention he was being denied equal protection of the laws because his restrictive covenant was not being enforced, the court stated the Constitution does not confer the right to demand action by the state that would result in the denial of equal protection of the laws to other individuals. Therefore, in granting judicial enforcement of the restrictive agreement, the state has denied the Shelleys (D) equal protection of the laws and the action of the state courts cannot stand. The court noted the enjoyment of property rights, free from discrimination by the states, was among the objectives sought to be effectuated by the framers of the Fourteenth Amendment. Reversed.

ANALYSIS

The Court in its post-*Shelley v. Kraemer* decisions has given this decision a fairly narrow reading. A broad reading of this case requires that whenever a state court enforces a private racial restrictive covenant such action constitutes state action that is forbidden by the Fourteenth Amendment. In cases where the ruling in this case could have been found to be applicable, the Court has used a different rationale. Some of the Court's statements suggest that more state involvement than evenhanded enforcement of private biases was necessary to find unconstitutional state action. Justice Black, in a dissenting opinion, stated the decision in this case only is applicable in cases involving property rights.

Continued on next page.

Quicknotes

CONDITION PRECEDENT The happening of an uncertain occurrence which is necessary before a particular right or interest may be obtained or an action performed.

EQUAL PROTECTION CLAUSE A constitutional provision that each person be guaranteed the same protection of the laws enjoyed by other persons in like circumstances.

FOURTEENTH AMENDMENT Declares that no state shall make or enforce any law that shall abridge the privileges and immunities of citizens of the United States. No state shall deny to any person within its jurisdiction the equal protection of the laws.

Burton v. Wilmington Parking Authority

Customer (P) v. Lessor public authority (D)

365 U.S. 715 (1961).

NATURE OF CASE: Action seeking declaratory and injunctive relief for racial discrimination.

FACT SUMMARY: Wilmington Parking Authority (D) leased space in a parking facility to Eagle Coffee Shoppe for use as a restaurant and they refused to serve Burton (P), a black man.

> ## RULE OF LAW
> Racial discrimination by a business that is located in and constitutes part of a state-owned public facility is considered to be state action and is forbidden by the Fourteenth Amendment.

FACTS: Wilmington Parking Authority ("the Authority") (D) was going to erect a public parking facility, but before it started construction it was advised the anticipated revenue from the parking of cars and proceeds from the sale of its bonds would not be sufficient to finance the construction costs of the facility. To secure additional capital, the Authority (D) decided to enter into long-term leases with responsible tenants for commercial use of some of the space available in the projected garage building. A 20-year lease was entered into with Eagle Coffee Shoppe, Inc. (Eagle), for a space to be used as a restaurant. Even though the Authority (D) had the power to adopt rules and regulations requiring the restaurant services be made available to the general public, the lease contained no such requirement of Eagle Coffee Shoppes. Under a Delaware statute, Eagle Coffee Shoppe was classified as a restaurant and not an inn and, therefore, was not required to serve all persons entering their shop. Burton (P) attempted to enter the restaurant but was refused service because he was black. As a result, Burton (P) filed an action seeking declaratory and injunctive relief against Wilmington Parking Authority (D), claiming that as the restaurant was the Authority's (D) lessee, and the Authority (D) was an agency of the state, the discrimination was therefore state action. However, the Supreme Court of Delaware held Eagle was acting in a purely private capacity under its lease and the action was not that of the Authority (D) and was not, therefore, state action. The court based its conclusion on the fact only 15 percent of the total cost of the facility was advanced from public funds and the revenue from parking was only 30.5 percent of the total income. Eagle had expended considerable amounts of its own funds on furnishings and there was no public entrance direct from the parking area. The only connection Eagle had with the public facility was the payment of $28,700 in rent annually. The decision was appealed to the Supreme Court.

ISSUE: Is racial discrimination by a business that leases facilities from the state considered to be state action?

HOLDING AND DECISION: (Clark, J.) Yes. Racial discrimination by a business that is located in and constitutes part of a state-owned public facility is considered to be state action and is forbidden by the Fourteenth Amendment. The Court held the restaurant was so closely tied in with the Parking Authority (D) that the discriminatory action by the restaurant was considered to be state action. The Court pointed out the land and building were publicly owned and the costs of land acquisition, construction, and maintenance were defrayed entirely from donations by the City of Wilmington from loans and revenue bonds, and from the proceeds of rentals and parking services out of which the loans and bonds were payable. The Court did not feel the figures used by the Delaware Supreme Court were very accurate. The Court also noted the restaurant operated as an integral part of a public building devoted to a public parking service and part of the facility was open to the public while in another part blacks were refused service. The fact that the Parking Authority (D) did not require in the lease that the restaurant be open to the public doesn't allow the restaurant to discriminate against blacks with impunity. By its inaction, the Authority (D) (and through it the state) made itself a party to the refusal of service. Because of the financial interdependence between the Authority (D) and the restaurant, and because of the physical relation of the facility, the discriminatory action by the restaurant cannot be considered purely private action. The Court also pointed out it is impossible for the Court to create a formula by which it can be determined what is and is not state action. It is necessary to look at the facts in each case in order to determine if state action is involved. Reversed and remanded.

⟩ ANALYSIS

As Justice Stewart pointed out in his dissent, the Court in this case did not clearly define the requirements for a finding of state action. In subsequent cases, however, it became clearer the critical factor in the *Burton* case was the leasing of public property to a private enterprise for its exclusive use. The City of Montgomery, Alabama, rented or granted the exclusive use of certain public recreation areas to private groups that practiced racial discrimination. The Court found no difficulty in invalidating this practice. But a

Continued on next page.

more troublesome problem was presented by the grant of non-exclusive permits to such groups. A case involving such non-exclusive use was remanded for further findings on how much restriction was placed on free public access by these non-exclusive permits. Finally, in *Moose Lodge No. 107 v. Irvis*, 407 U.S. 163 (1972), the Court found the granting of a liquor license to a private fraternal organization that discriminated was not sufficient state action to involve the Equal Protection Clause.

Quicknotes

EQUAL PROTECTION CLAUSE A constitutional provision that each person be guaranteed the same protection of the laws enjoyed by other persons in like circumstances.

FOURTEENTH AMENDMENT Declares that no state shall make or enforce any law that shall abridge the privileges and immunities of citizens of the United States. No state shall deny to any person within its jurisdiction the equal protection of the laws.

Moose Lodge No. 107 v. Irvis

Private club (D) v. Guest (P)

407 U.S. 163 (1972).

NATURE OF CASE: Constitutional challenge against racial discrimination in a private club.

FACT SUMMARY: The Moose Lodge (D) refused to serve liquor to the black guest of a member solely on the basis of his race.

🏛 RULE OF LAW
Merely granting a liquor license to a private club that engages in discriminatory practices is not sufficient state action to invoke the Fourteenth Amendment.

FACTS: Irvis (P), a black man, was invited to the Moose Lodge ("the Lodge") (D) by a member. The Lodge (D) refused to serve liquor to Irvis (P) solely because he was black. Irvis (P) brought an action in federal district court alleging the state was authorizing and furthering discrimination. Irvis (P) requested the Court to enjoin the Lodge's (D) discriminatory practices. Irvis's (P) claim of state action under the Fourteenth Amendment was based solely upon the granting of a liquor license to the Lodge. The district court found state action present based on the state's total control over the granting of licenses.

ISSUE: Is the issuance of a liquor license alone sufficient state action to invoke the Fourteenth Amendment?

HOLDING AND DECISION: (Rehnquist, J.) No. Merely granting a liquor license to a private club that engages in discriminatory practices is not sufficient state action to invoke the Fourteenth Amendment. For state action to be found, it must be shown the state, through an exercise of its power and authority, encouraged discrimination. Merely granting a permit enabling a private club to serve liquor to its members and their guests is essentially neutral conduct. It cannot be said such conduct either fosters or encourages discriminatory practices. It also cannot be said the state is lending either its prestige or support to a discriminatory group. Merely regulating the physical aspects of the club or granting a liquor license is not sufficient state action to invoke the prohibitions of the Fourteenth Amendment. The case might be decided contra if the rules and bylaws of the club required racial discrimination. Here they do not. Reversed and remanded.

DISSENT: (Douglas, J.) Liquor licenses in Pennsylvania are not freely available, and are subject to a complex quota system. The state-enforced scarcity of licenses restricts the ability of blacks to obtain liquor. I would affirm the judgment below.

▶ ANALYSIS

Granting a lease in a public facility has been held to be sufficient governmental involvement to invoke the Fourteenth Amendment. *Burton v. Wilmington Parking Authority*, 365 U.S. 715 (1961). Another example of state action is where a private discriminatory facility contracts with the police to hire deputies to enforce the discriminatory practices. *Griffin v. Maryland*, 378 U.S. 130 (1964).

◼◼◼

Quicknotes

FOURTEENTH AMENDMENT Declares that no state shall make or enforce any law that shall abridge the privileges and immunities of citizens of the United States. No state shall deny to any person within its jurisdiction the equal protection of the laws.

◼◼◼

Jackson v. Metropolitan Edison Co.

Customer (P) v. Power company (D)

419 U.S. 345 (1974).

NATURE OF CASE: Appeal of constitutional challenge to termination of electrical service for non-payment.

FACT SUMMARY: Metropolitan Edison Co. (D), a privately owned, regulated power company, terminated service to Jackson (P) for nonpayment.

🏛 RULE OF LAW
A privately owned utility may cease providing service without raising due process concerns, even if it is highly regulated.

FACTS: Metropolitan Edison Co. (D) was a privately-owned utility company. It was regulated by the State Utility Commission. The evidence tended to show Metropolitan Edison (D) was a legal monopoly, although this issue was inconclusive. Metropolitan Edison (D) terminated service to Jackson (P) for alleged nonpayment, a practice sanctioned by the utilities commission. Jackson (P) brought suit, alleging a violation of due process. The court of appeals held for Metropolitan Edison (D).

ISSUE: May a privately owned utility cease providing service without raising due process concerns, even if it is highly regulated?

HOLDING AND DECISION: (Rehnquist, J.) Yes. A privately owned utility may cease providing service without raising due process concerns, even if it is highly regulated. A decision made by a business that is highly regulated involves state action only if the state was actively involved in the decision or otherwise coerced it. The mere fact of regulation or approval does not give rise to state action. Here all the state did was regulate Metropolitan Edison (D) and approve its procedures. The state did not actively involve itself in decision-making. Therefore, no state action existed. Affirmed.

▶ ANALYSIS

It would seem the key concept in this area is governmental neutrality. As long as the government takes a passive role in decision-making, no state action is involved. Of course, there are those, such as Justice Marshall in dissent here, who believe licensing and regulation is more than neutrality, but rather is imprimatur necessary for state action.

▬▬■

Quicknotes

DUE PROCESS The constitutional mandate requiring the courts to protect and enforce individuals' rights and liberties consistent with prevailing principles of fairness and justice and prohibiting the federal and state governments from such activities that deprive its citizens of life, liberty, or property interest.

▬▬■

Marsh v. Alabama

Distributor of literature (P) v. State (D)

326 U.S. 501 (1946).

NATURE OF CASE: Appeal from a criminal conviction.

FACT SUMMARY: Marsh (D) attempted to distribute religious literature in a company-owned town.

🏛 RULE OF LAW
When private property is the equivalent of a public "business block," it ceases to be strictly private and First Amendment rights may not be arbitrarily curtailed.

FACTS: Chickasaw was a company-owned town in Alabama (D). Its business district was open to the public and public highways ran through it. The company prohibited all solicitation or distribution of literature without a permit. Marsh (P), a Jehovah's Witness, attempted to pass out religious literature on the sidewalks of the business district. Marsh (D) was arrested and convicted of a misdemeanor for remaining on private property after being asked to leave. Marsh (D) alleged this violated her First and Fourteenth Amendment rights and the sidewalks in the business block were quasi-public.

ISSUE: Where private property has taken on the public character of a public business block, may First Amendment rights be arbitrarily curtailed?

HOLDING AND DECISION: (Black, J.) No. When private property is the equivalent of a public "business block," it ceases to be strictly private and First Amendment rights may not be arbitrarily curtailed. Certain property becomes quasi-public as it becomes opened to the general public. The greater the access to and encouragement of public use, the less arbitrary freedom is granted to the owner as to the use and condition of his property. Where the property becomes the equivalent of a public business block, private ownership will not excuse arbitrary curtailment of First Amendment rights. The public's right to free access to information and Marsh's (D) right to practice her First Amendment rights cannot be arbitrarily interfered with by the company. It cannot allow the distribution of certain material and arbitrarily deny access to others. Those living in company towns have a right to receive free access to divergent views. When the company's right to the free use of its quasi-public property is balanced against these other rights, the company's rights must give way. Reversed and remanded.

DISSENT: (Reed, J.) We permit company towns and there is no compelling reason to accommodate trespasses. Absent public dedication there is no reason to treat company towns any differently than other private property.

▶ ANALYSIS

Marsh has subsequently been limited to cases involving company towns and public dedications. Private property rights are still deemed superior to First Amendment rights in other situations. The rationale in *Marsh* is basically that the inhabitants of the town or those interested in influencing them have no other means to reasonably do so since the company can restrict newspapers, etc. In other situations, many public areas are available for distribution to the citizens of a community without requiring private property owners to suffer unwanted intrusions.

Quicknotes

FIRST AMENDMENT Prohibits Congress from enacting any law respecting an establishment of religion, prohibiting the free exercise of religion, abridging freedom of speech or the press, the right of peaceful assembly and the right to petition for a redress of grievances.

Common Latin Words and Phrases Encountered in the Law

A FORTIORI: Because one fact exists or has been proven, therefore a second fact that is related to the first fact must also exist.

A PRIORI: From the cause to the effect. A term of logic used to denote that when one generally accepted truth is shown to be a cause, another particular effect must necessarily follow.

AB INITIO: From the beginning; a condition which has existed throughout, as in a marriage which was void ab initio.

ACTUS REUS: The wrongful act; in criminal law, such action sufficient to trigger criminal liability.

AD VALOREM: According to value; an ad valorem tax is imposed upon an item located within the taxing jurisdiction calculated by the value of such item.

AMICUS CURIAE: Friend of the court. Its most common usage takes the form of an amicus curiae brief, filed by a person who is not a party to an action but is nonetheless allowed to offer an argument supporting his legal interests.

ARGUENDO: In arguing. A statement, possibly hypothetical, made for the purpose of argument, is one made arguendo.

BILL QUIA TIMET: A bill to quiet title (establish ownership) to real property.

BONA FIDE: True, honest, or genuine. May refer to a person's legal position based on good faith or lacking notice of fraud (such as a bona fide purchaser for value) or to the authenticity of a particular document (such as a bona fide last will and testament).

CAUSA MORTIS: With approaching death in mind. A gift causa mortis is a gift given by a party who feels certain that death is imminent.

CAVEAT EMPTOR: Let the buyer beware. This maxim is reflected in the rule of law that a buyer purchases at his own risk because it is his responsibility to examine, judge, test, and otherwise inspect what he is buying.

CERTIORARI: A writ of review. Petitions for review of a case by the United States Supreme Court are most often done by means of a writ of certiorari.

CONTRA: On the other hand. Opposite. Contrary to.

CORAM NOBIS: Before us; writs of error directed to the court that originally rendered the judgment.

CORAM VOBIS: Before you; writs of error directed by an appellate court to a lower court to correct a factual error.

CORPUS DELICTI: The body of the crime; the requisite elements of a crime amounting to objective proof that a crime has been committed.

CUM TESTAMENTO ANNEXO, ADMINISTRATOR (ADMINISTRATOR C.T.A.): With will annexed; an administrator c.t.a. settles an estate pursuant to a will in which he is not appointed.

DE BONIS NON, ADMINISTRATOR (ADMINISTRATOR D.B.N.): Of goods not administered; an administrator d.b.n. settles a partially settled estate.

DE FACTO: In fact; in reality; actually. Existing in fact but not officially approved or engendered.

DE JURE: By right; lawful. Describes a condition that is legitimate "as a matter of law," in contrast to the term "de facto," which connotes something existing in fact but not legally sanctioned or authorized. For example, de facto segregation refers to segregation brought about by housing patterns, etc., whereas de jure segregation refers to segregation created by law.

DE MINIMIS: Of minimal importance; insignificant; a trifle; not worth bothering about.

DE NOVO: Anew; a second time; afresh. A trial de novo is a new trial held at the appellate level as if the case originated there and the trial at a lower level had not taken place.

DICTA: Generally used as an abbreviated form of obiter dicta, a term describing those portions of a judicial opinion incidental or not necessary to resolution of the specific question before the court. Such nonessential statements and remarks are not considered to be binding precedent.

DUCES TECUM: Refers to a particular type of writ or subpoena requesting a party or organization to produce certain documents in their possession.

EN BANC: Full bench. Where a court sits with all justices present rather than the usual quorum.

EX PARTE: For one side or one party only. An ex parte proceeding is one undertaken for the benefit of only one party, without notice to, or an appearance by, an adverse party.

EX POST FACTO: After the fact. An ex post facto law is a law that retroactively changes the consequences of a prior act.

EX REL.: Abbreviated form of the term "ex relatione," meaning upon relation or information. When the state brings an action in which it has no interest against an individual at the instigation of one who has a private interest in the matter.

FORUM NON CONVENIENS: Inconvenient forum. Although a court may have jurisdiction over the case, the action should be tried in a more conveniently located court, one to which parties and witnesses may more easily travel, for example.

GUARDIAN AD LITEM: A guardian of an infant as to litigation, appointed to represent the infant and pursue his/her rights.

HABEAS CORPUS: You have the body. The modern writ of habeas corpus is a writ directing that a person (body) being detained (such as a prisoner) be brought before the court so that the legality of his detention can be judicially ascertained.

IN CAMERA: In private, in chambers. When a hearing is held before a judge in his chambers or when all spectators are excluded from the courtroom.

IN FORMA PAUPERIS: In the manner of a pauper. A party who proceeds in forma pauperis because of his poverty is one who is allowed to bring suit without liability for costs.

INFRA: Below, under. A word referring the reader to a later part of a book. (The opposite of supra.)

IN LOCO PARENTIS: In the place of a parent.

IN PARI DELICTO: Equally wrong; a court of equity will not grant requested relief to an applicant who is in pari delicto, or as much at fault in the transactions giving rise to the controversy as is the opponent of the applicant.

IN PARI MATERIA: On like subject matter or upon the same matter. Statutes relating to the same person or things are said to be in pari materia. It is a general rule of statutory construction that such statutes should be construed together, i.e., looked at as if they together constituted one law.

IN PERSONAM: Against the person. Jurisdiction over the person of an individual.

IN RE: In the matter of. Used to designate a proceeding involving an estate or other property.

IN REM: A term that signifies an action against the res, or thing. An action in rem is basically one that is taken directly against property, as distinguished from an action in personam, i.e., against the person.

INTER ALIA: Among other things. Used to show that the whole of a statement, pleading, list, statute, etc., has not been set forth in its entirety.

INTER PARTES: Between the parties. May refer to contracts, conveyances or other transactions having legal significance.

INTER VIVOS: Between the living. An inter vivos gift is a gift made by a living grantor, as distinguished from bequests contained in a will, which pass upon the death of the testator.

IPSO FACTO: By the mere fact itself.

JUS: Law or the entire body of law.

LEX LOCI: The law of the place; the notion that the rights of parties to a legal proceeding are governed by the law of the place where those rights arose.

MALUM IN SE: Evil or wrong in and of itself; inherently wrong. This term describes an act that is wrong by its very nature, as opposed to one which would not be wrong but for the fact that there is a specific legal prohibition against it (malum prohibitum).

MALUM PROHIBITUM: Wrong because prohibited, but not inherently evil. Used to describe something that is wrong because it is expressly forbidden by law but that is not in and of itself evil, e.g., speeding.

MANDAMUS: We command. A writ directing an official to take a certain action.

MENS REA: A guilty mind; a criminal intent. A term used to signify the mental state that accompanies a crime or other prohibited act. Some crimes require only a general mens rea (general intent to do the prohibited act), but others, like assault with intent to murder, require the existence of a specific mens rea.

MODUS OPERANDI: Method of operating; generally refers to the manner or style of a criminal in committing crimes, admissible in appropriate cases as evidence of the identity of a defendant.

NEXUS: A connection to.

NISI PRIUS: A court of first impression. A nisi prius court is one where issues of fact are tried before a judge or jury.

N.O.V. (NON OBSTANTE VEREDICTO): Notwithstanding the verdict. A judgment n.o.v. is a judgment given in favor of one party despite the fact that a verdict was returned in favor of the other party, the justification being that the verdict either had no reasonable support in fact or was contrary to law.

NUNC PRO TUNC: Now for then. This phrase refers to actions that may be taken and will then have full retroactive effect.

PENDENTE LITE: Pending the suit; pending litigation under way.

PER CAPITA: By head; beneficiaries of an estate, if they take in equal shares, take per capita.

PER CURIAM: By the court; signifies an opinion ostensibly written "by the whole court" and with no identified author.

PER SE: By itself, in itself; inherently.

PER STIRPES: By representation. Used primarily in the law of wills to describe the method of distribution where a person, generally because of death, is unable to take that which is left to him by the will of another, and therefore his heirs divide such property between them rather than take under the will individually.

PRIMA FACIE: On its face, at first sight. A prima facie case is one that is sufficient on its face, meaning that the evidence supporting it is adequate to establish the case until contradicted or overcome by other evidence.

PRO TANTO: For so much; as far as it goes. Often used in eminent domain cases when a property owner receives partial payment for his land without prejudice to his right to bring suit for the full amount he claims his land to be worth.

QUANTUM MERUIT: As much as he deserves. Refers to recovery based on the doctrine of unjust enrichment in those cases in which a party has rendered valuable services or furnished materials that were accepted and enjoyed by another under circumstances that would reasonably notify the recipient that the rendering party expected to be paid. In essence, the law implies a contract to pay the reasonable value of the services or materials furnished.

QUASI: Almost like; as if; nearly. This term is essentially used to signify that one subject or thing is almost analogous to another but that material differences between them do exist. For example, a quasi-criminal proceeding is one that is not strictly criminal but shares enough of the same characteristics to require some of the same safeguards (e.g., procedural due process must be followed in a parole hearing).

QUID PRO QUO: Something for something. In contract law, the consideration, something of value, passed between the parties to render the contract binding.

RES GESTAE: Things done; in evidence law, this principle justifies the admission of a statement that would otherwise be hearsay when it is made so closely to the event in question as to be said to be a part of it, or with such spontaneity as not to have the possibility of falsehood.

RES IPSA LOQUITUR: The thing speaks for itself. This doctrine gives rise to a rebuttable presumption of negligence when the instrumentality causing the injury was within the exclusive control of the defendant, and the injury was one that does not normally occur unless a person has been negligent.

RES JUDICATA: A matter adjudged. Doctrine which provides that once a court of competent jurisdiction has rendered a final judgment or decree on the merits, that judgment or decree is conclusive upon the parties to the case and prevents them from engaging in any other litigation on the points and issues determined therein.

RESPONDEAT SUPERIOR: Let the master reply. This doctrine holds the master liable for the wrongful acts of his servant (or the principal for his agent) in those cases in which the servant (or agent) was acting within the scope of his authority at the time of the injury.

STARE DECISIS: To stand by or adhere to that which has been decided. The common law doctrine of stare decisis attempts to give security and certainty to the law by following the policy that once a principle of law as applicable to a certain set of facts has been set forth in a decision, it forms a precedent which will subsequently be followed, even though a different decision might be made were it the first time the question had arisen. Of course, stare decisis is not an inviolable principle and is departed from in instances where there is good cause (e.g., considerations of public policy led the Supreme Court to disregard prior decisions sanctioning segregation).

SUPRA: Above. A word referring a reader to an earlier part of a book.

ULTRA VIRES: Beyond the power. This phrase is most commonly used to refer to actions taken by a corporation that are beyond the power or legal authority of the corporation.

Addendum of French Derivatives

IN PAIS: Not pursuant to legal proceedings.

CHATTEL: Tangible personal property.

CY PRES: Doctrine permitting courts to apply trust funds to purposes not expressed in the trust but necessary to carry out the settlor's intent.

PER AUTRE VIE: For another's life; during another's life. In property law, an estate may be granted that will terminate upon the death of someone other than the grantee.

PROFIT A PRENDRE: A license to remove minerals or other produce from land.

VOIR DIRE: Process of questioning jurors as to their predispositions about the case or parties to a proceeding in order to identify those jurors displaying bias or prejudice.